Dear David,

Thank you for allowing me to share your vision of leadership in action @ PrintPac

Belinda
3/16/2018
Psalm 127:1

BELINDA JOHNSON WHITE, PH.D.

FOCUS IN ACTION

IS GREAT LEADERSHIP

10 TENETS OF LEADERSHIP
& PROFESSIONAL EXCELLENCE

WESTBOW
PRESS®
A DIVISION OF THOMAS NELSON
& ZONDERVAN

Scripture quotations are taken from the Holy Bible, New Living Translation, copyright ©1996, 2004, 2007, 2013, 2015 by Tyndale House Foundation. Used by permission of Tyndale House Publishers, Inc., Carol Stream, Illinois 60188. All rights reserved.

THE HOLY BIBLE, NEW INTERNATIONAL VERSION®, NIV® Copyright © 1973, 1978, 1984, 2011 by Biblica, Inc.® Used by permission. All rights reserved worldwide.

This book is a work of non-fiction. Unless otherwise noted, the author and the publisher make no explicit guarantees as to the accuracy of the information contained in this book and in some cases, names of people and places have been altered to protect their privacy.

WestBow Press books may be ordered through booksellers or by contacting:

WestBow Press
A Division of Thomas Nelson & Zondervan
1663 Liberty Drive
Bloomington, IN 47403
www.westbowpress.com
1 (866) 928-1240

Because of the dynamic nature of the Internet, any web addresses or links contained in this book may have changed since publication and may no longer be valid. The views expressed in this work are solely those of the author and do not necessarily reflect the views of the publisher, and the publisher hereby disclaims any responsibility for them.

Any people depicted in stock imagery provided by Thinkstock are models, and such images are being used for illustrative purposes only.
Certain stock imagery © Thinkstock.

ISBN: 978-1-5127-7099-5 (sc)
ISBN: 978-1-5127-7101-5 (hc)
ISBN: 978-1-5127-7100-8 (e)

Library of Congress Control Number: 2017900127

Print information available on the last page.

WestBow Press rev. date: 02/01/2017

To my family: Your love and happiness are
the only things that truly matter.
To my Morehouse College students: Your destiny
of greatness is the inspiration for my work.
To twenty-first-century global leaders everywhere: Thank you.

Acknowledgments

Book writing is a team endeavor, and my book is no exception. My book has integrated ideas and support from many people, and I sincerely want to acknowledge them. Being part of the Morehouse College family for more than twenty years has allowed me to develop deep and rich relationships with many wonderful people.

I especially thank my friends, colleagues, and mentors in the Division of Business Administration and Economics, Morehouse College—Drs. Willis B. Sheftall, John E. Williams, Cheryl L. Allen, Keith Hollingsworth, and Carolyn Davis; Douglas Cooper, Patricia Allen-Jackson, Patricia Bowers, Claudia Smalls, the late Benjamin P. McLaurin, and Dr. Walter E. Fluker, former executive director of the Leadership Center at Morehouse College. Their intellectual stimulation and support enabled me to pursue my dream of creating and publishing a leadership and professional development model and book.

I acknowledge the encouragement and support of the thousands of students I have taught and their accounts of the positive difference that my teachings have had on their personal and professional success. I would be remiss if I did not recognize and give thanks to the hundreds of corporate representatives, including Morehouse alumni, who have given so much of their time and expertise to the students of Morehouse College and the Atlanta University Center. A considerable amount of their firsthand experiences and practical insights are woven into my work.

I also want to acknowledge and extend special thanks to my friends and supporters Sandra Edmonds, Bernice W. Kirkland, Lavonya Jones, Dana McLaurin, and Calvin Williams.

Without the love, support, and encouragement from my "sister friends," this book would not be a reality. These are the fabulous women who make up my circle of sisters from my church, Hoosier Memorial United Methodist Church; my Christian group, Women After God's Own Heart Ministry, Inc.; my sorority, Delta Sigma Theta Sorority, Inc.; my undergraduate school, Spelman College; my Niskey Lake Falls neighbors; my professional organization, the Academy of Management; and the unshakeable friendship, support, love, and care from my dear sister friend, Thelma.

Finally, I want to acknowledge my loving and beloved family. I have always received much love, support, and guidance from my husband Bob, son Robert, and daughter Bethany. I am eternally grateful for my parents, the late Mr. Benjamin and Mrs. Ozelle Sanders Johnson, whose example of Christian faith, focus, and action are the foundation on which I stand; my wonderful sister, Rebecca and her beautiful daughter Alona, whom I miss so deeply; my lovely nieces, Nicolle and Rechelle, and handsome grandnephews Ivan and Aaron, who have been and are always there to cheer me on. To my extended Johnson, Sanders, Shuford, and White family network of grandparents, aunts, uncles, cousins, and in-laws, living and deceased, I acknowledge you also as being the wind beneath my wings.

Contents

Preface

An age-old question in academia of whether leaders are born or made begs the question, "Can leadership be taught?" Those who study the field of leadership often say, "You may not be able to teach it, but it can be learned."

My view is that it is irrelevant whether a person is born a leader or made a leader, is taught leadership or learns leadership. What is relevant is that development and training continue with speed and diligence to provide lessons and opportunities that challenge us all to become leaders and professionals of excellence.

The world desperately needs faithful men and women who will embrace and nurture the principles, philosophies, skills, traits, and behaviors that will enable them to improve their lives and their organizations. With passion, compassion, commitment, and dedication, these men and women will use their gifts and talents ultimately to improve society as a whole.

Belinda Johnson White, PhD
Atlanta, Georgia
September 2016

Introduction

With the hundreds of books and textbooks published on the subject of leadership development, you may be asking, "Why another one?" To that question, I answer, "Because there is not a book that blends into one whole the what, when, how, and why of leadership *and* professional development for emerging leaders *and* shares the secrets of executive-level leadership." This gap is filled in my book through the introduction of my leadership model, which I named the Johnson White Leadership Model (JWLM).

This book is intended for leadership and professional development courses at the secondary, undergraduate, and graduate levels of schools. It is suitable for curricular and co-curricular courses, workshops, and seminars. This book also meets the needs of profit and nonprofit companies and organizations to assist them in maintaining their competitive advantage within their industry through the intentional leadership and professional development of their employees at all levels of the organization and/or clients.

Goals

The overarching goal of this book is to build leaders whose focus and action will result in the great leadership needed to address twenty-first-century issues and challenges. Now, more than in any other time in history, effective leaders will have to master four hallmarks of leadership and professionalism: relationships built on integrity; work grounded in excellence; service that meets the needs of local, regional, national, and international customers; and a commitment to the resolution of social issues and the protection of our global resources through outcomes that result in the betterment of all stakeholders and humankind.

I prayerfully trust that this book will accomplish my goal of building twenty-first-century global leaders through *"motiva-cation."* Motiva-cation is a term I coined that represents a blend of motivation and education that I seek to accomplish and inspire through the pages of this book.

Organization

The book is organized around the Johnson White Leadership Model (JWLM). The JWLM is developed from my research conducted over the more than twenty years I have served as a leadership professor at Morehouse College. During this time, I developed and taught a core business course entitled Bus 321 Leadership and Professional Development (LPD). The JWLM was created as a result of the class, which has been taken by more than three thousand Morehouse business students.

Part I explains JWLM Module 1, "FOCUS," which consists of the *intrapersonal* TASKBs (traits, abilities, skills, knowledge, and behaviors) and principles needed for personal leadership, a prerequisite to public leadership.

Part II explains JWLM Module 2, "ACTION," which consists of the *interpersonal* TASKBs and competencies needed for public leadership.

Part III explains JWLM Module 3, "Great Leadership." Great Leadership discusses the overarching goal of the JWLM—to build twenty-first-century leaders who view leadership as "an influence process between team members (leaders and followers) resulting in the attainment of group goals for the betterment of the group, the organization, and/or society as a whole."

Overview of the Johnson White Leadership Model

For leaders to get results, they need all three kinds of
focus. Inner focus attunes us to our intuitions, guiding
values, and better decisions. Other focus smooths our
connections to the people in our lives. Outer focus lets
us navigate in the larger world. A leader tuned out of
his or her internal world will be rudderless; one blind to the
world of others will be clueless; those indifferent to the larger
systems within which they operate will be blindsided.

----Daniel Goleman, FOCUS

Daniel Goleman is most widely known in leadership development
circles for his 1995 book *Emotional Intelligence: Why It Can Matter
More Than IQ.* Approximately two decades later, he has written
another book, which is even more groundbreaking. The book is
FOCUS: The Hidden Driver of Excellence.

In *FOCUS,* Goleman supports the premise of my leadership
model, which is the absolute necessity for effective leaders to be
focused in three areas: inner focus, other focus, and outer focus,
which is also defined as a world-systems focus. The Johnson White
Leadership Model, "FOCUS in ACTION Is Great Leadership," concurs
with Goleman's inner, other, and outer view (Figure Overview 1.
JWLM Summary).

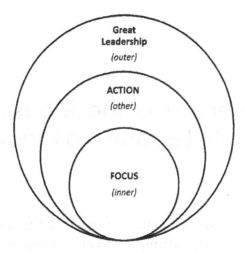

Figure Overview 1. JWLM Summary

JWLM Modules

The JWLM consists of three modules. The first module, *FOCUS*, targets the development of *intrapersonal* skills through five principles: find your power source, open your internal systems, connect to external systems, understand the big picture, and sell yourself as excellence.

The second module, *ACTION*, targets the development of *interpersonal* skills through five competencies: awesome professionalism, courageous character, tenacious inclusion, optimal service, and noble leadership.

The third and final module, *Great Leadership*, presents the overarching goal of the JWLM, targeting development of an emerging leader's worldview toward twenty-first-century leadership, which the JWLM defines as "an influence process between team members (leaders and followers) resulting in the attainment of group goals for the betterment of the group, the organization, and/or society as a whole." The ability to deliver great leadership is based on the leader's adoption of FOCUS principles and mastery of ACTION competencies.

The JWLM is based on both the theory and practice of effective leadership and professionalism. Therefore, the five principles of

FOCUS and the five competencies of ACTION are collectively referred to as the "ten tenets of leadership and professional excellence." Webster defines tenet as "a principle, belief, or doctrine generally held to be true; *especially* one held in common by members of an organization, movement, or profession." The central goal of the JWLM is to develop students prepared to excel as leaders in the twenty-first-century global-leadership process by outlining tenets of leadership and professional excellence.

Researchers Hughes, Ginnett, and Curphy created a straightforward, comprehensive definition of leadership that takes into account the art and science aspects of leadership by defining it as "the process of influencing an organized group toward accomplishing its goals." This definition of leadership reminds us that leadership in and of itself is a neutral process; it could apply to the work of a government leader, pastor, corporate leader, elected official, community organizer, or leader of a band of armed robbers.

Leadership that results in humanity at its best, such as the goal of the JWLM, must be intentional in its purpose to accomplish something positive, intentionality grounded in moral values such as espoused in the 1995 article "Universal Human Values: Finding an Ethical Common Ground" by Rushworth Kidder.

Kidder's article shared the outcome of a study in which two dozen "men and women of conscience" were interviewed. The purpose of the interviews was to find the moral glue that will bind us together in the twenty-first century. "In our age of global interdependence, can there be a global code of ethics; a common core of values in the world?" The men and women interviewed were viewed as ethical thought leaders within their different cultures—a kind of ethical standard-bearer.

The eight values that emerged from their interviews as the core of moral values are as follows: love, truthfulness, fairness, freedom, unity, tolerance, responsibility, and respect for life. To help us better understand the role of these values in leadership effectiveness and outcomes, I present eight leaders of the twentieth century. As you read the short bio of each leader's life accomplishments, ask yourself whether the leader's actions demonstrated positive leadership (connection to the eight moral values) or negative leadership (disconnection to the eight moral values). Does your assessment agree with my assessment?

In politics, compare Winston Churchill, prime minister of the United Kingdom, and Adolf Hitler, chancellor of Germany. Churchill led Britain to victory against the Axis powers (Nazi Germany, Fascist Italy, and Imperial Japan) in World War II from 1939 to 1945. Churchill was noted for his speeches, which became a great inspiration to the British people and embattled Allied forces of Great Britain, the Soviet Union, and the United States. Hitler was the leader of the Nazi Party of Germany from 1933 to 1945. From 1939 to 1945, the Nazi military systematically killed somewhere between eleven and fourteen million people, including about six million Jews, in concentration camps, ghettos, and mass executions (the Holocaust).

- o Assessment: Winston Churchill, Positive Leadership; Adolf Hitler, Negative Leadership

In the realm of social justice, compare Rev. Dr. Martin Luther King Jr., Baptist minister and leader in the American civil rights movement, and George Wallace, four-term governor of Alabama in the 1960s, 1970s, and 1980s. In 1964, at thirty-five years of age, Dr. King became the youngest person to receive the Nobel Peace Prize for his work to end segregation and racial discrimination through civil disobedience and other nonviolent means. Governor Wallace, supporter of pro-segregation attitudes, was a symbol of bigotry during the American desegregation period. To stop desegregation by the enrollment of black students, he stood in front of doors at the University of Alabama in 1963.

- o Assessment: Dr. Martin Luther King Jr., Positive Leadership; George Wallace, Negative Leadership

In religion, compare Rev. Billy Graham, evangelist, evangelical Christian, and spiritual adviser to multiple American presidents and Jim Jones, founder and leader of the Peoples Temple, a religious movement and cult. Rev. Graham preached in person to more people around the world than anyone who has ever lived. As of 1993, more than 2.5 million people had stepped forward at his crusades to "accept Jesus Christ as their personal savior." As of 2002, Graham's lifetime audience, including radio and television broadcasts, topped two billion. In November 1978, Jones led one of the largest mass murder-suicides in history, perhaps the largest in more than 1,900 years, and the largest mass murder-suicide of United States citizens, when more than nine hundred of his followers died from cyanide poisoning in Guyana.

- o Assessment: Rev. Billy Graham, Positive Leadership; Jim Jones, Negative Leadership

In business, compare Bill Gates, American business magnate, philanthropist, investor, and one of the world's richest persons, and Ken Lay, CEO and chairman of Enron Corporation. Bill Gates is noted as the creator of the personal computer revolution. He is admired by many but also cited for anticompetitive business tactics. In the later stages of his career, he pursues philanthropic endeavors. Ken Lay is best known for his role in the widely reported corruption scandal that led to the downfall of the Enron Corporation. Lay and Enron have become synonymous with corporate abuse and accounting fraud.

- o Assessment: Bill Gates, Positive Leadership; Ken Lay, Negative Leadership

I trust your assessment for each leader agreed with mine. Humanity at its best is a fitting description for the positive leadership figures, and humanity at its worst appropriately describes the behaviors and/or results of negative leadership figures. The actions of the leaders (Winston Churchill, Martin Luther King, Billy Graham, and Bill Gates) I assessed as demonstrating positive leadership held true to Kidder's list of universal values: love, truthfulness, fairness, freedom, unity, tolerance, responsibility, and respect for life. The actions of the leaders (Adolf Hitler, George Wallace, Jim Jones, and Ken Lay) I assessed as demonstrating negative leadership did not. The goal of this book is to help build leaders whose legacies will be classified as positive.

JWLM Skill Sets

Through research and practice, it is commonly accepted that at the core of effective leadership are a set of competencies, requisite or adequate abilities or qualities, which are manifest through a leader's traits, abilities, skills, knowledge, and behaviors. The use of knowledge, skills, and abilities (KSAs) is prevalent in job postings to indicate the work behaviors desired in the individual an organization is looking to hire for a particular position. However, leadership research and practice adds to KSAs desired traits and behaviors for leader effectiveness (see chapter 10), which dictate a need for the inclusion of traits and behaviors as distinct components of a leadership development model.

Traits refer to a variety of individual attributes, including aspects of personality, temperament, needs, motives, and values. They form the foundation for skills and behaviors. Skills refer to the ability to do something in an effective manner. Behaviors center on what a person does. Knowledge is the circumstance or condition of apprehending truth or fact through reasoning. Along with experience, knowledge bridges behaviors and skills to our foundational attributes. The foundational attributes are difficult to change and predispose a leader to act in a certain, and usually distinctive, way.

The JWLM uses the term TASKBs (traits, abilities, skills, knowledge, and behaviors) to collectively represent all of these characteristics. The TASKBs are divided into three skill sets needed for effective leadership: intrapersonal, interpersonal, and leadership. *Intra*personal relates to the internal aspects of a person. Possessing *intra*personal skills means access to one's own feelings, one's range of affects or emotions with the capacity instantly to effect discriminations among these feelings and, eventually, to label them, decode them, and draw upon them as a means of understanding and guiding one's behavior. Possessing *inter*personal skills means having the ability to notice and make distinctions among other individuals and in particular, among their moods, temperaments, motivations, and intentions in order to build meaningful relationships. Possessing *leadership* skills enables one to motivate and inspire a team with the vision of better, and through artful communications, influence the team to achieve great goals.

Regardless of their field or industry, leaders need to master intrapersonal, interpersonal, and leadership skills in order to be effective. A fourth set of skills necessary for effective leadership is technical skills. Technical skills are primarily concerned with things in regard to knowledge in conducting a specialized activity. Because the JWLM is designed as a leadership and professional development model that can be used as a universal framework for leadership development regardless of one's occupation or field of study, it does not cover the development of specific technical skills.

Many researchers feel the most important of these four skill sets for effective leadership are intrapersonal (private principles) and interpersonal (public competencies) and agree they are the most difficult to effect. This may explain why individuals who are solid performers in the area of technical skills find themselves challenged to reach executive levels of the organization.

Research conducted by Hughes, Ginnett, and Curphy in the area of managerial derailment—whereby individuals who were on the fast track but have had their careers derailed—show that these individuals exhibited one or more behavioral patterns not evident in the high-potential persons who succeeded. Of the four derailment themes identified, the number one was "problems with interpersonal relationships." The other three themes were failure to meet business objectives, the inability to build and lead a team, and the inability to develop or adapt.

It seems reasonable to conclude that excellence in intrapersonal skills precedes the ability to excel in interpersonal relationships, which in turn precedes the ability to excel in leadership. Therefore, the modules are presented in that order: first, the *intra*personal skills module, FOCUS, followed by the *inter*personal skills module, ACTION, and lastly the Great Leadership module.

Developing and sharpening your intrapersonal skills via FOCUS will assist you in respecting, submitting, and obeying authority, even when it's uncomfortable. Developing and sharpening your interpersonal and leadership skills via ACTION will assist you in being the authority and gaining support from others to overturn immoral authority. The execution of FOCUS *and* ACTION results in an outcome of Great Leadership—a change for the betterment of all.

A pictorial representation of the JWLM is found in Figure Overview 2. JWLM Components.

The Johnson White Leadership Model

"FOCUS in ACTION is Great Leadership"

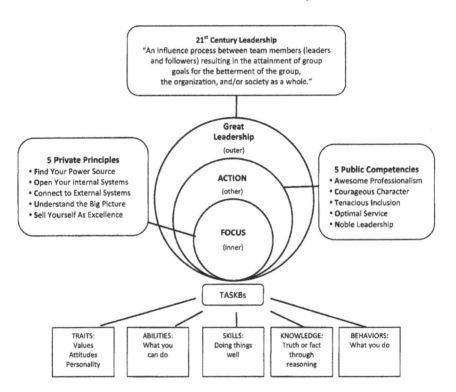

Figure Overview 2. JWLM Components

The Johnson White Leadership Model

Module 1 FOCUS

Introduction

Focus entails being single-minded in the pursuit of a goal,
along with an obsessive attention to the details of the task at
hand. Having focus means being able to set priorities and
recognize new assets while filtering out any and all diversions.

—Price M. Cobbs and Judith L. Turnock,
Cracking the Corporate Code

The first module of the JWLM identifies the intrapersonal skills
needed for effective twenty-first-century leadership (Figure
Module 1. JWLM Summary). These skills are presented as FOCUS—a
mnemonic that serves a dual purpose. First, FOCUS aides in the
memory retrieval of the multiplicity of information that comprises
*intra*personal TASKBs. Secondly, the meaning of the word focus
succinctly defines the essence of success in the building of
intrapersonal skills for effective leadership and professionalism—
intentional intensity. Just as high-level athletes train for years to
perfect the smallest aspects of their performances and synchronize
their emotional, mental, physical, and spiritual states into a whole
in order to achieve success on the playing field, effective leaders
must do the same.

Figure Module 1. JWLM Summary

Building Intrapersonal Skills: FOCUS

In *On Becoming a Leader,* Warren Bennis—master practitioner, researcher, theoretician, and prolific author in the area of leadership—shares the advice top executives said they would give younger executives. Three basic themes came from their responses: take advantage of every opportunity, aggressively search for meaning, and know yourself.

Developing the skills identified by Bennis takes concentrated effort, commitment, and dedication to the task at hand—in other words *focus.* Practitioners and researchers agree that focus is a critical component for leadership success. FOCUS was chosen as the name of the intrapersonal skills module of the JWLM. It expands into a mnemonic to assist students in recalling, retrieving, and using the intrapersonal skills of effective leaders.

FOCUS identifies five key *intrapersonal* skill areas, also called principles or tenets, needed for effective leadership. The five FOCUS principles are as follows:

#1. Find your power source.

Having a support system from which you draw strength and encouragement, including faith/spirituality, fitness, finances, freedom, future, family, friends, forgiveness, forgetting, freedom, failure, and fun.

#2. Open your internal systems.

Knowing one's values, attitudes, personality, and principles; strengths and weaknesses; life purpose, calling, mission, and vision; setting and achieving goals based on accurate, reflective self-assessment; emotional intelligence.

#3. Connect to external systems.

Building and sustaining networks consisting of a personal board of directors comprised of sponsors, mentors, life coaches, and advisors; mastermind groups and brain trusts; participation in civic organizations, nonprofit board memberships.

#4. Understand the big picture.

Acquiring a sensitivity and awareness of environmental, political, regulatory, societal, technological, globalization, and competitive trends and forces that affect all demographic groups of developed and developing economies, local and foreign.

#5. Sell yourself as excellence.

Learning the ABCs of professional presence—appropriate, believable, and credible through appearance, body language, communication, deliverables (work ethic and work product), and etiquette (business and social).

Because successful people have successful habits, make *FOCUS*, both literally and figuratively, a habit in your life. Chapters 1–5 provide you with details about how to instill the FOCUS principles into your life.

CHAPTER 1

Find Your Power Source

This is the single most powerful investment we can ever
make in life—investment in ourselves, in the only instrument
we have with which to deal with life and to contribute.
We are the instruments of our own performance, and to
be effective, we need to recognize the importance
of taking time regularly to sharpen the saw in all four
[physical, mental, social/emotional, and spiritual] ways.

—Stephen Covey, *The 7 Habits of Highly Effective People*

The first principle of the FOCUS module of intrapersonal skills development centers on keeping the leader whole and sane. Wholeness and balance in life provide the leader with the power and support to identify the tasks and complete the work he or she is called to do as a leader and a professional in four circles of influence: home, workplace, community, and place of worship (Figure Chapter 1-1. Four Circles of Influence).

Figure Chapter 1-1. Four Circles of Influence

One of the most challenging aspects of personal leadership is being the same person in all four circles. The term "code switching" is used to describe a way of doing and being aimed at justifying the use of different behaviors depending on the situation.

When choosing code switching as a leadership and professionalism strategy, ensure that what does not get switched is your strict adherence to a personal set of standards, higher than the norm, that you refuse to violate or compromise. Your standards should be based on Kidder's universal, common core of moral values of love, truthfulness, fairness, freedom, unity, tolerance, responsibility, and respect for life.

A Winning Support System: The "F" Series

A support system from which you can draw strength and encouragement is a must for the twenty-first-century global leader. A strong support system, at the minimum, should cover the basics of human existence, starting with self-preservation in the areas of spiritual, physical, personal choice, finances, and hope. Your support system must also include significant relationships with family and friends along with the preservation of relationships with others and self through forgiveness and forgetting. And lastly, your support system must provide sanctuaries that allow you to live a fulfilled life that includes safe passage in times of fun as well as failure.

Components of a Winning Support System, Level 1: Self-Preservation

One's survival is a top priority in life for any individual. For the emerging leader, this means getting your house in order! Your house must have a strong foundation built on faith, steel beams of personal fitness, open windows of freedom, hardwood floors of financial stability, and doors that lead to a successful future.

Faith allows human beings to find personal strength through a belief in a higher power or spiritual connection. A spiritual center gives your life purpose and meaning, and it establishes a moral compass when faced with ethical dilemmas. A moral compass always points north to Kidder's universal, common core of moral values—love, truthfulness, fairness, freedom, unity, tolerance, responsibility, and respect for life.

Staying healthy is a dire necessity for leaders. Mental and physical *fitness* through exercise, smart eating, adequate sleep, and when prescribed, use of doctor-approved medication is work that is to be done on a daily basis. Eliminating drugs and tobacco and alcohol moderation are keys to healthy living and longevity along with regular medical checkups from physicians, dentists, and other health-care professionals.

The importance of guarding and maintaining one's *freedom* cannot be overemphasized. You have voice and choice. Be proactive in the construction of your life. Know the difference between a victim mentality (reacting to what others do and say to you) and a victor mentality (proactively directing your own life); always operate with a victor mentality. Never react to anyone else's words or actions in such a way that causes you to lose your composure. Stay calm and, if necessary, respond with respect.

Money will not buy you happiness, but the lack of money will cause you pain. Strive to keep your *finances* and spending habits under control. Make budgeting your BFF! Your credit score will be an asset or a liability. In our capitalistic society, credit is a power tool; it is the difference between the haves and the have-nots. Good credit means the ability to have the good things in life.

The *future* will come, and things will be better. It is the hope in a better tomorrow that keeps us sane and gives life meaning. With hope, all things are possible; without hope, nothing is. Dream big, think big, do big, be big. And let the spirit of hope in the future drive you to the realization of your self-defined big.

Components of a Winning Support System, Level 2: Relationship Preservation

No man is an island. Life is meant to be enjoyed with, through, and because of family, friends, forgiveness, and forgetting.

Your primary and extended *family* members, including parents, siblings, grandparents, spouses, children, aunts, uncles, cousins, nieces, nephews, and in-laws can offer a place of unconditional love and support. Enjoy their company.

Develop close relationships with a select group of *friends* who serve as your inner circle of supportive comrades. Choose friends who share your same goals and aspirations. If you hang out with five broke friends, you stand a good chance of becoming number six.

Stop feeling angry or resentful toward someone for an offense, flaw, or mistake. Emotionally holding onto pain from the past will significantly decrease your ability to move on in life and achieve the success and significance that is waiting for you. *Forgiveness* is not for others; it's for you. Forgiveness allows you to release your heart from the pain caused by toxic encounters. Let go of the past and focus on your future: forgive and forget!

Train your mind to not dwell on toxic encounters. Choose not to remember. *Forgetting* is an act of will that releases your mind from the oppression caused by others. Learn quickly from the experience, file it immediately in your "no return, no repeat" mental folder, and move on!

Components of a Winning Support System,
Level 3: Life Happens!

You only live once, and if you do it right, once is enough! Enjoy every moment as you experience fulfillment, failure, and fun.

You make a living by what you do (success); you make a life by those you touch (significance). *Fulfillment* comes through both. Make it your goal to achieve both success and significance in your life.

Failure is too often viewed as the uncle in the family who no one wants to acknowledge as part of the family. It's time to let Uncle Failure out of the locked room. So it didn't work out "this time" as you had planned. Stuff happens. View every experience as moving you one step closer to your ultimate life purpose, providing you more knowledge and wisdom to add to the understanding of your existence. When you fall down, "keep calm, get up, and carry on!"

We can all agree that *fun* is the favorite uncle in the family. Uncle Fun reminds us to stop and smell the roses. Let's stop taking ourselves so seriously; lighten up and enjoy a good laugh! Have fun, be happy, and share your happiness with others.

While all twelve "Fs" in principle 1 ("Find Your Power Source") are critical components of a leader's foundation, the interaction of the five factors that comprise Level 1 Self-Preservation—faith, fitness, finances, freedom, and future—deserves additional discussion.

There is an interdependent relationship between our faith, fitness, finances, freedom, and future. Our faith is our connection to our Creator, who has given us a purpose and calling for our lives. The Creator also designed our miraculous bodies, made up of miles of blood vessels, coordinated muscles, and life-sustaining organs. Our bodies give us ways to experience the beauty of the world through the human senses of sight, touch, smell, taste, and hearing. It is through our complex brain and heart system that we make sense of the world and experience the beauty of our joyful emotions as well as the hurt of an occasional pain. Our bodies are a gift from God that allow us to interact with the world and other people and honor him by living out our purpose. When we neglect and misuse our bodies, we limit our ability to live a life that honors our faith.

The same is true regarding our finances. The misuse of our finances through overindulgence, poor money-management habits, and wasteful spending results in the inability to take care of our obligations and responsibilities. These behaviors bring undue stress to our physical, emotional, and mental states, further hindering our ability to carry out our life purpose.

Choosing to live within the moral and ethical statutes of society protects our freedom, allowing us the ability to claim our civil rights, which include nondiscrimination in employment, financial transactions, housing, and voting; the liberty to run and serve in an elected office; and potentially safeguards us from legal adversities. (My discussion here in no way attempts to overlook or trivialize the many disparities in society and the criminal-justice system. They are real and should not be minimized. Also real is the need for consistent moral and ethical decision making in all of our daily lives, a level of personal responsibility to which our Creator will hold us all accountable.)

The degree to which we connect our faith to our fitness, finances, and freedom, ensuring we remain whole and healthy, directly impacts our future. One's future is designed to be a place where you are enjoying the relationships of family and friends, walking in your calling, living out your purpose, and honoring your Creator, the source of your faith. This is the circle of life, starting and ending with your faith.

As emerging leaders from all walks of life enter the twenty-first century with a wealth of opportunities at their disposal, the unfortunate reality that the ugliness of humanity's past remains ever present must also be addressed. Economic, racial, ethnicity, gender, and lifestyle divisions continue to plague American society. Emerging leaders must be able to hold on when the worst is happening in life. It is for this reason that the JWLM begins with "finding your power source."

Chapter Summary

This chapter covers the first principle of the FOCUS intrapersonal skills module ("Find Your Power Source"). Knowing, developing, and using your power source is step one in becoming an effective leader. Your power source is where you will derive your strength to accomplish the tasks and manage the stress of leadership in order to achieve the goals of the people and organizations you serve. It is similar to the aircraft-survival instruction: "In case of an emergency, place the airbag over your mouth and nose first before attempting to help others." Finding, developing, and using your power source first enables you to help others.

Twelve areas are identified as sources of power and comprise the "F" series: faith, fitness, finances, freedom, future, family, friends, forgiveness, forgetting, fulfillment, failure, and fun. Your journey to becoming a twenty-first-century global leader is made smoother when you diligently seek, *find* (and use) *your power source*.

Leadership and Professional Development Exercises

Key Terms

- circles of influence
- the "F" series
- winning support system

Questions to Discuss

1. What is the first principle of the FOCUS module?
2. What is the role of a winning support system in a leader's life?
3. What is the relationship between the five components (faith, fitness, finances, freedom, and future) that comprise Level 1: Self-Preservation?
4. What is the relationship between the four components (family, friends, forgiveness, and forgetting) that comprise Level 2: Relationship Preservation?

5. What is the relationship between the three components (fulfillment, failure, and fun) that comprise Level 3: Life Happens?

Questions to Consider

1. Do you have a winning support system? Are all twelve components of FOCUS principle 1 operating in your life?
2. Which components of the "F" series are active in your life? What are the three most important components for you?
3. Great leaders throughout history have relied on strong faith/spirituality as the foundation from which they were able to fulfill their life purpose. Strong faith develops over time through intentional focus on spiritual disciplines. Do you regularly practice the spiritual disciplines of your faith, i.e., prayer, fasting, scripture reading and memorization, meditation, worship, hospitality, and service? If not, which three will you commit to regularly practicing today?
4. The JWLM starts with faith and is built on the premise that "effectiveness in every other aspect of the model and one's life relates back to one's faith." Do you agree or disagree with the premise? Why or why not?
5. What will you stop doing today because it hinders your ability to effectively use your power source? What will you intentionally start doing today so that you can focus on finding your power source?

Books to Stimulate Your Mind

- The religious text of your faith. Examples include Judaism, the *Hebrew Bible*; Christianity, the *Christian Bible*; Islam, the *Quran*; Mormonism, The *Christian Bible* and *Book of Mormon*
- *The Wonderful Wizard of Oz* by L. Frank Baum (1900)
- *The Alchemist* by Paul Coelho (1988)

CHAPTER 2

Open Your Internal Systems

Successful leaders are those who can access
and then express their true selves.

—Warren Bennis, *On Becoming a Leader*

When asked what I do for a living, I proudly say I am a professor in the Department of Business at Morehouse College. The next question is always, "What do you teach?" My response, of course, is leadership and professional development. The response to my response, nine out of ten times is, "Oh, you teach the 'soft' skills." I am then left to wonder what my conversation partner is thinking. Is he or she mentally classifying my teaching expertise as strategically significant or possibly insignificant? Is he or she astutely aware of the importance of mastering *soft* skills? Does he or she know that *soft* skills provide a leader with knowledge in the art and science of flexibility in order to adapt effectively and skillfully in order to lead the *people* of the organization through change? Or is the comment a reflection of a mental dismissal of the critical role of self-knowledge, emotions, and subjectivity in the twenty-first-century organizational maze?

Manfred Kets De Vries, author of *The Leadership Mystique*, notes that "soft" matters can actually be "hard," and that soft matters can kill a career. Kets De Vries, whose professional training is in management and clinical psychology, states that his main objective in studying leadership is to bring the *person* back into the organization. From his research on organizational behavior, Kets De Vries concludes that companies possess a conspicuous neglect of the people who are the principal actors in their organizations. Often they give structures and systems precedence over people, operating under the mantra of "what you can't see doesn't exist." Because people are complex and hard to change, it becomes easier to deal with structures and systems than with people. De Vries writes, "As I sometimes like to say, it's easier to change *people* than to *change* people."

Kets De Vries's work provides the backdrop and rationale that supports the second principle in the FOCUS module of intrapersonal skills ("Open Your Internal Systems"). He demonstrates that an individual's leadership style, which is a synthesis of the various roles that he or she chooses to adopt, is a complex outcome of the interplay of the person's inner theater. One's inner theater is where core issues of cognition, affect, and behavior (which are influenced by personality traits and temperament) exist and the competencies that the person develops over the course of the life span.

From his clinical psychology background, Kets De Vries works from numerous behavior premises that are based in two actualities: all human behavior, no matter how irrational it appears, has a rationale, and we're all products of our past.

Behavior that appears irrational to an observer may be rational to the doer since it may exist outside of the doer's awareness, serving as a defensive structure. Kets De Vries describes a character disorder as a secret you don't know you're keeping in that it operates outside consciousness. Examples of these "character disorders" found in the workplace include personality types and characteristic behaviors such as narcissistic (grandiosity), paranoid (distrustful), obsessive-compulsive (overly conscientious), dependent (submissive), depressive (pessimistic), borderline (impulsive and unstable), avoidant (socially insecure), schizoid (detached and reclusive), antisocial (unreliable), sadist (abrasive behavior), masochistic (self-sacrificing), and passive-aggressive (say yes, mean no, don't act). In order to change this type of behavior, one must start with awareness resulting from intentional self-reflection and feedback.

We are all a direct result of our early environment modified by our genetic endowment. Understanding our past and its connection to who we are in the present allows us to be more aware of things that happen around us resulting in an extra layer of intelligence—an "emotional intelligence." The three primary components of emotional intelligence are getting to know our own emotions, learning to manage these emotions, and learning to recognize and deal with the emotions of others. Research has shown that people who possess emotional intelligence are more effective at motivating themselves and others; they also do better in leadership positions because they are better equipped to track down the rationality behind irrational behavior.

Understanding Your Internal Systems

Our internal systems are the source of our thoughts, words, and actions. These internal systems are a conglomeration of many things, including our values, attitudes, personalities, and principles. Because twenty-first-century global leaders will be responsible for taking culturally diverse organizations and groups to higher levels of "being and doing," it is imperative that these leaders have a clear understanding of who they are based on their values, attitudes, personalities, and principles, which are then represented as a whole through character. (Character is one of the competencies of the ACTION module of the JWLM and is discussed in more detail in chapter 7).

Twenty-first-century global leaders must intentionally seek to understand who they are. The next step is making an honest assessment of that reality to determine if who they are will allow them to be effective. Following an accurate self-assessment, leaders must measure their "state of being and doing" against acceptable moral and ethical ways of being and doing. Finally, they must seek ways to make the necessary changes and adjustments to their values, attitudes, principles, personalities, and ultimately their character in order to be effective. The twenty-first-century leader, when faced with situations outside his or her personal comfort zone, will not be able to operate from the paradigm of "that's just the way I am," and refuse to make decisions that are ethically and morally sound in a world of diverse people and cultures.

Values

Values play an important role in the lives of leaders because they affect how leaders lead. The fundamental beliefs an individual considers to be important are relatively stable over time and have an impact on attitudes and behaviors. These values represent long-lasting personal views about what is worthwhile and desirable, right and wrong, good and bad.

Values can be thought of in terms of instrumental and terminal. Instrumental values are beliefs about the types of behaviors that are appropriate for reaching goals, including being helpful to others, being honest, or exhibiting courage. These values can be viewed as ways and means by which desired goals or outcomes are realized. Terminal values, also referred to as *end values*, are beliefs about the kinds of goals or outcomes that are worth trying to pursue, including security, a comfortable life, good health, and freedom. Our values are generally well established by early adulthood and can also change throughout life.

Everyone possesses instrumental and terminal values, but people differ in the way they prioritize the values. Part of the difference is based on culture. However, as mentioned in the introduction, researchers have identified eight universal values that transcend cultures. These values according to Kidder are love, truthfulness, fairness, freedom, unity, tolerance, responsibility, and respect for life.

Attitudes

Attitudes are positive or negative feelings about people, things, and issues. They affect what we say, how we think, and how we act as evidenced through our performances, behaviors, and expectations. They often result in biases, prejudices, and a willingness to accept or reject stereotypes. Our attitudes impact how we feel about ourselves and others.

Our attitudes toward ourselves are referred to as "self-concept" and can be positive or negative. People who have a positive view of themselves as capable tend to possess the self-confidence trait. If you think you can, you can. People who have a negative view of themselves tend to possess the self-doubt trait. If you think you can't, you can't. Self-efficacy is a related concept and is the belief in your own capability to perform in a specific situation.

A manager's attitude toward others in the workplace can be described as Theory X and Theory Y Management Styles. Theory X attitudes hold that employees dislike work and must be closely supervised in order to do their work. Theory Y attitudes hold that employees like to work and do not need to be closely supervised in order to do their work.

The Pygmalion effect is a theory proposing that leaders' attitudes toward and expectations of followers, and their treatment of them, explain and predict followers' behavior and performance. The theory proposes that followers' behavior mirror the attitudes and expectations of the leader. If the leader's attitude and expectations of the follower is high, the behavior and performance will be high and vice versa.

Personality

The term *personality* is often used with two different meanings. One meaning refers to the impression a person makes on others, emphasizing the person's social reputation, reflecting not only a description but also an evaluation of the person in the eyes of others. (This meaning is associated with the concept of personal branding and is also discussed in chapter 7.) Our discussion here will cover the second meaning of personality, emphasizing the underlying, unseen structures and processes inside a person that explains why we behave as we do.

An understanding of what constitutes personality requires an understanding of the concept of traits. Lussier and Achua define traits as distinguishing personal characteristics and personality as a combination of traits that classify an individual's behavior. Because there are literally hundreds of personality traits, research efforts have organized them into a smaller number of broadly defined categories. A popular model is the "Big Five Model of Personality," which categorizes traits into the dimensions of openness to experience, conscientiousness, extraversion, agreeableness, and neuroticism, also referred to as adjustment.

The openness to experience personality dimension consists of those traits related to being willing to change and try new things. The openness to experience continuum ranges from a high of seeking change and trying new things (curious, inquisitive, liberal, impractical, open-minded, learning oriented) to a low of avoiding change and new things (practical, conservative, traditional, efficient).

The conscientiousness personality dimension includes traits related to achievement. Its continuum ranges from a high of being responsible/dependable (on time, prepared, organized) to a low of being irresponsible/undependable (spontaneous, impulsive, fickle, unconcerned with deadlines). Additional traits associated with high conscientiousness are disciplined, cautious, stubborn, personal integrity, need for achievement, resilient, credibility, and conformity. Conscientious people pride themselves in a strong work ethic/habits and are willing to put in the extra time and effort to accomplish goals and achieve success.

The extraversion personality dimension includes leadership and assertiveness traits. Also called dominance and surgency, people strong in extraversion want to be in charge. Dominant behavior ranges from having a strong interest in getting ahead and leading to competing and influencing. People weak in extraversion are comfortable being followers, not competing, and not influencing. Extraversion as a dimension consists of traits that range from the high end—extravert behavior, including being outgoing and enjoying meeting new people—to introverted behavior such as shyness, the low end of the dimension.

In contrast to extraversion behavior to get ahead of others, the agreeableness personality dimension is comprised of traits related to getting along with people. A person on the high end of this dimension is called warm, easygoing, compassionate, friendly, and sociable. A person on the low end of this dimension is called cold, difficult, uncompassionate, unfriendly, and unsociable.

The neuroticism, also known as adjustment, personality dimension includes traits related to emotional stability and is on a continuum between being emotionally stable and unstable. A person who is on the low end of the neuroticism (or high end of adjustment) dimension is considered stable and seen as possessing self-control, being calm under pressure, relaxed, secure, and positive. A person who is on the high end of the neuroticism dimension (or low end of adjustment) is considered unstable and seen as out of control, bad under pressure, nervous, insecure, and negative.

Principles

The last component of our internal systems is principles. People will have a set of personal principles based on their personal values. Effective leaders strive to have their personal principles concurrent with *universal* principles. Whereas values, attitudes, and personality can be made more or less through personal choices, principles cannot. Individuals and organizations ought to be guided and governed by a set of proven principles, having universal application.

Universal principles are natural laws and governing social values that have gradually come through every great society and every responsible civilization over the centuries. They surface in the form of values, ideas, norms, and teachings that uplift, ennoble, fulfill, empower, and inspire people. Kidder's eight universal values—love, truthfulness, fairness, freedom, unity, tolerance, responsibility, and respect for life—can also be classified as universal principles that transcend cultures.

According to Covey, principles are guidelines for human conduct that are proven to have enduring, permanent value. They are fundamental and essentially unarguable because they are self-evident. He states:

> One way to quickly grasp the self-evident nature of principles is to simply consider the absurdity of attempting to live an effective life based on their opposites. I doubt that anyone would seriously consider unfairness, deceit, baseness, uselessness, mediocrity, or degeneration to be a solid foundation for lasting happiness and success. Although people may argue about how these principles are defined, manifested, or achieved, there seems to be an innate consciousness and awareness that they exist.

Covey wrote *Principle-Centered Leadership* (1990) as a follow-up to *The 7 Habits of Highly Effective People* (1989). He found that while people knew the seven habits and wanted to use the seven habits, they were having a hard time breaking their old habits and replacing them with the new habits. They could not escape the pull of the past and recreate themselves to achieve meaningful change in their lives. In *Principle-Centered Leadership*, Covey addressed this issue by stating that lasting solutions to problems resulting in happiness and success must be inside out (versus outside in), principle centered and character based.

Inside out means to start with self—the most inside part of self that includes your paradigms (ways of thinking), character, and motives. Outside-in approaches result in unhappy people who feel victimized and immobilized. They focus on the weaknesses of other people and the circumstances they feel are responsible for their own problem. Covey's position is that, in reality, the problem is not "out there" but "in here."

An inside-out approach to life requires one to educate and obey the conscience—our internal governance structure that senses congruence or disparity with correct principles and guides our behaviors toward them. Obeying the conscience results in one having a sense of stewardship about everything in life, including one's time, talents, money, possessions, relationships, family, and bodies. (This point is in concert with FOCUS principle 1, "Find Your Power Source"). Individuals who obey their conscience use their resources for positive purposes and expect to be held accountable. They return kindness for offense and patience for impatience and strive to bring out the best in other people.

A leader of character and competence operates from the inside out, educating and obeying his or her conscience while being guided by universal principles. The principled-centered leader trusts the people of the organization to do the work of the organization. The need for constant monitoring, evaluating, correcting, or controlling is eliminated because principles are understood and people are empowered to operate based on the principles. As a result, the leader and the people reap the achievement of the organization's goals and vision.

Values, Attitudes, Personality, and Principles: A Prescription for Self-Confidence

If asked to identify one word that could be used to describe the collective intrapersonal TASKBs (traits, abilities, skills, knowledge, and behaviors) needed in order to be an effective leader, I would vote for *self-confidence*. Defined as a feeling of trust in one's abilities, qualities, and judgment, self-confidence is the outer manifestation of a person's values, attitudes, personality, and principles. For this reason, nurturing and protecting the development and growth of our values, attitudes, personality, and principles is critically important for emerging leaders. When self-doubt takes hold, your inner theater can become your enemy.

The result of opening your internal systems is to be fully aware of your "inner theater." Kets De Vries uses this term to describe an individual's leadership style as expressed in his or her core issues of cognition, affect, and behavior (which are influenced by personality traits and temperament), and the competencies that the person develops over the course of his or her life span. By being consciously aware of the "real movie and play" that is taking place in your inner theater, you can proactively grow and develop in the direction of becoming a twenty-first-century global leader whose end goal is success and significance.

One's inner theater can be a murky and even scary place. For some, it consists of hidden traits and attitudes that we may not know are there. For others, it is a place in which we refuse to go such that we do not have to see what is behind the curtains. In either case, an unrealistic view of the play that is happening in your inner theater may cause you to be unavoidably looped and detained in "stagnation station." You will find yourself in stagnation station when your nonproductive habits, destructive behaviors, and/or pathological (unreasonable or unable to control) tendencies are preventing you from achieving your goals and objectives.

Possible reasons to justify your presence in stagnation station include personal preferences (this is just the way I am), cultural preferences (this is just the way "we" do things), ancestral legacy (the ills of hundreds of years of oppression still govern my life), and institutionalized obstacles (the "system" is holding me back). Reason one is a personal choice that you have direct control over. Reasons two, three, and four are examples of Covey's outside-in approach to life. While they may be real, you don't have to choose to allow them to cripple your life, stifling your chances for success and significance.

An inner theater that is playing scenes of self-imposed defeat is not a winning life strategy. It's a play that releases you from your obligations of responsibility and accountability. By making allowances for bad choices, your cycle of failure and lost potential continues. This is the time to engage your power source (FOCUS principle 1) and activate your agency—an inside-out approach.

Remember you have a voice and a choice. Choose a new way through principle-centered self-leadership. Instead of an outside-in view of life, choose an inside-out life view. Create a plan, build a brand, and believe that you can operationalize a new paradigm in your life that leads to success and significance. Leave stagnation station behind and let self-confidence be your ticket to board the JWLM ACTION train (see chapter 6 through chapter 10 for details).

Chapter Summary

The purpose of this chapter is to help you understand the critical importance of self-awareness, self-confidence, and self-identity to your ability to become an effective twenty-first-century global leader. The second principle of the FOCUS module ("Open Your Internal Systems") presents four states of being and doing of which effective leaders are consciously aware.

The four states of being and doing are *values*, defined as constructs representing generalized behaviors or states of affairs that are considered by the individual to be important; *attitudes*, defined as positive or negative feelings about people, things, and issues; *personality*, defined as the underlying, unseen structures and processes inside a person that explain why we behave as we do; and *principles*, defined as natural laws and governing social values that have gradually come through over the centuries to every great society and every responsible civilization.

The three states of being and doing—values, attitudes, and personality—are individualistic in nature and origin. While developed early in life, they can also be changed throughout life. The fourth state of being and doing—principles—is entirely different.

Principles are not individualistic. Principles are natural laws held as enduring and endearing universal social values. Kidder's universal social values—love, truthfulness, fairness, freedom, unity, tolerance, responsibility, and respect for life—have been the foundation on which great peoples have built great societies. Let these eight universal social values become your guiding principles as you *open your internal systems.*

Leadership and Professional Development Exercises

Key Terms

- attitudes
- Big Five Model of Personality
- emotional intelligence

- inner theater
- Inside out versus outside in
- personality
- principles
- self-confidence
- stagnation station
- TASKBs
- values

Questions to Discuss

1. What is the second principle of the FOCUS module?
2. How does a person's *inner theater* affect his or her outlook on life?
3. What is the role of values, attitudes, personality, and principles in the life of a leader?
4. What is the Big Five Model of Personality and what are its dimensions?
5. What is the impact of "stagnation station" on one's ability to achieve personal and professional success?

Questions to Consider

1. What is the relationship between who you are, how you feel, what you think, and what you do? What role does your past play in your present and future thoughts, actions, and feelings?
2. Will your current values, attitudes, personality, and principles support the achievement of your personal and professional goals? If not, what are you willing to do to change?
3. What is your level of self-confidence: low, average, or high? Is it a realistic assessment of your TASKBs? Are you using self-confidence as a strategic tool to accomplish your personal and professional goals? If not, what are you willing to start doing *today* to build a strategically healthy level of self-confidence?

4. Do you believe that having values, attitudes, and personality traits, based on a principled life, honors your faith as well as other components of your winning support system? Why or why not?

5. What will you stop doing today because it hinders your ability to honestly assess your internal systems? What will you intentionally start doing today so that you can focus on opening your internal systems?

Books to Stimulate Your Mind

- *Principle-Centered Leadership* by Stephen Covey (1990)
- *Attitude is Everything for Success* by Keith Harrell (2004)
- *Think and Grow Rich* by Napoleon Hill (1937)
- *Think and Grow Rich: A Black Choice* by Dennis Kimbro and Napoleon Hill (1991)

CHAPTER 3

Connect to External Systems

No matter how ambitious, capable, clear-thinking
competent ... and witty you are, if you don't relate well to
other people, you won't make it. No matter how professionally
competent, financially adept, and physically solid you
are, without an understanding of human nature,
a genuine interest in the people around you, and the
ability to establish personal bonds with them, you
are severely limited in what you can achieve.

—Deborah A. Benton, *Lions Don't Need to Roar*

Displayed prominently in my office are replicas of large ships. Students visiting my office inquire about my affinity to ships. I do enjoy the serenity of the sea, but I have no special attachment to the sea or to ships. As I explain to my students, seeing the ships is a simple reminder to me of the importance of others in the leadership process. Ships, unlike boats, are built to carry a multitude of people. The success of the ship from the start of its voyage to its destination is determined by its skillful leader along with a large capable crew, all connecting to each other for a common cause, which is to safely get the passengers and cargo to the destination. For me, the large ships in my office are visual metaphors of the catalyst for leadership success—relationships! When I glance at my ships, I am reminded that "leadership without relationship is a sinking ship; leadership with relationship is a championship."

Building relationships is one of the most important jobs of the leader. And it is certainly one of the most difficult. As discussed in the previous chapter, human beings are all unique, each with their own set of values, attitudes, and personalities. In organizational settings, Kets De Vries states that when issues occur, it is often easier to change (replace) people than to change (adjust) people. Stephen Covey speaks to the difficult process of changing people by describing the process as "slow is fast and fast is slow" when attempting to change people.

Successful leaders recognize the importance of connecting to a multitude of others and building mutually beneficial networks. Strong, positive, interactions with strangers; deep, abiding relationships with family members, friends, associates, coworkers, and clients; and service to others make living a joy and working a pleasure.

Many people endorse the phrase, "Your network is your net worth." Net worth, defined as the amount assets exceed liabilities, is used in the financial arena to indicate a person's worth based on a monetary value. To associate net worth to your networks suggests that your ability to amass financial wealth is largely dependent upon the people you know and those who know you and are willing to assist you in achieving your goals and objectives. I would like to add, "Use your networks to increase your net worth *and* your net reach." Net reach is defined as the ways in which you can touch the lives of others in a positive manner (see Figure Chapter 3-1. Power of Networks).

There is a Bible story about a poor widow who put two very small copper coins, worth only a fraction of a penny, in the offering. Jesus said, "This poor widow has put more in the treasury than all the others. They gave out of their wealth; but she, out of her poverty, put in everything—all she had to live on" (Mark 12:43–44, NIV). If a poor widow could give out of her poverty, surely we can give out of our abundance—be it time, talents, or treasures—in order to make life better for someone else. Emerging leaders must view net reach as a more important measure of success than net worth since only what you do for others will last.

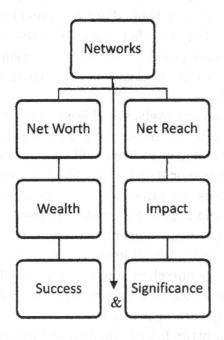

Figure Chapter 3-1. Power of Networks

This chapter will share three big acts of "being and doing" that are foundational in helping you connect and build relationships. Once mastered, they enable you to extend your networks and ultimately your net worth *and* net reach across all dimensions of your personal and professional life. The three big acts of being and doing are: "Be the authentic you, be likeable, be strategic."

Be the "Authentic You"

You were challenged in chapter 2 to carefully examine your values, attitudes, personality, and governing principles. This is who you are. If you were asked to assess yourself in these areas, how would you rate yourself on a scale of 1 to 10 with 1 representing the low end of the scale and 10 representing the high end of the scale? An exercise I have my students complete is to list three traits that they feel best describe them, three traits that other people use to describe them, and three traits that they would like others to use to describe them. The overwhelming choices that students list for all three sections are positive, glowing, and exceptional. Even the student who never talks in class will list extrovert as a trait that best describes him.

Most people see themselves as shining examples of humanity: caring, friendly, and easy to get along with. We claim these traits because we know they most likely will help us achieve our goals and objectives in personal and professional success. If we are not achieving our goals, we often take the "outside-in" approach of self-assessment and assign the problem to the "other." This may make us feel okay for the moment, but it does not move us closer to achieving our goals. We all know we can't change the "other." We can only change ourselves. And that's the good news because you have complete control over yourself, your values, attitudes, personality, and governing principles.

If your values, attitudes, personality, and governing principles are not resulting in personal and professional success, you owe it to yourself to adopt new ones that will lead to your success. It is the you that is achieving success that is the *authentic you.* Don't settle for anything less. Continuously ask, "Is this working for me? Does this action lead to the accomplishment of my goals? And does this action also leave me healthy and whole emotionally, socially, physically, mentally, and spiritually in all four spheres of my influence—home, workplace, community, and place of worship?" If the answer is no to any of these questions, you are not being the authentic you. You must change what you are doing.

The authentic you will attract prosperity, success, health, and happiness by being able to draw others to you with ease and comfort. And to your surprise, the authentic you can do this effortlessly and will enjoy the journey. You cannot achieve personal and professional success alone. Success is achieved with and through others. The journey starts by learning how to be likeable.

Be Likeable

How do you feel about the statement, "People buy from people they like." Or the statement, "People like people who are like them." True? False? Think about making a major purchase. Would you prefer a salesperson who was friendly and helpful or rude and argumentative? Think about going to dinner with a group of people. Would you rather spend your evening with people who you share mutual interests or people who you have nothing in common? My guess is your preference is to have a friendly, helpful salesperson and dinner with people who you can easily relate. Just as this is your preference, so it is for other people. Being likeable is a must for all leaders and professionals. Being likeable is what allows the authentic you to connect to others.

Undoubtedly, the most recognizable name in the genre of how to be likeable and connect to people is Dale Carnegie. Dale Carnegie, born in 1888 to a Missouri farming family, became a salesman and unsuccessful actor before he hit upon the idea of teaching public speaking. In 1936, he literally wrote the book on networking: *How to Win Friends and Influence People*. Carnegie demystified the process of making friends out of strangers and inspired legions of business coaches to carry on his message. His book has been translated into dozens of languages and been sold to millions around the world.

In the early twentieth century, Carnegie discovered research that revealed that even in such technical lines as engineering, about 15 percent of one's financial success is due to one's technical knowledge and about 85 percent is due to skill in human engineering—personality and the ability to lead people. The research showed, Carnegie writes, "the person who has technical knowledge *plus* the ability to express ideas, to assume leadership, and to arouse enthusiasm among people—that person is headed for higher earning power."

Carnegie's *How to Win Friends and Influence People* contains a set of core principles on how to connect with others effectively. Regarding effective ways to handle people, Carnegie says not to criticize, condemn, or complain; instead, give honest, sincere appreciation. If you want people to like you, you must first become genuinely interested in them. "People don't care about how much you know until they know how much you care." You show your interest with a smile as you remember and say a person's name. Be a good listener and encourage others to talk about themselves. Make the other person feel important—and do it sincerely.

A critical connection skill that leaders must develop is winning people over to your way of thinking. Engaging in an argument with someone is the fastest way to lose a person to your way of thinking. Carnegie cautions that the only way to get the best of an argument is to avoid it. Show respect for the other person's opinions and never say, "You're wrong." However if you are wrong, admit it quickly and emphatically. Always let the other person do a great deal of the talking and get the other person saying, "yes, yes" immediately. A surefire way to win someone over to your way of thinking is to let the other person feel that the idea is his or hers.

Another connection skill leaders must develop is being able to change people without offending or stirring up resentment. In order to change others' attitudes and behaviors, begin with praise and honest appreciation. Call attention to people's mistakes indirectly by talking about your own mistakes before criticizing the other person. Ask questions instead of giving direct orders and let the other person retain respect and avoid humiliation. Praise the slightest improvement—and every improvement. Encourage the other person and give the person a fine reputation to live up to. Your goal is to make the other person happy about the thing(s) you suggest.

Dale Carnegie's early twentieth-century research and writing on the critical role of connecting to people set the foundation for work in building relationships for the entirety of the twentieth century and into the twenty-first century. Hundreds of researchers, authors, motivational speakers, and practitioners over the past hundred years support Carnegie's philosophy on the importance of connecting with others for personal and professional success.

Included in this group are researchers Jo-Ellan Dimitrius and Mark Mazzarella who wrote *Put Your Best Foot Forward.* Dimitrius and Mazzarella frame their position on connecting with people from the work of Dale Carnegie and William James. Dale Carnegie said, "When dealing with people, let us remember we are not dealing with creatures of logic. We are dealing with creatures of emotion; creatures bristling with prejudices and motivated by pride and vanity." William James, a nineteenth-century psychologist and philosopher, said, "The deepest principle in human nature is the craving to be appreciated."

Dimitrius and Mazzarella suggest the best way to be likeable and connect to people is by addressing their emotional needs— their yearning to feel important and worthwhile. Their principles for how to make an emotional connection with people begin with the assumption that everyone craves the appreciation of others, including the closest people to you who are often overlooked. When you get home after a long day at the office, try "kissing the cat instead of kicking the cat." Recognizing significant achievements is absolutely necessary. In bad times, a person most needs you to bolster his or her self-esteem.

Always remember two key points about likeability: "people buy from people they like" and "people like people who are like them." Dimitrius and Mazzarella write, "Personal and professional relationships that are the strongest, most fulfilling, and longest lasting are those in which the people involved share basic values, life experiences, ideals, goals, mannerisms, and even a common level of physical attractiveness."

Be Strategic

As discussed by Dale Carnegie and researchers Dimitrius and Mazzarella, connecting with people in business and in everyday life cannot be understated. Possessing the traits, abilities, skills, knowledge, and behaviors (TASKBs) to demonstrate that you value others is valuable to you. There are no downsides to connecting to people in an honorable manner. Connecting with people to establish and enhance your career is no exception. It is a strategic move that will result in a competitive advantage for the authentic you.

As an emerging leader, building relationships that will result in your career advancement is more than a nice idea—it is an absolute must! In *Strategize to Win*, Carla Harris, vice chairman, managing director, and senior client advisor at Morgan Stanley, provides step-by-step strategies that she has used to launch and sustain her successful career. Harris uses the term *relationship currency* to describe the importance of building professional relationships.

Relationship currency is "the medium of exchange you use to further your professional agenda; to acquire more responsibility, more senior roles, and better assignments; and even to have your voice heard." Your work will not be the only deciding factor in compensation and career advancement. Other factors that will weigh heavily in the decision to promote you to more senior levels include your management skills, your ability to influence, and your ability to organize, motivate, and execute. Harris says, "The way in which assessments are made about your capabilities in these areas is by the decision makers observing you, working with you, spending time with you—in other words having a relationship with you."

Part of the strategic offense the authentic you will put into play is identifying the people with whom you should have relationships. Your networks should be horizontal (connecting with your peers) and vertical (connecting with your bosses and senior-level management in all areas of your organization). This strategy, according to Harris, provides you with "access to people you need to know; information you need in order to successfully execute an assignment and move ahead; and the assurance that you need when you are not sure how to read a particular situation." Once identified, seek to build your relationship currency with the individuals by spending time with them, getting to know them, sharing ideas, and working with them on internal task forces and company projects. Because senior-level employees are typically sponsors of the company's community outreach projects, such as the Red Cross blood drive, Habitat for Humanity, and United Way, volunteering to work with or lead these efforts is a tactical way to build relationship currency. Through these "high-touch" encounters, Harris says you will build the relationship currency that can give you the ability "to make a request of someone, connect to someone else's relationships, and when necessary, recover from a mistake."

Strategic Networks: Board of Directors, Mastermind Groups, and Brain Trusts

Board of Directors

Your networks will need to extend beyond the floors, walls, and ceilings of your organization. In *Breaking Through: The Making of Minority Executives in Corporate America*, David Thomas and John Gabarro write, "Thriving in one's career is the result of being able to get the career and psychological support that mentors, sponsors, and special peers can provide." What is great about this and works to your advantage is successful people, people whom you look up to and want to be like—leaders in your communities, schools, places of worship, corporate organizations, government, public, and private institutions—want to help you!

With this fact in mind, aggressively create a network of supporters—a personal board of directors—that includes sponsors, mentors, coaches, and advisors. Each has a specific function and will play a different role.

Sponsors

Compare these individuals to a "godfather." They are at the senior level in the organization, and their purpose is to assist in your career placement and advancement by serving as behind-the-scene door openers and vocal promoters. Their work is done without your knowledge in closed-door talent-management meetings. Seldom is personal contact made, and it is typically initiated by the sponsor. These high-level sponsors will be required in order for the protégé to access the highest levels of organizational advancement.

A sponsor is an active booster or advocate for any number of people—all at the same time. An individual may have many sponsors at the same time. The sponsoring relationship is informal, and neither person makes any commitments or takes responsibility for interaction. The sponsor knows who is being sponsored; the sponsored person may or may not know who the sponsor is. Sponsor activities include making introductions to top people in the organization and others with influence in the industry or profession, making recommendations for advancement, reflecting power on the sponsored person by publicly praising accomplishments and abilities, and facilitating entry into meetings and activities usually attended only by high-level people.

Mentors

Of the four member groups on your personal board of directors—sponsors, mentors, coaches, and advisors—the work of mentors has become internationally researched and practiced. When used effectively, it becomes a critical tool that contributes to the positive growth and development of individuals. The work is called mentoring.

The concept of mentoring can be traced back to ancient Greek literature as described by Homer in *The Odyssey*. Around 1200 BC, Odysseus was preparing to leave for the siege on Troy. He appointed a guardian, named Mentor, to act as a teacher, advisor, friend, and surrogate father to his son until his return. It was customary in ancient Greece for young males to be paired with older males in hopes that the boys would learn and emulate the values of their mentors. In her book *Beyond the Myths and Magic of Mentoring*, Margo Murray states, "The Greeks based these relationships on a basic principle of human survival: Humans learn skills, culture, and values directly from other humans whom they look up to and admire."

Murray discusses two types of mentoring: informal and facilitated or formal mentoring. Informal mentoring occurs when a senior person takes interest in the professional career of a junior person. Examples of successful informal mentoring relationships include the apostle Paul (mentor to Timothy in the early church), Ralph Waldo Emerson (mentor and friend to Henry David Thoreau in the mid-1800s), Apple founder Steve Jobs (mentor to Mark Zuckerberg, cofounder and CEO of Facebook), businessman and investor Warren Buffett (mentor to Bill Gates), and Raven Wilkinson who in 1955 became the first black ballerina in the illustrious Ballet Russe de Monte Carlo (mentor to Misty Copeland, who in 2015 became American Ballet Theater's first female African-American dancer to reach principal status).

Compare these individuals to favorite uncles or aunts. Their level in the organization could be senior, but they are more likely to be middle manager. Their purpose is to provide career/life strategy advice, encouragement, and mediation in times of trouble. Personal contact is usually initiated by the protégé on a monthly/bimonthly basis. Checking in may take the form of regularly scheduled fifteen-minute conversations over coffee, phone conversations, event shadowing to high-level meetings, company outings and home visits, or e-mail updates. The mentor typically assists in career development or guides the protégé through the political pathways of a profession or an organization. Both parties reap benefits from the relationship; the protégé receives increased professional recognition or job effectiveness, and the mentor receives a sense of accomplishment from having made a contribution to the growth of another person.

In the organizational environment, the mentor—the senior person in the relationship—acts as a source of information on the mission and goals of the organization. The mentor tutors specific skills, effective behavior, and proper functions in the organization, gives feedback on observed performances, serves as a confidant in times of personal crisis and problems, and assists in plotting a career path.

The names associated with the junior person in the mentoring relationship include protégé, mentee, candidate, apprentice, aspirant, advisee, counselee, trainee, and student. Desirable characteristics of the candidate for protégé include willingness to assume responsibility for his or her own growth and development, assessed potential to succeed at one or more levels above the present position in the organization, ability to perform in more than one skill area, a record of seeking challenging assignments and new responsibilities, and actionable receptivity to feedback and coaching.

When you are the protégé, be proactive in making the mentoring relationship work. Ask your mentor for a fifteen-minute coffee talk. Express your appreciation for his or her time. Ask your mentor to assess your strengths and areas for improvement and ask for developmental assignments. Follow through on all assignments given by the mentor and provide feedback to your mentor on what you learned from the assignments.

If you do not have a mentor, get one! Remember that your goal is to become an effective twenty-first-century global leader. Therefore, actively seek mentoring relationships with individuals who are culturally different from you.

Coaches

Compare coaches to drill sergeants. Coaches are middle- or first-level managers in an organization. They may be senior colleagues or peers with experience. Coaches provide on-the-job training, tactical advice, and answer specific how-to questions. Your contact with a coach could be daily or weekly, and sessions might last from fifteen minutes to an hour or more.

Advisors

Everyone needs a trusted friend, and that is the role of an advisor. Your advisors are individuals outside the organization. They serve as service providers, problem solvers, and/or confidants. Advisor titles include lawyer, doctor, real estate broker, financial planner, stockbroker, insurance agent, clergy/spiritual advisor, image consultant, personal trainer, spouse/partner, or significant other.

Personal contact with advisors is on an as-needed basis and is typically initiated by the junior person.

Role Models

While not a member of an individual's board of directors, role models play an important function in the emerging leader's life. Role models are individuals who are held in high regard by any number of people without even knowing that they are viewed in this favorable light. Role models typically do not know the people who view them as role models. (Millions of young people list President Barack Obama as a role model.) Role models may be historical figures or current figures. (President Barack Obama lists Abraham Lincoln as a role model.)

Individuals typically have several role models at a time. There is no particular structure to the role-modeling relationship, and it lasts as long as the observers see behaviors they desire to emulate. When deciding who you will look to as a role model, look for individuals who demonstrate behaviors such as success in their chosen field, exemplary behavior in achievement and style, an ability to get things done, knowledge of organizational policy and philosophy, and apparent enjoyment of position and accomplishment.

Mastermind Groups and Brain Trusts

As the focus on innovation and technology advances, two new networks have been identified as beneficial and necessary for success in one's professional life: *mastermind groups* and *brain trusts*.

Mastermind groups are typically on the same level and offer a combination of brainstorming, education, peer accountability, and support in a group setting. The purpose is to help all group members succeed through mutual encouragement. The focus is sharpening your business and personal skills. A level of expertise is expected from each group member, and the purpose of the group is "give and take" from each member.

Participants challenge each other to set powerful goals and accomplish them. Critical to the success of the group is each member's commitment to the success of the others, holding discussions in confidentiality, and being willing to both give and receive advice and ideas. Mastermind groups are built on total honesty, respect, compassion, and care. Networking for business expansion and financial gain is not the purpose of the mastermind group. However it can be a by-product as a result of mutual interests.

Brain trust groups are made up of close advisers to a decision maker. They are highly respected and highly valued for their expertise and experience in particular fields. When a person is making a major decision that has potential to impact and cause ramifications to his or her professional *and* personal lives, this group is called into play. The concept originated in the political arena with individuals considering entering political races assembling brain trusts. Others such as executives in senior administration in business, education, health care, and religion are now using this group to assist them in making high-level strategic decisions and career moves.

"Net Reach" Networks: Civic Causes, Nonprofit Boards, and Professional Organizations

Connecting to people inside and outside of your organization will serve you by helping grow and enhance your professional and personal life. This is also known as networking. In addition, emerging leaders have an obligation to connect with external systems such that instead of being served, they can serve others. I call this "net reaching," and it is equally important. This is an obligation we all have to humanity and can be satisfied in numerous ways such as doing volunteer work in your community (see chapter 9 "Optimal Service").

A way in which to blend networking with "net-reaching" is through pro bono service on nonprofit boards and through your professional organizations. As an emerging leader, you have time, energy, and expertise that would add significant value to nonprofit organizations, charitable foundations, and civic causes. By volunteering your time and efforts to these groups, you will meet a variety of people with extended professional and personal networks. You might even be asked to join them as a board member. By building strong relationships with these board members, you position yourself to be connected to members of their networks. The same holds true with joining and working in professional and community organizations.

Scripture says, "By this kind of hard work we must help the weak ... 'It is more blessed to give than to receive'" (Acts 20:35, NIV). Faithfully establish your "net reach" networks and see this scripture come true in your life.

Chapter Summary

The most effective and efficient way of getting what you want out of life is by developing meaningful relationships with others who are willing and able to assist you in making your personal and professional dreams come true. The key to being able to develop meaningful relationships with others is found in three big acts of being and doing: be the "authentic you," be likeable, and be strategic. The importance of these three intrapersonal skills is supported by insights from authors Dale Carnegie, *How To Win Friends and Influence People;* Jo-Ellan Dimitrius and Mark Mazzarella, *Put Your Best Foot Forward;* and Carla Harris, *Strategize to Win.*

The "authentic you" is the version of yourself that is genuinely interested in other people and is a good listener—a version of self that everyone is capable of being. The "authentic you" is likeable and strategic without being seen as brown-nosing or manipulative.

To be likeable, Carnegie warns against criticizing, condemning, and complaining. Dimitrius and Mazzarella's advice on how to be likeable includes validating the worth of others, bolstering others' self-esteem, and showing appreciation to others for their unique contributions to your life. Harris shares her thoughts on how to be strategic by explaining her concept of the role of "relationship currency" for professional success, concluding with a three-part response to the question, "What can relationship currency do for you?" According to Ms. Harris, "Relationship currency can give you the ability to 1) request something or some action of someone else; 2) connect to other relationships; and 3) recover from a mistake."

The effective execution of these three "be-attitudes" enables the emerging leader to construct networks that lead to increased net worth and net reach. Your board of directors is a network that includes sponsors, mentors, coaches, and advisors. Intentionally create a board that is made up of a diverse network across races, genders, ages, ethnicities, religions, and lifestyles. Mastermind groups and brain trusts were also presented.

Members of your networks should come from inside *and* outside your organization. In order to maximize the effectiveness of your networks, ensure that they create mutually beneficial relationships so that *all* members of your networks reap desired benefits as you *connect to external systems.*

Leadership and Professional Development Exercises

Key Terms

- advisors
- board of directors
- brain trusts
- coaches
- connection-based big acts of being and doing
- mastermind group
- mentor
- net reach
- net worth
- network
- nonprofit boards
- protégé
- relationship currency

- role models
- sponsors

Questions to Discuss

1. What is the third principle of the FOCUS module?
2. What are five strategies (proven tips and techniques) to effectively connect with others?
3. How does the concept of relationship currency apply to a person's personal and professional success?
4. What is a personal board of directors and what can it do for you?
5. What is mentoring? What are its ancient origins? How is it used as a strategic tool in organizational behavior today?

Questions to Consider

1. Can you get to where you want to be all by yourself? If yes, explain how? If no, explain why not?
2. Do you have a personal board of directors? Are all positions (sponsors, mentors, coaches, and advisors) currently occupied? If so, who are they? If not, who will you ask *today* to become a member of your board of directors?
3. What level is your relationship-building skill: low, medium, or high? Is this a realistic assessment of your TASKBs? Are you using relationship building as a strategic tool to accomplish your personal and professional goals? If you are, how can you improve? If not, what will you do *today* to start?
4. Do you believe that connecting with others honors your faith as well as other components of your winning support system? Why or why not?
5. What will you stop doing *today* because it hinders your ability to connect with others? What will you intentionally start doing *today* so that you can focus on connecting to others and developing your external systems?

Books to Stimulate Your Mind

- *How to Win Friends and Influence People* by Dale Carnegie (1936)
- *Put Your Best Foot Forward* by Jo-Ellan Dimitrius and Mark Mazzarella (2000)
- *Strategize to Win* by Carla Harris (2014)

CHAPTER 4

Understand the Big Picture

Mother, mother,
There's too many of you crying;
Brother, brother, brother,
There's far too many of you dying
You know we've got to find a way
To bring some lovin' here today

—Marvin Gaye, "What's Going On" (1971)

One of my most vivid memories of growing up in the 1960s in Hueytown, Alabama, a small town twelve miles west of Birmingham, is the civil rights movement. Specifically, my memories center on the work of one man, the Reverend Dr. Martin Luther King Jr. It was Dr. King's commitment to leadership through his personal standards and public beliefs rooted in faith, ethics, values, and integrity that compelled him to risk his life to come to Birmingham. Dr. King is quoted by Phillips as saying, "I am in Birmingham because injustice is here."

In 1963, the SCLC (Southern Christian Leadership Conference), under the leadership of Dr. King, came to Birmingham. It was a place he called "the most thoroughly segregated city in the country." Dr. King came with one goal in mind: to "awaken the moral conscience of America" and produce federal legislation that would force desegregation everywhere. His goal was achieved with the passing of the Civil Rights Act of 1964. This federal legislation ended segregation in public places and banned employment discrimination on the basis of race, color, religion, sex, or national origin and is considered one of the crowning legislative achievements of the civil rights movement.

Dr. King's legacy is an exemplary representation of "FOCUS in ACTION Is Great Leadership." King was a twentieth-century great leader who was able to focus America's attention on the rampant societal issue of racism and bring its leadership to act on the passage of laws to address this evil. The twenty-first century continues to need great leaders who, like King, will seek to understand the big picture and ask, "What's going on?"

The Pew Research Center published a report on the "Top 10 Global Trends in 2014," based on a poll of 1,592 experts and thought leaders from academia, business, government, and nonprofits. The following list is a summary of their findings published by the World Economic Forum:

1. Rising societal tensions in the Middle East and North Africa
2. Widening income disparities with the gap between rich and poor
3. Persistent structural unemployment, inflation, inequality, and debt
4. Intensifying cyber threats
5. Inaction on climate change
6. Diminishing confidence in economic policies
7. A lack of values in leadership
8. The expanding middle class in Asia
9. The growing importance of megacities
10. The rapid spread of misinformation online

As an emerging leader, I hope this list caused some sort of intellectual and emotional response by you, seeding questions such as, "How do these trends affect my circles of influence? How will these trends affect my ability to succeed in my chosen career field? What will be the long-term implications of these trends?

What impact do they have on the sustainability of a stable global society? What responsibility do I have to address these issues? How can I make a difference that will positively impact the trends? What issues not on this list do I see as major challenges to my life and the lives of those I connect and intersect with culturally, socially, economically, politically, and professionally? How can I affect a positive change in society such that I live a life of service that honors my faith?"

The World in Perspective

Twenty-first-century global leaders *must* be prepared for a workplace that has no borders. The realization of a global economy dictates the need for leaders to be deliberate in their understanding of economic, political, and social systems throughout the world and to develop an appreciation for the strength that currently lies dormant in the world's cultural diversity.

While thinking globally, emerging American leaders have to be prepared to live and act within the national, regional, and local structures of the United States. Therefore, an understanding of the state of America's economic, political, and social systems as they affect minorities within the framework of the larger American economic, political, and social systems defined by the majority is also needed. Statistical information on the problem areas identified as worldwide social ills by Dr. King in 1968—issues of racism, poverty, and overpopulation in relationship to allocation of resources areas—for the world and for America follows.

The World Wide Web is an excellent source of statistical information and facts on world issues. The following data were retrieved from a variety of Internet-based sources including Our World in Data and NationMaster, a massive central database obtained from such sources as the Central Intelligence Agency World Factbook, United Nations, and Organization for Economic Co-Operation and Development.

World Population Data

According to the Population Reference Bureau (PRB), in 2015, the top three countries with the largest population were 1) China—1,372 million; 2) India—1,314 million; and 3) the United States—321 million. The next four were Indonesia—256 million; Brazil—205 million; Pakistan—199 million; and Nigeria—182 million. The PRB predicts that by 2050, the top three countries will continue to be the largest in population with 1) India—1,660 million; 2) China—1,366 million; and 3) the United States—398 million. Nigeria will move up to fourth place with a population of 397 million; followed by Indonesia with 366 million; Pakistan with 344 million; and Brazil with 226 million.

The United Nations Department of Economic and Social Affairs reports that the projected total world population, which in 2011 was reported at 7 billion, will reach 9.6 billion by 2050. The growth will be mainly in developing countries with more than half in Africa.

Overall, life expectancy is projected to increase in developed and developing countries in future years. At the global level, it is projected to reach seventy-six years in the period 2045–2050 and eighty-two years in 2095–2100. By the end of the century, people in developed countries could live on average around eighty-nine years, compared to about eighty-one years in developing regions.

World Poverty Data

In the early 1800s, most people lived in poverty. However, industrialization and economic growth benefitted developing nations and left other countries in poverty. Poverty remains in those regions in which the accumulated economic growth is still small and industrialization is still at the early stages.

Disturbing but not surprising is Max Roser's list of people in poverty. Roser reports in Our World In Data, an online publication that presents empirical evidence on the development of human living conditions at a global scale, the highest poverty percentages in African countries, including Liberia, 80 percent; Zimbabwe, 80 percent; Chad, 80 percent; Democratic Republic of the Congo, 71 percent; Sierra Leone, 70.2 percent; Nigeria, 70 percent; Suriname, 70 percent; Swaziland, 69 percent; and Burundi, 68 percent. The decades-long–and in some cases century-long—turbulences caused by genocide, war, lack and pilferage of natural resources, poor farm management, poor government structures, and colonization by Western societies has resulted in systemic poverty.

The sobering reality of the inhumane effects of poverty can be seen by looking at the life expectancy data of the citizens of a country. Life expectancy is defined as the average number of years to be lived by a group of people born in the same year, if mortality at each age remains constant in the future. Life expectancy at birth is also a measure of overall quality of life in a country and summarizes the mortality at all ages.

An analysis of the data shows an inverse relationship between the percentage of population below the poverty line and the years of life expectancy, i.e., the higher the poverty level, the lower the years of life expectancy. The nine high-poverty African countries identified by Roser have an average poverty rating of 73 percent of the population living below the poverty line, with a country range of 68 percent in Burundi to 80 percent in Liberia, Zimbabwe, and Chad. The average life expectancy is 52 years, with a range of 49.81 years in Chad to 72 years in Suriname.

In comparison, the average poverty rating of the United States, France, Japan, United Kingdom, and Germany is 13.96 percent, with a country range of 8.1 percent in France to 16.1 percent in Japan. The average life expectancy for these five countries is 81.5 years, with a range of 79.7 years in the United States to 84.7 years in Japan.

In summary, the nine African countries average a 73 percent poverty level and 52 years of life expectancy. The five countries from North America, Europe, and Asia average a 13.96 percent poverty level and 81.5 years of life expectancy. The difference in poverty level is 59 percentage points. The difference in longevity of life is 29.5 years.

United States Social Structure: Statistical Facts

Our discussion now moves to providing insight into the social structure on the national level. While enjoying the status of being the richest and most powerful nation in the world, America is not without its economic problems and social ills, especially for members of the minority populations.

According to the 2015 US Census (estimated), the total US population is 321,418,820. Approximately 40 percent of the US population identifies as part of the minority population (17.6 percent Hispanic or Latino; 13.3 percent black or African American; 5.6 percent Asian; and 1.2 percent American Indian and Alaska Native) and 61.6 percent identify as white. The gender composition is 50.8 percent female and 49.2 percent male. The age composition is persons under 18 years, 22.9 percent; persons 18 years old and under 65 years, 62.2 percent; and persons 65 years and over, 14.9 percent.

American Quality of Life

A balcony view of America in terms of economic distribution, education, and employment of demographic groups provides a factual perspective on the huge disparity in the quality of life of Americans based on race and ethnicity. The following data are based on published reports from the Pew Research Center, a nonpartisan fact tank that informs the public about the issues, attitudes, and trends shaping America and the world. Much of the data comes from a Pew 2013 report titled, "King's Dream Remains an Elusive Goal: Many Americans See Racial Disparities."

Employment

The unemployment rate among blacks is about double that among whites, as it has been for most of the past six decades. In 1954, the earliest year for which the Bureau of Labor Statistics has consistent unemployment data by race, the white rate averaged 5 percent and the black rate averaged 9.9 percent. In July 2013, the jobless rate among whites was 6.6 percent; among blacks, it was 12.6 percent. Over that time, 1954 to 2013, the unemployment rate for blacks has averaged about 2.2 times that for whites. According to Pew Research Center senior writer Drew DeSilver the black-white unemployment gap appears to have emerged in the 1940s, with no consensus among labor economists, sociologists, and other researchers on the causes.

Income

The median household income for whites was $67,175 in 2011, as reported in the Census Bureau's March 2012 Current Population Survey. For blacks, it was $39,760; for Asians, $68,521; and Hispanics $40,007. Comparative income data for Asians is available only since 1987, when Asian income was about equal to white income. In 2011, Asian income was 102 percent of white income.

Homeownership

In 2012, 73 percent of white households owned their own homes, compared with 44 percent of black households, 57 percent of Asian households, and 46 percent of Hispanic households, according to the Census Bureau's Annual Social and Economic Supplement.

Wealth

In 2011, the typical white household had a net worth of $91,405; compared with $6,446 for black households; $7,843 for Hispanic households; and $91,203 for Asian households. The figures for net worth—also known as wealth—are based on assets minus liabilities. In 1984, black households had a median net worth equal to 9 percent that of white households, compared with 7 percent in 2011. Hispanic net worth also is notably smaller than white net worth, and the gap has widened over time. In 1984, the typical Hispanic household had 13 percent of the wealth of the typical white household. In 2011, the typical Hispanic household had 9 percent of the wealth of the typical white household. Figures for Asian wealth are available only since 2004; in 2011, the typical Asian and white households had about equal net worth.

Net worth accounts for the values of items such as a home and car, checking and savings accounts, and stocks, minus debts such as mortgage, car loans, and credit card bills. Greater wealth means a great ability to weather a job loss, emergency home repairs, illness, and other unexpected costs, as well as being able to save for retirement or a child's college tuition.

Education

Today's high school completion rates are similar for adults ages 25 and older who are white, black, or Asian, but they lag for Hispanics. In 2012, 92 percent of white adults, 86 percent of black adults, and 89 percent of Asian adults had at least a high school education, as did 65 percent of Hispanic adults. Looking at adults ages 25 and older, the gap in college completion between whites and blacks, as well as the gap between whites and Hispanics, is larger than that in high school completion. In 2012, 34 percent of white adults had finished college, compared with 21 percent of black adults and 15 percent of Hispanic adults. Among Asians, 51 percent had completed college, a higher share than for whites.

Poverty

Black Americans are nearly three times as likely as white Americans to live in poverty, according to the 2012 March Current Population Survey. Among whites, 10 percent were poor in 2011, compared with 28 percent of blacks, 25 percent of Hispanics, and 12 percent of Asians.

Marriage and Births

Marriage is considered an indicator of well-being in part because married adults are economically better off, although that may reflect the greater propensity of affluent adults to marry. In 2011, 55 percent of white adults ages 18 and older were married, compared with 31 percent of black adults ages 18 and older, according to Census Bureau statistics. Thus, the marriage rate for black adults was 56 percent that of the white rate. In 2011, 47 percent of Hispanic adults were married, 85 percent of the marriage rate for white adults that year. The share of births to unmarried parents also has risen for all groups, accounting for 41 percent of births in 2011, according to the National Center for Health Statistics. In 2011, 72 percent of births to black women were to unmarried mothers, compared with 29 percent of births to white women.

Voter Turnout

Census Bureau estimates of voter turnout by race indicate that black voters have not only closed the gap with white voters in participation but they exceeded whites on this measure in the 2008 and 2012 presidential elections. In 2008, the year Barack Obama ran for president as the first black major-party nominee, 76 percent of black eligible voters participated, compared with 74 percent of whites. In 2012, 67 percent of eligible black voters cast ballots, compared with 64 percent of eligible white voters. Hispanic participation was 48 percent in 2012 and Asian-American voter participation was 73 percent that of white participation in 2012.

Incarceration

In 2010, the incarceration rate for white men under local, state, and federal jurisdiction was 678 inmates per 100,000 white US residents; for black men, it was 4,347. According to the Bureau of Justice Statistics, black men were more than six times as likely as white men to be incarcerated in 2010 (4,347 versus 678 respectively). The incarceration rate for Hispanic men in 2010 was 1,775 per 100,000 US Hispanic residents. Hispanic men were nearly three times as likely as white men to be incarcerated in 2010 (1,775 versus 678 respectively).

Statistics for female prisoners show black women are more likely to be incarcerated than white women. In 2010, the incarceration rate for white women was 91 per 100,000 white residents; for black women it was 260.

Life Expectancy

White life expectancy at birth exceeds black life expectancy at birth by nearly four years, according to data from the National Center for Health Statistics. A white baby born in 2010 could expect to live to 78.9 years of age, while a black baby could expect to live 75.1 years. Data for Hispanic life expectancy are more limited because of a variety of data quality issues. Hispanic life expectancy at birth in 2006, the earliest year available from the National Center for Health Statistics, was higher than white life expectancy, and it remained so in 2010.

Health and Vitality

Research conducted by Majid Ezzati, professor at Harvard School of Public Health, shows that, in America, the length of your life might depend on where you reside and to which racial group you belong. Based on his findings, Ezzati states, "There are very large inequalities in mortality and health in American people; inequalities that can be mapped and described using a small number of socio-demographic and geographical indicators."

From a 2006 research project in which he was the lead researcher, Dr. Ezzati has identified what he terms "Eight Americas." The Eight Americas are life-expectancy categories based on a person's race, local surroundings, and other community characteristics. The Eight Americas are: 1) Asians; 2) northland low-income rural whites; 3) Middle-Americans; 4) low-income whites in Appalachia and the Mississippi Valley; 5) western Native Americans; 6) black Middle-Americans; 7) southern low-income rural blacks; and 8) high-risk urban blacks.

Ezzati and his team found big differences in life expectancy between the eight groups. One example noted Ezzati is the life expectancy gap between the best-off men and women and the worst-off groups. For males, the best-off group is Asians, and the worst-off group is high-risk urban blacks—life expectancy difference, 15.4 years. For females, the best-off group again is Asians and the worst-off group is low-income rural blacks in the South—life expectancy difference, 12.8 years.

Dr. Ezzati shares observations that should be of special interest to twenty-first-century leaders:

- The conditions responsible for the differences—heart disease, diabetes, and injuries—are preventable with specific interventions.
- The gaps between best-off and worst-off groups were similar in 2001, fourteen years later, to what they were in 1987.
- Inequalities in health care must be corrected, and at the same time, disease prevention should have a major role.
- Instead of thinking about how many lives are going to be saved by lowering blood pressure, cholesterol, etc., we should think about *whose* lives we are saving.

According to *HealthDay* senior staff reporter Steven Reinberg, additional observations on Ezzati's research findings were made by Dr. David L. Katz, a professor at Yale University School of Medicine:

How sobering it is to learn that we live in as many as eight different worlds—and all within the United States. The United States is the world leader in biomedical advances, high-tech care, and health care expenditure, but we are also the world leader in health disparities. Within the borders of just this one country, the health experiences of diverse populations are truly worlds apart. Culturally tailored interventions that take messages of disease prevention and health promotion to the places they are most urgently needed should be a national public health priority. A system that allocates both health care and health as inequitably as ours cannot be considered anything but a failure.

The above overview of life-quality issues in the world and the United States solidifies the fact that much work is still needed to be done to close the gap between the rich and the poor. This is the work that emerging leaders of all nations and faiths must be committed.

Chapter Summary

This chapter covers the critical twenty-first-century issues and challenges facing the world house identified almost five decades ago by Dr. King in 1968—issues of racism, poverty, and overpopulation in relationship to allocation of resources—which are strongly rooted in the economic, political, and social structures of the world. Chapter 4 presents statistical facts of the impact on a world with such a disparity between the haves and the have-nots.

Country poverty rates suggest the majority of the countries in the world have 10 percent or more of their populations living below the poverty level. The relationship between country population poverty levels and life expectancy data indicate an inverse relationship between the percentage of population below the poverty line and the years of life expectancy, i.e., the higher the poverty level, the lower the years of life expectancy. This effect is very evident in the high poverty rate countries of Africa.

Research done by the Pew Research Center gives a balcony view of a variety of economic, educational, health, political, and social indicators, comparing the quality of life and relative well-being of American demographic groups since the beginning of the twenty-first century. Overall, whites and Asians have better outcomes in all of these areas in comparison to blacks and Hispanics.

Of particular note is a study done by researchers at Harvard University, which identifies large inequalities in mortality and health in American people based on socio-demographic and geographical indicators. The term "Eight Americas" is used in the study and identified life-expectancy categories based on a person's race, local surroundings, and other community characteristics. The Eight Americas are: 1) Asians; 2) northland low-income rural whites; 3) Middle-Americans; 4) low-income whites in Appalachia and the Mississippi Valley; 5) western Native Americans; 6) black Middle-Americans; 7) southern low-income rural blacks; and 8) high-risk urban blacks.

Poverty, mortality, and health disparities are just a few of the many problems that comprise the twenty-first-century "big picture." While many of the problems of the world are caused by "generation-old" vestiges of the classical "isms," including racism and sexism (addressed in chapter 8 "Tenacious Inclusion"), the solution to the problems will lie in "generation-new" attitudes and a revolution of values. The key to addressing these problems lies in a commitment of twenty-first-century global leaders to continually ask themselves the question, "What's going on?" such that they can *understand the big picture.*

Leadership and Professional Development Exercises

Key Terms

- classical "isms"
- Eight Americas
- life expectancy
- net worth
- poverty
- Top 10 Global Trends (2014)
- world house
- world population

- worldwide social ills

Questions to Discuss

1. What is the fourth principle of the FOCUS module?
2. Of what significance is it for twenty-first-century emerging leaders to have an understanding of environmental and societal forces?
3. What are worldwide social ills named by Dr. Martin Luther King Jr. in 1968?
4. How does poverty correlate to life expectancy?
5. According to the "Eight Americas," what is the relationship between (1) where someone lives; (2) the racial group they belong; and (3) their life-expectancy?

Questions to Consider

1. Are you concerned by the current state of affairs in your community, region, and nation? If so, what concerns you? If not, why not? What global issue(s) causes you the most alarm? If there are none, why not?
2. Do you believe that you have a personal responsibility to aggressively seek solutions to what concerns you in your community, region, nation, and globally? If you do, why? If you do not, what new attitudes and values will you incorporate as intrapersonal skills such that you will become and remain enraged at the problems of the world and aggressively seek to participate in solving them?
3. What will you do differently *today* to ensure that you are part of the solution and not the problem?
4. Do you believe that understanding the big picture honors your faith as well as other components of your winning support system? Why or why not?
5. What will you stop doing today that hinders your ability to understand the big picture? What will you intentionally

start doing today so that you can focus on understanding the big picture?

Books to Stimulate Your Mind

- *The New Jim Crow: Mass Incarceration in the Age of Colorblindness* by Michelle Alexander (2010)
- *Where Do We Go From Here: Chaos or Community?* by Martin Luther King Jr. (1968)
- *Losing the Race: Self-Sabotage in Black America* by John McWhorter (2000)

CHAPTER 5

Sell Yourself as Excellence

"Finally, brothers and sisters, whatever is true,
whatever is noble, whatever is right,
whatever is pure, whatever is lovely, whatever
is admirable—if anything is
excellent or praiseworthy—think about such things."

—Philippians 4:8 (NIV)

When you do your work professionally, people take notice.
People notice because professionals perform what often are
ordinary jobs in extraordinary ways. Professionals add a little
extra to everything they do. They put enthusiasm into every
move they make. They smile more, seem happier, act more
confidently, move quicker, and take special pride in their work.

—James R. Ball, *Professionalism is for Everyone*

Up to this point, the FOCUS module has demonstrated the need
for emerging leaders to 1) find their power source; 2) open their
internal systems; 3) connect to external systems; and 4) understand
the big picture. The fifth and final principle of the intrapersonal
foundation of the JWLM—sell yourself as excellence—will lay the
foundation for emerging leaders to execute at the highest levels of
personal and professional success.

Principle 5 encompasses the "what, why, how, when, and where" of the skills needed to be and be seen as a true professional. My operational definition of principle 5 reads as follows:

> *Sell Yourself as Excellence* occurs everyday, all day, as you present yourself to the public as a person who respects others and, in turn, deserves the respect of others. It is a process of cultivating goodwill in momentary encounters, short interactions, informal meetings, or formal structured consultations. The goal is to develop meaningful relationships by discovering needs, matching one's appropriate skills and abilities with these needs, and communicating benefits through informing, reminding, or persuading. Increasingly, to *sell yourself as excellence* is viewed as a process that *adds value.*

Principle 5 will cover the TASKBs you will need to enter into a professional organizational setting, sell yourself as excellence, and add value by first "fitting in." For many of you, the term "fitting in" has caused your defensive emotions to rise. You might be thinking, "Why do I have to fit in? I don't want to conform. I don't want to lose my individuality. Who made the rules? Why can't I break them? You just want me to lose my identity and look like 'the man.'"

These questions and concerns are rather interesting in that they are typically coming from young persons who have been "conforming" for much of their lives. These same young persons eagerly pursue membership and participation in social clubs, sports teams, bands, choirs, fraternities, sororities, schools, colleges, and universities—with the ultimate goal of acceptance and fitting in. Young people who eagerly jump the highest hurdles and swim the deepest oceans just to be on the team and be considered one of "them." In doing so, they fit in gladly by adopting the cultural norms of the group and proudly wear the groups' colors and paraphernalia. They will learn the mottos and slogans and intentionally seek to hang out with other members of the group without any complaints.

Why do people conform so easily? A possible reason is they know if they complain, rebel, or go against the cultural norms, they will not be selected to be part of the group. If they are somehow selected and do not conform, they will be ostracized, marginalized, and probably kicked out of the group or off the team. Their desire to belong to the group and be a member of the team is much greater than the perceived inconvenience of conformity.

But when it comes to "fitting in" on a job, in an organization that will *pay you* to be a contributing member, somehow or another, these same young persons find it perfectly acceptable to complain, rebel, and commence to go against the cultural norms. So the question that begs to be addressed is, once again, "What's going on?"

Ron Alsop provides some insights into the thinking patterns of today's young persons in his 2008 book *The Trophy Kids Grow Up*. Through extensive conversations with millennials, their parents, major student recruiters, and employers in management consulting, accounting, and investment banking firms, Alsop provides insights into the generation born between 1980 and 2001.

He found that millennials have a strong desire to reshape the work environment to conform to their personal goals and lives. Their preference for flip-flops, ripped jeans, and text messages over face-to-face communication is causing conflict with older colleagues and managers. According to Alsop:

> Millennials also are a polarizing generation. They have many fans who admire their optimism, intelligence, ambition, and commitment to make the world a better place, but they also come in for some stinging criticism for their inflated expectations. Employers, in particular, have mixed feelings about millennials. While respecting their aptitude for technology and their ability to work well in teams, many recruiters and managers find millennials far too demanding when it comes to needing guidance, frequent performance appraisals, rapid career advancement, and work-life balance. Although many of them are well educated, millennials strike employers as being book

smart but suffering from a deficit of common sense. How else to explain the job candidate who showed up late for an interview at a public relations agency with chewing gum in her mouth and blue, chipped fingernails?

Without a doubt the millennial generation is causing a perplexing situation in the workplace. As organizations look to fill their talent pool with young employees who will take their organization to new heights in the future, the question being asked is, "Will millennials mature into strong leaders who can give direction rather than depend on others for guidance?" While it may be decades before that question is answered, I have full confidence that there will be strong, mighty cadres of millennials who answer the call to great leadership. I trust you are up to the challenge of being part of the great leadership movement.

The strategy for anyone preparing to lead in the twenty-first-century global society is to adopt the same openness to "fitting in" as a well-respected, contributing member of social clubs, fraternities and sororities, and colleges and universities, to "adding value" as a well-respected, contributing member of companies and institutions. You are needed as a valued employee. You can make a positive difference in your organization, your community, and ultimately in society as a whole. This journey starts with fitting in on your job as a professional who adds value to his or her workplace setting.

Chapter 5 shares the many rules, nuances, and secret codes that professionals in the workplace are expected to know. Please don't get hung up on the whys. "Why a blue suit, white shirt, black socks, and minimal to no facial hair is the standard interview attire/look for a man? Why should a woman wear flesh-colored hose and a clear, short manicure for an interview? Why is the bottom button of a man's suit coat never buttoned? Why is standing deemed the appropriate posture when shaking someone's hand?" The list of whys goes on and on.

I usually reply to these questions from my students with a question: "Why do drivers in England drive on the left side of the street and drivers in America drive on the right side?" The answer, "That's just the way it is. Neither way is better than the other. But you do need to know and abide by the way of the country you are in so that you can get to where you are going alive and in one piece." Similarly, learn and exhibit the ways that demonstrate you are a professional of excellence such that you can bypass the detours and roadblocks of organizational life and arrive safely at your leadership destiny.

Stages in the Growth of Professional Skills

One of the most difficult transitions emerging leaders face is moving from an educational success mind-set to a professional success mind-set. Alexandra Levit explains it this way in her 2009 book, *They Don't Teach Corporate in College.*

> We're [college graduates] comfortable with the concept of school. We know how the story goes: if you work hard, you get good grades and everyone is happy. The business world, however, is another animal entirely. Politically motivated and fraught with nonsensical change, the corporate world is not a natural fit for graduates who leave school expecting results from a logical combination of education and effort. Suddenly, the tenets of success we were taught since kindergarten don't apply, because getting ahead in the business world has nothing to do with intelligence or exceeding a set of defined expectations. In our first corporate jobs, we come up against rules no one ever told us about. We feel lost. It's like we were whisked away on a spaceship and have landed on an alien planet where we have to eat oxygen and breathe vegetables.

As Levit so colorfully described, an interesting phenomenon about professional work skills is that you are expected to know them, but most colleges and workplaces don't teach them. In fact, once you are in the workplace, your first indication that you are not exhibiting professional behavior may well come during a performance review when the rating you are being given by your manager is clearly below the rating you have been giving yourself.

If the concern is in your dress attire or grooming habits, the manager will not directly point out the problems. It is easy for managers to identify job performance deficiencies but next to impossible for them to discuss professionalism concerns in the areas of personal appearance, communication skills, and behaviors. An employee's poor or nonexistent professional skills present an uncomfortable situation for both the manager and the employee. Who wants to tell or be told that what you are wearing to work does not fit the culture of the organization or the image the company wants to portray to its client base?

What managers look for, and twenty-first-century leaders should strive to deliver, is a mastery in the art of professionalism— employees who are *unconsciously competent* in their professionalism skills. This level, unconsciously competent, is the fourth and highest level of development that a professional can reach. For a professional athlete, such as LeBron James, Kawhi Leonard, or Stephen Curry, it is demonstrated when he makes shooting a three-pointer at the buzzer to win a NBA championship game seem easy. Or Russell Wilson when he completes a forty-yard pass to win the Super Bowl. For a professional in the workplace, it is demonstrating professional excellence in appearance, communication skills, and behaviors with ease and confidence—style *and* substance. You, like millions of other college athletes, will be "going pro" in something other than athletics. Be ready!

The four stages of competence is a learning model that relates to the psychological states involved in the process of progressing from "don't know what you don't know" (incompetence) in an area to knowledge of and some level of "can do" (competence) in the area. Developed in the 1970s, this model suggests that individuals are 1) initially unaware of how little they know; 2) recognize their incompetence; 3) consciously acquire knowledge in the area and use it; and 4) move to a state of utilization without it being consciously thought through.

- *Unconscious Incompetence.* "You don't know that you don't know." This is the most difficult stage to be in because the persons are unaware of the rules they are breaking because they are not aware that there are rules. But as is often said in life, "Ignorance of the law is no excuse."
- *Conscious Incompetence.* "You know that you don't know." This is the most important step to learning. You are now aware that there is a "secret code" and are also aware that by not knowing the secret code, your chances of obtaining your employment goals will be significantly lowered.
- *Conscious Competence.* "You know that you know." At this point, you have done your homework and learned the "secret code." You are still a novice so you have to remind yourself to look, talk, and act like a professional. It may seem a little unnatural for you, but you are willing to put in considerable practice knowing that it will pay off in the realization of your goals.
- *Unconscious Competence.* "You don't know that you know." You are now the consummate professional. You *always* look, talk, and behave like a professional. Professional behavior is not an act or an inconvenience. It is a way of life for you; you willingly embrace and internalize the "secret code" because you know it is the "breakfast of champions."

So just what is the secret code? The answer to this question is made perfectly clear in this chapter. This chapter covers the TASKBs entry-level professionals are expected to know and exhibit. Employers use the presence or absence of professionalism skills to evaluate whether a prospective new hire possesses good judgment skills and therefore can be trusted to make good decisions. No one willingly adds to their team someone who is perceived as having questionable judgment and decision-making skills.

This principle is intentionally geared to provide the most salient information an emerging leader needs to know in order to enter into the professional arena of the employed—whether in an established for-profit organization, i.e., corporate America; the public service fields, i.e., government, health care, education, philanthropy, religion; the entertainment fields, i.e., music, arts, theater, sports management; or self-employment, i.e., entrepreneurship. Don't be fooled. *Professionalism is expected and required anyplace money is exchanged for services rendered.*

Employers are looking for people who can add value as a contributing member of an organizational team—not someone who will be a distraction. Knowing this, the wise prospective employee gladly uses the simple yet significant (like driving on the "right side" of the road, which can be different from one country/culture to another) tools available to demonstrate his or her ability to be a value-add member of a team. I refer to these tools as the *ABCs of professional presence.* Before I explain in detail the ABCs of professional presence, let's take a quick look at the origins of professionalism.

Professionalism Guiding Principles

The basic foundation of professionalism is profession. *Webster's* dictionary defines profession as:

> A calling requiring specialized knowledge and often long and intensive preparation including [1] instruction in skills and methods as well as in the scientific, historical, or scholarly principles underlying such skills and methods, [2] maintaining by force of organization or concerted opinion high standards of achievement and conduct, and [3] committing its members to continued study and [4] to a kind of work which has for its prime purpose the rendering of a public service.

In the early twentieth century, the professions stood on the formalities of education, admission, ordination, and licensing. Recognition as a profession was confined to the three "learned professions"—theology, law, and medicine. The professions are respectable because they did not strive for money. The professional man was not thought of as engaged in the pursuit of his personal profit but in performing services to his patients or clients, or to impersonal values like the advancement of science.

The behavior of the professional man was labeled as "altruistic" as opposed to "egoistic." The professions were respectable because they did not strive for money. But they could only remain respectable if they succeeded in making quite a lot of money—at least enough to support the needs and wants of a prosperous lifestyle.

The "altruistic versus egoistic" dichotomy is no longer a matter of debate when determining the professional status of an occupation or an individual. Money as the medium of exchange for services rendered is the norm. Professional assessment is now based on ethical standards of the occupation and performance of its practitioners.

In 1969, Harvard Business School professor Kenneth Andrews examined the long-standing debate on whether business in our society can be characterized as a profession. In his article "Towards Professionalism in Business Management," Andrews identified five criteria to evaluate the professional quality of any occupation.

The first is knowledge. In addition to information and historical fact, the knowledge has been subjected to disciplined analysis, tested to extend its usefulness and possible meanings, and capable of being extended further by systematic research. Next is competent application of the knowledge as it is applied to a class of practical yet complex problems of major concern to society by responsible individuals using judgment and skill tempered by pride and pleasure in the field with sympathy for the individuals or groups being served.

The third criteria is social responsibility. Practitioners must be motivated less by self-elevation and more by the desire to satisfy needs, solve problems, or accomplish goals appropriate in the field. Material and monetary rewards are not to be valued primarily for their own sake.

Self-control must be evident in the profession where members of a profession monitor itself through standards of conduct, influencing behavior, and disciplining poor performance.

Examples of monitoring organizations within a profession include American Institute of Certified Accountants (accounting); Chartered Financial Analyst (finance); Academy of Management (management); American Marketing Association (marketing); American Bar Association (law); and American Medical Association (medicine). The last criterion is community sanction. As a result of knowledge, skill, responsibility, and self-control, the individuals and segments of society served by a profession grant its practitioners respect, authority, considerable freewill to practice, and high positions in the hierarchy of occupations.

Andrews's position is that an impressive degree of professionalism marks the management of business and makes a case for reframing the twentieth-century question, "Is business a profession?" He continues by stating, "More important questions that should be addressed as we prepare for the twenty-first century are how business and the established professions can better serve society and what are the circumstances in which the people in an occupation attempt to turn it into a profession, and themselves into professional people."

In response to Andrews's questions regarding the human/ people side of profession, Touro College management professor Patrick McGuigan states, "Whether or not the occupation itself has attained professional status, according to the definition of profession, the individual can attain the attributes of professionalism." The attributes of professionalism that should be exhibited by the individual—the professional, as listed by McGuigan are as follows:

1. Reliance on a high personal standard of competence in providing professional services.
2. Promotion and maintenance of the image of the profession.
3. Willingness to pursue development opportunities that improve skills.
4. Pursuit of quality, competence, and ideals within the profession.
5. Presentation of a sense of pride about the profession.

The work of Andrews and McGuigan lays the foundation on which the ABCs of professional presence stand. As confirmed by Andrews's criteria to evaluate the professional quality of any occupation and McGuigan's attributes of professionalism for the individual, the expectations for an occupation and the individuals who practice the occupation are high. A mind-set of mediocrity (ordinary, average, uninspired, undistinguished, indifferent, unexceptional, unexciting, unremarkable, pedestrian, lackluster, forgettable, amateur, amateurish) has no place in a profession or the life of a professional.

Professionals are *unconsciously competent in selling themselves as excellence.* Today's professionals pride themselves on adhering to the behaviors that society deems distinctive. For Western society, those behaviors include being on time, dressing appropriately, conducting oneself appropriately with others without being offensive in verbal or body language, keeping promises on the delivery of work products, and conducting work in an ethical manner. These behaviors of excellence and more comprise the ABCs of professional presence.

Why Sell Yourself as Excellence?

To begin our discussion on the ABCs of professional presence, I return to the work of Dimitrius and Mazzarella, first discussed in chapter 3. In that chapter, I examined the importance of building strong relationships to assist in achieving your personal and professional goals, including career advancement. In this chapter, I will examine the role of impression management in turning the adage "perception is reality" into a positive, winning strategy for achieving your personal and professional goals. Through personal and professional excellence, you will be able to create a favorable perception of who you are and the value you can add to an organization or situation. This strategy is known as *impression management.*

You can't judge a *book* by its cover, but people judge *people* by how they look, act, talk, walk, and smell. In *Put Your Best Foot*

Forward, Dimitrius and Mazzarella write, "Every day, every person you meet sizes you up within the first few seconds. They form impressions about who you are, what you think and how you are likely to act. Once those impressions are set in their minds, they are difficult to change." Use this idiosyncratic trait of human beings to your advantage by adopting and demonstrating personal and professional excellence through the execution of the ABCs of professional presence.

Components of the ABCs of Professional Presence

To convey the fact that there is nothing difficult or unattainable in the area of personal and professional excellence, I purposely organized the subject matter around a familiar elementary topic. The ABCs of professional presence require that a person demonstrates the specific TASKBs (traits, abilities, skills, knowledge, and behaviors) of professional excellence in appropriateness, believability, and credibility through appearance, body language, communication skills, deliverables, and etiquette/social skills.

Appropriateness, Believability, and Credibility

- Appropriateness encompasses a person's decorum in a particular occasion or setting. "Do you look, talk, and act like a professional?"
- Believability encompasses a person's workplace knowledge, expertise, and competencies. "Can you do the job excellently with both effectiveness and efficiency?"
- Credibility speaks to a person's character—integrity, ethics, honesty, and credentials—training, and continuous development. "Can you be trusted to deliver your work? Can you be trusted with confidentialities? Can you be trusted with relationships? Can you be trusted with finances? Can you be trusted ... period? Do you have the formal training—qualifications and certifications— needed to do the job? Are your skills relevant and up to date?

Appearance, Body Language, Communication Skills, Deliverables, and Etiquette/Social Skills

- Appearance covers aspects of attire, grooming, and personal hygiene.
- Body language covers aspects of posture, facial expressions, eye contact, and handshake.
- Communication includes talking skills—tone of voice, pronunciation, enunciation, accent, and rate of speech; writing skills; presentation skills; and technology skills—proper use of land phones, cell phones, Internet products such as e-mail, Facebook, Instagram, YouTube, and Twitter.
- Deliverables refer to one's work products—doing what you are asked to do; doing what you say you can or will do; providing excellent customer service; goal setting, planning, and time-management skills.
- Etiquette/social skills include dining etiquette, business etiquette, reception and networking savvy, and gender considerations.

Using the familiar concept of the ABCs should make it easy for you to remember the desired and profitable outcome of professionalism—*impression management through personal excellence as conveyed through socially acceptable, correct behaviors.* You are in control of how and what others think of you. Through excellence in appearance, body language, communication, deliverables, and etiquette/social skills, you can be seen as a person who is appropriate, believable, and credible—a person of professional excellence.

The heart of effective impression management rests in your recognition of the "significance of the insignificant." The chapter continues with detailed explanations of the correct behaviors in each of the following five areas:

- *a*ppearance
- *b*ody language
- *c*ommunication

- *d*eliverables
- *e*tiquette/social skills

Appearance: Dressing for Today's Business Environment

Personal and professional excellence starts with looking the part: wearing the appropriate attire for the occasion, according to a set of generally accepted standards or rules defined by organizational culture. Usually these standards evolved over decades as a result of identifying the attire choices that resulted in the "know, like, and trust" factor of people interactions. Smooth and efficient organizational operations result from the collaborative efforts of people who "know, like, and trust" each other.

Often the standard of professionalism was created at the discretion of the founder of an organization. A perfect example is the standard blue suit, white shirt, and wing tips for IBM salesmen. This dress standard was created by IBM's founder, Thomas J. Watson, shortly after the company was founded in 1911. From studies in human relations in the early 1900s, Mr. Watson learned the navy blue suit/white shirt/red tie combination built trust faster. Therefore, he dressed in this manner and institutionalized this dress combination for the entire company.

It was certainly the dress culture I experienced throughout my thirteen-year career in sales and marketing with IBM during the 1980s and early 1990s. IBM, a century-old company originating in 1911 and retaining more than 400,000 worldwide employees in the 1980s, is recognized globally as one of the largest, most profitable, respected, and admired companies in business. Because of its reputation for success and excellence, IBM's organizational culture nuance of navy suit/white shirt/red tie uniform for its sales force became the dress standard for salespersons throughout all of industry. This look remains today as the most definitive and professional dress in business and politics—two "selling" professions.

Recent research by Dimitrius and Mazzarella shows that color of clothing is equated with people's assumptions as to someone's professionalism or honesty. Navy blue consistently scores higher than bright, flashy colors, and solids receive higher ratings than plaids or dramatic patterns. A general societal perception based on years of experience is that those who are more professional and honest tend to dress more conservatively and those who dress in flashy clothes tend to be less professional and less honest.

The professional attire discussion would be incomplete if it did not address the contrary view to standard business attire. The "appropriate" attire and grooming—dark suit, white shirt, tie, absence of facial hair, minimal head hair, no earrings—is viewed by many in the millennial generation as "selling out." Students holding this view often express their disdain for having to give up their individuality and creativity in order to conform to "the man." Dimitrius and Mazzarella make the following observation on the subject.

> There's nothing inherently wrong with being individualistic, creative or expressive; but few people hold nonconformity, even if it reflects creativity and expressiveness, in high esteem if it detracts from the four points of the Compass [trustworthiness, caring, humility, and capability]. And that conflict can be expected when your appearance deviates from others' expectations. Many people think that they'll get ahead if they break from the pack. This is seldom true. We are not unlike the other members of the animal kingdom whose suspicions are immediately drawn to anything unusual or unexpected in our environment.

When deciding what dressing image you want to be known for in your professional setting, choose classic fashion over trends and fads. An example is the wearing of denim items. Denim is a classic fabric, which never goes out of style and is acceptable for casual wear in the office workplace. Distressed denim (holey, frayed, torn, and worn) is a denim fad, in today and out tomorrow, and would likely raise eyebrows if worn in the office workplace. Observe how the top performers dress and emulate their style. Be cautious of duplicating their style as your workplace clothing choices and brands should be in line with your salary level.

Professional Attire

Earlier in this chapter, I presented a discussion on the guiding principles of professionalism. Included in the discussion was McGuigan's list of five attributes of professionalism for the individual who works in a specific occupation. These attributes are as follows:

1. Reliance on a high personal standard of competence in providing professional services.
2. Promotion and maintenance of the image of the profession.
3. Willingness to pursue development opportunities that improve skills.
4. Pursuit of quality, competence, and ideals within the profession.
5. Presentation of a sense of pride about the profession.

One sure way for an individual to demonstrate the attributes of professionalism is through his or her dress attire. When an individual within an occupation adheres to the dress code of the occupation, he or she is adhering to attribute #2 (promote and maintain the image of the profession) and attribute #5 (presentation of a sense of pride about the profession). As one of my astute students says, "You look like success."

The dress code in some occupations expresses itself in some type of uniform. Examples include sports teams, judges, police, clergy, medical profession, and airplane pilots. Have you ever noticed how individuals when dressed in their uniforms seem to exude a sense of self-confidence? The way they walk and talk demonstrates a degree of authority and competence in their ability to do their jobs (attributes #1 and #4). They wear their uniforms as badges of honor, signaling they have achieved something significant in their professional lives. I trust the wearing of the "business uniform" will have the same effect on you.

The first definitive book on the business uniform was written in 1961, fifty years after the founding of IBM, by John T. Molloy, a scientific image consultant and clothing researcher. *Dress for Success* started the image consulting industry and was used as a textbook by business schools and the management of America's blue chip corporations, such as General Motors and Merrill Lynch. *Dress for Success* became a phenomenal best seller and paved the way for his second book on the topic, *John T. Molloy's New Dress for Success*, published in 1988.

Molloy's work was not without its challengers. Molloy states, "Many critics charge that my approach to successful dress is snobbish, conservative, bland, and conformist." However, he confronts his critics' charges. "People who look successful and well-educated receive preferential treatment in almost all of their social or business encounters."

Some of Molloy's advice on business dress, unlike the "uniforms" of some of the professions previously mentioned, has evolved over time. As an example, personal taste in colors is allowed in a much greater degree in the business uniform as opposed to occupations where the color of the uniform must be the team's color, e.g. sports teams or the company's color, e.g., flight attendants. What has not changed over time in business dressing is that the rules of business dressing exist to enforce and reinforce the occupational status of "business" as a profession and adhering to the rules of business professional dressing signals one has a sense of pride about themselves as well as the profession and organization being represented.

Let's examine specific details of business professional attire, the first component of the ABCs of professional presence. There are four categories of business professional attire, all beginning with the word business. These four categories are:

1) *Business Strict Interview.* The most conservative and traditional dress standard. Very few personal choices

are inserted in the standard interview attire, also referred to as the "interview uniform." This uniform look for the interviewee is the expectation of the interviewer. The benefit of wearing the uniform is that the appearance expectations of the interviewer are immediately matched when the interviewee is greeted by the interviewer. If the appearance matches, the interviewer is open to see if there are other matches between the interviewee and job position. Because the interviewer is not distracted by the interviewee's appearance, he or she can focus on the interviewee's skills, resume, and conversation. Not wearing the uniform may be perceived as a signal that you don't want to be part of the team. Dressing appropriately says, "Put me in, Coach. I'm ready to play *today!*"

2) *Business Dress.* This second category is very similar to interview attire but has more color options and personal choices than strict interview attire. This category is also called client-facing attire. Additions and deviations in personal choices are acceptable over time as you prove yourself to be a valuable asset to the organization.

3) *Business Casual.* Suits and ties are not required or expected for men. This third category is very organizational culture specific. Jeans, T-shirts, and flip-flops may be okay at Google or Apple but not at Goldman Sachs. Effective impression management dictates that you have your own high standards of professionalism regardless of the organizational culture.

4) *Business Relaxed Casual.* The last category of business dressing is the appropriate choice for business functions that do not take place at the company site or a client's site. Attire in this category is worn at weekend company outings such as sporting events and company picnics.

Business Strict Interview Attire for Men

When preparing for the interview, a suit is your first choice of attire. The colors that are permissible and/or acceptable are navy blue, gray, and coffee beige (hot summer climates only)—in that order. Black, brown, and forest green should *never* be worn in an interview situation. A lightweight tropical wool fabric is the most functional year-round option. It is very resistant to wrinkling, while also needing a minimal amount of maintenance—cleaning and pressing between wears. A solid suit is ideal. If a pin-strip is worn, the maximum width is no larger than one-sixteenth of an inch. If a suit is not available, a navy blue blazer and a pair of gray or beige pants are acceptable but should be avoided if at all possible.

The preferred jacket (suit coat) style for an interview is a two-button single-breast, notch lapel jacket with side vents. The number of buttons should never be more than three. When wearing a two- or three-button suit (no vest), always unbutton the last button. The pockets should be made in the jacket and not sewn onto the jacket like patch pockets. The two side pockets should be flapped, and the flaps remain outside.

The basic rule regarding pants is that if the pants are pleated, they should be cuffed, and if the pants are non-pleated, they should be plain bottomed. If wearing cuffs, 1.25 inches is the standard cuff width. Pants should have a medium break. (The break is where your pants fall on your shoes, creating a horizontal crease in the fabric across the front of your pant leg. The break is created when the tailor hems your pants. Ask your tailor to adjust the length of your pants to hit midway between the top of your dress shoe and the top of your shoe sole.)

Know the difference between braces and suspenders. Traditionally, the term "braces" refers to button-on suspenders, generally made of high-quality materials. The term "suspenders" refers to the clip-on variety. Adult men wear braces; boys wear suspenders. Neither is worn when wearing a belt. Unless you are interviewing in a very formal profession, do not wear braces to the interview.

Shirt should be white, long-sleeved, no-cuff, and 100 percent cotton; a white undershirt is worn underneath. Tie should be 100 percent silk, solid, or patterned. Solids, stripes, and pin dots are all good pattern choices for interviews. Unless you are interviewing in the specialized professions of law or academia, refrain from wearing a bow tie to an interview.

Shoes may be black, dark brown, or cordovan (burgundy). Tan and light brown shoes should be avoided. Shoes must be shined, heels and soles in perfect condition, and no ornamentation. Lace-ups and wing tips are the preferred shoe styles. The color of your shoes and your belt should match. Socks should be dress socks that are black and plain—never in the red family (burgundy or maroon) striped, patterned, or with cartoons. Never wear athletic (cotton) socks in any color to an interview. (Consult the websites of men's business clothiers such as Brooks Brothers, JoS. A. Bank, and Men's Wearhouse for examples of appropriate business clothing for an interview before purchasing at budget-friendly stores, i.e., T. J. Maxx and Goodwill.)

Limit jewelry to a medium, plain-face (one-inch diameter) watch with black leather band and one ring, preferably a wedding band or class ring, on left ring finger. No earrings, collar bars, cuff links, lapel pins, bracelets, wristbands, or necklaces are to be worn.

Business Dress Attire for Men

Suit colors remain the same as for strict interview attire— navy blue, grays, and coffee beige. Avoid black and brown and assign an absolute "no" to green, maroon, and other colors. However, the choice of colors and patterns for your shirts, ties, and socks are slightly broader. Ties are not to be worn with button-down shirts. You can add "soft" colors to your shirt selections—pastel blues and yellows. Dark shirt colors—maroon, green, black, red, brown, and purple—are considered less professional choices. You may wear two-toned shirts (white collar and cuffs with pastel color body). Shirts with French cuffs, spread collars, and bold stripes are also acceptable—but never short-sleeved shirts. Always wear a 100 percent cotton undershirt (T-shirt), either V-neck or crew-neck, under your dress shirt.

You may wear pocket squares and collar bars. An additional ring on ring finger (not the pinkie) and/or bracelet on the right hand are also appropriate. Earrings are seldom appropriate. Use extreme caution when deciding whether to wear earrings. Be mindful of the culture of the organization and your status in the office. Wearing earrings can be one of those "silent killers" to career mobility. Just because you are not told to take out your earrings doesn't mean it is viewed positively in your workplace.

The well-dressed junior executive professional wardrobe consists of three or four "good" suits: one navy blue suit, one gray suit, one coffee-beige suit, and one navy or gray pinstripe. Have your suits tailored to fit such that they do not appear to be too little or too big. Suits may be two- or three-button; single- or double-breasted. The cross suit (sport jacket and contrasting pant color) along with a shirt and tie is accepted as business dress attire in certain professional fields including medicine, sales, media, manufacturing, academia, city and county government, and law enforcement. This cross suit look is not considered business dress in the corporate business setting or law profession. Suits with "extra" decorations (pleats in the back, top-stitching, contrasting chevrons, straps, and insignias on the sleeves, snaps and epaulets on shoulders) are also not viewed as business professional in the corporate business setting or law profession.

Button Your Jacket!

As a man walks, his suit coat is buttoned as follows:

- ➤ *Three-Button Suit*
- Top Button—Sometimes
- Middle Button—Always
- Bottom Button—Never

➤ *Two-Button Suit*
- Top Button—Always
- Bottom Button—Never

As a man sits in his chair, he unfastens all buttons. This allows for comfort while sitting and the preservation of his attire from wrinkles. As a man rises from his chair, he begins to fasten the "always" button. When he reaches his destination in the room, the fastening action should be completed. He is now ready to begin the business at hand (presenting, presiding, accepting an award, etc.).

Business Casual Attire for Men

If your office is formal—a bank, a law office, or a brokerage firm— your business casual attire consists of button-down-collar shirts, polo-style shirts, sport shirts, and sweaters with collars. A tie is not worn for business casual. Always wear a 100 percent cotton undershirt (T-shirt), either V-neck or crew-neck. Because your collar will be open, be sure to not expose chest hair or your undershirt.

A sports jacket or blazer should always be worn or easily accessible in the office. You will wear a sport coat in a solid color or muted plaid such as herringbone or tweed. The classic navy, gray, or beige blazer is also a good choice. Trousers made from light-weight wool in plain colors, such as browns, olives, navy, and gray are best choices. Other choices include subtle tweed wool and gray flannels. Combine textures for an interesting fabric mix. Shoe choices include suede lace-ups or soft leather loafers.

If your office is semiformal—meaning you have little to no dealings with clients and the atmosphere is relaxed, acceptable business causal attire includes sport cardigan sweaters or pullovers, jackets without linings, vests, corduroy trousers, or khakis, open-shirt collars, and no ties. Avoid jogging suits, sweatshirts, shorts, distressed jeans, T-shirts, sleeveless shirts, sandals, and flip-flops. Avoid bold patterns or garish colors. Never show tattoos or body art. Remember, the emphasis in business casual dressing is still on *business*.

Business Relaxed Casual Attire for Men

This category is reserved for business activities that take place outside of the office building. Khakis and Dockers are good choices for pants. Jeans are allowed, but they should not have more than the two standard pockets in front and back and no holes, rips, or tears. Shorts are to be worn with extreme caution. Pants and shirts must be wrinkle free. Never show tattoos or body art. Sneakers and shirts should be clean, solid colored, and non-assuming. None of the items should have prominent designer labels or thoughts expressed in words or pictures (unless it is or relates to the company logo). This is similar to discussing taboo topics such as religion, politics, or race. You never want to risk offending people or making them uncomfortable with your views.

Business Strict Interview Attire for Women

Simplify the dressing option by investing in an "interview uniform." Your uniform should be a navy blue, gray, or black skirt suit (a pantsuit is also acceptable as is a dress with a jacket). The fabric choice is light-weight wool with no patterns. The suit should fit well—not too tight or too big. Purchasing a suit with a small amount (less than 10 percent) of stretch fabric (nylon, polyester, rayon, Lycra, or spandex) helps provide a more tailored, comfortable professional fit to one's body type. Under the suit jacket, wear a white or cream blouse. Undergarments (bra and camisole) should be worn but not visible to the eye.

The skirt length should not be so short (not above the knee) that when you sit or cross your legs, your thigh shows. Your skirt should have a split (three or four inches) in the back (not the front or side). The purpose of the split is to allow for ease of movement when you walk, climb stairs, sit in a chair, and enter or exit a car.

Special Note

Unfortunately, women in business have an extra hurdle to face in business encounters—being perceived as a professional colleague and not a social opportunity. The good news is that through your dressing choices, you are in charge of how you are perceived. Adopt a proactive mind-set when choosing how to dress—and do not fall victim to the negative side of the "perception is reality" coin. Use your choice of interview attire as a strategy to advance your career agenda and achieve your professional goal. Avoid bare skin (always wear a jacket and hose), avoid showing cleavage (cleavage starts at the point of breast separation), and avoid showing the intricate details of your body shape and undergarments (nothing too tight, too short, or see-through). Wear good support clothing, such as Spanx undergarments, to give a clean, no-line profile to your look.

Always remember that you want to look businesslike, not sexy. Long hair should be pulled away from the face and not interfere with your eyesight. Your makeup should be for daytime wear only. Keep nails neat, short, and manicured.

The most appropriate jewelry set consists of a fourteen-to-nineteen-inch strand of white pearls and white pearl stud earrings. Any earrings worn should be studs or a small clip-on—never anything dangling. If you have more than one hole in your ear(s), wear only one set of earrings. Bracelets should not make noise when moving your arms around in normal conversation. Neck chains should remain simple and few.

Run-free stockings are a must and should be the color of your legs or slightly darker—nothing too light. If you do not want to wear pantyhose, wear a pantsuit with knee-high hose. Your shoes should be leather pumps (not suede or pattern), with a heel height of two to three inches—no stilettos. Shoe color is black for dark clothes and taupe for light clothes.

The purse you carry should be of good-quality leather, medium size, with the inside contents organized neatly such that your professional appearance is consistently maintained. Have pen and pad in hand so as not to "go fishing" in your purse. (Consult the websites of business clothiers for women such as Brooks Brothers or department stores such as Nordstrom and Macy's for examples of appropriate business clothing before purchasing at budget-friendly stores, i.e., T. J. Maxx and Goodwill.)

Business Dress Attire for Women

Women's standards for business dress attire vary and depend greatly on whether you work in a large metropolitan area or a small town, and in which region of the country you live. Corporate attire in large cities, such as New York, Chicago, Detroit, and Los Angeles, tends to be less conservative than in the South or smaller towns. For instance, in New York, more vibrant colors, such as red, gold, purple, yellow, and green, when used appropriately, are acceptable. It also must be noted that women in certain professions, such as finance and law, as well as female executives in major corporations, are expected to dress more conservatively than those in creative fields, such as the media, advertising, and public relations. However, the standards for professional attire are continuously evolving. Colored and coordinated pantsuits, dresses, and skirt suits are all acceptable, along with the traditional dark pant and skirt suits.

Body type/size must always be taken into consideration when selecting dress attire. Skirts more than two inches above the knee are not appropriate for any body type. The "no-hose" look has become very popular in business. Your age, body type/size, and length of dress or skirt should be taken into consideration when deciding whether to wear hose. Dark-colored opaque hose that complements your attire is a chic, classy business dress choice for women of all ages and body types/sizes who want to be seen as professional *and* fashionable in the workplace. Shoes are the same as business interview attire.

Women who have found a niche in corporate America agree that you must dress for the position you hold—but also for the position to which you aspire. Good taste is the key. If an outfit is questionable, don't wear it. Avoid a situation in which you have to be told what *not* to wear to work.

Business Casual Attire for Women

Outer dress options include pants and skirts; crisp button-down, collared shirts, polo shirts, shells; tailored jackets; cashmere sweater sets, and knit separates. As with men, jackets should always be worn; they can be belted or zipped for variety. Instead of pumps, heels with sling backs or slips-ons (mules) are acceptable— but no stilettos. When wearing sandals and open-toe shoes, be sure feet have been freshly pedicured and toes polished. Loafers and flats work well with casual attire. Ankle-high or calf-high (no thigh-high) boots with matching opaque tights work well with skirts and dresses.

Avoid jogging suits, sweatshirts, shorts, distressed jeans, T-shirts, sleeveless shirts, sandals, and flip-flops. Avoid bold patterns or garish colors. Never show tattoos or body art. Remember, the emphasis in business casual dressing is still on *business.*

Business Relaxed Casual Attire for Women

This category is reserved for business activities that take place outside of the office building. Jeans and city shorts are allowed but should not be skin-tight or have holes, rips, or tears. Choices for shoes include flats, heels, and sandals showing a moderate amount of skin—but again, no stilettos.

None of the items you wear should have noticeable designer labels or thoughts expressed in words or pictures (unless it is or relates to the company logo). Extremely revealing tops showing midriff, cleavage, or a large portion of your back are not suitable. Never show tattoos or body art. Again, I caution the showing of bare skin. Perceptions vary widely in this area. However, it never hurts to play it safe. Save revealing ensembles for personal engagements.

Dress for Success Tips for Women

- If you want to get ahead, emulate those women who are moving up in the company.
- Dress appropriately and blend in, yet maintain your personal style. If you are in a traditional corporate setting, wear

the navy suit and white pearls; individualize your outfit through accessories such as a colorful scarf or suit pin.

- Dress classically—suits, dresses, and sensible heels or flats. Stick to the basics. Never wear tennis shoes and socks with your business attire. This is not a power look!
- Save dressy shorts sets, tight skirts, leggings, jogging suits, stretch pants, and other casual attire for non-business-related leisure activities.
- Stay away from clothes that wrinkle easily such as 100 percent linen.
- If you are in a conservative environment, choose suits and dresses with jackets rather than sweaters. Jackets are perceived as a power look. Sweaters are perceived as an administrative look.
- Avoid situations in which you have to be told what *not* to wear to work.
- Always demonstrate personal leadership. Maintain a set of standards that is higher than the norm that you refuse to violate or compromise.

Gender-Neutral Professionalism Topics

- *Technology.* In this age of technology, many millennials are choosing not to wear a watch or carry paper and pen, preferring to use their iPhones or similar devices to check the time or take notes. I advise against using this tactic, especially in a job interview, for two main reasons. First, to have your phone out during the interview may appear that you are attending to personal matters—texting, reading e-mails, checking Facebook—and not focused on the business at hand, which should be to get the job. Secondly, if your interviewer is not a member of the millennial generation, which will probably be the case, he or she may prefer the use of paper and pen for taking notes as the professional choice. Using pen and paper suggests you are engaged and interested in the matter at hand, which is to get the job.

- *Tattoos.* If you have body art, tattoos, and piercing in places other than your earlobes, be intentional about wearing clothing that will keep your tattoos covered and remove visible body-piercing jewelry. Dressing tastefully in this category sends a positive signal that you have good judgment and will use it to make good decisions as a member of the organization.

- *The Office Gym.* Many companies have included on-site gyms for their employees. If you choose to take advantage of this perk, dress appropriately. Invest in fashionable, coordinated fitness attire, from head to toe, including your sport bag. Although wonderful for convenience, how you present yourself in the office gym has the potential, positively or negatively, to contribute to your progression in the organization. Remember, every contact with your workplace is a contact that can make or break your career. Keep in mind you are still on the playing field of the game, so adhere to the rules of the game—business etiquette and appropriate attire.

- *Grooming.* Immaculate, impeccable grooming is a must for men and women. Positive attributes that others project onto a professionally groomed individual is that he or she pays attention to details, takes pride in his or her appearance, and enjoys the fine art of impression management. Professional grooming is a "silent promoter" that can result in positive public recognition. Unprofessional grooming can be a "silent killer" to your dream job or promotion.

Facial Hair

- Men: Mustache, sideburns no longer than length of ear hole, and thin beard, all neatly trimmed are acceptable. Shave chin hair or hair underneath your bottom lip. (Adjustments to this standard based on culture and skin type are becoming more acceptable. Tread cautiously.)

- Women: None. Have hairs that appear over the lips (mustache), side of face (sideburns), or under chin (beard) professionally removed.

Head Hair

- Men: Short, combed, neat; fresh maintenance regardless of length.
- Women: Short or medium in length; long hair should be neatly restrained. All styles combed and regularly maintained is a must.

Other Body Hair

- Men: Chest and underarm hair never exposed.
- Women: Shaved legs and underarms.

Nails/Makeup

- Men: Nails short and clean; buffed manicure. No makeup on face.
- Women: Makeup a must. A light application of lipstick, eye shadow, liner, mascara, and rouge gives a mature, professional look for all ages. Nails are short to moderate in length, manicured, and neutral in color. Save multicolored nails, nail art—including designs, glitter, and sparkles—for vacation and holiday time.

Body Art/Body Piercings

- Men and Women: Completely covered.

Diversity and Professionalism

Hairstyles for Men and Women of Color. Many young professionals of color are choosing to wear braids, cornrows, Afros, twists, and locs.

Some men are choosing to wear shoulder-length hair and ponytails. While these hairstyles are not the traditional choices for corporate America, they are becoming more acceptable in the twenty-first-century workplace. This evolution is due to the desire of corporate America to become more inclusive and diverse in its workforce.

If you choose to wear a hairstyle viewed as nontraditional for the corporate environment, be prepared for comments and looks that you may perceive as negative and insensitive. You may also encounter consequences that are detrimental to your career as a result of your hairstyle choice, including unfavorable decisions in hiring, promotions, job assignments, and client decisions. Regardless of the hairstyle you choose, be sure it is always neat, clean, and combed.

Warning! The proliferation of long and sometimes un-styled hair on professional athletes and entertainers has become a style of choice for a significant number of young men of color. As a choice for professional athletes and entertainers, long hair may be of no consequence to their multimillion-dollar paychecks. Professional athletes make their brands by the stats they acquire on the basketball court, football, and baseball fields; musicians depend on record sales. If their stats are exceptional, their jobs are secure—regardless of hair or clothing styles.

Unfortunately for the young men of color who are not athletes or entertainers, wearing this same hairstyle and clothing may *prevent* them for being able to accumulate the "stats" necessary to get, keep, and/or move up in their jobs or their entrepreneurial careers. Perception is the reality of the perceiver. The perception held by the decision makers in the room when assessments are being made regarding hiring, firing, and promotions will take into account appearance, including grooming. You will never be told you were not hired, not promoted, fired, or didn't get the contract because of your appearance and/or hairstyle, but it can and does happen.

Voice of Experience

> If you are wearing a hairstyle or dress style that is not the norm in corporate America, you have a decision to make. If the hairstyle or dress style is a conviction, i.e., a part of your spiritual center, keep them and don't go into corporate America. If the hairstyle or dress style is a habit, i.e., you are wearing it just because you always have or you just like it, get rid of it if you want to work in corporate America. I am wearing a full beard and double-breasted suit today because I have earned the right to wear them; decades of producing millions of dollars in revenue for the company gives me the right, and until you do the same, stay clear of attire and appearance that is not the norm in corporate America.
>
> —Jeffrey Humber, SVP, Merrill Lynch
> Conversation with Morehouse Students, 2002

Body Language: Basic Business Behaviors

Knowing and utilizing proper body language is as essential as knowing and using proper English and diction and is therefore a critical component of the ABCs of professional presence. Relationships can be forged through proper body language, and relationships can be hindered through improper body language. In daily interactions with people—whether with coworkers and executives, clients and customers, or neighbors, friends, and even strangers, body language plays a role. Knowing how to communicate effectively through body language will make you a relationship magnet—attracting people to an engaging style that puts them at ease. Poor body language yields the same detrimental results as kryptonite to Superman—weakening your ability to build relationships. Here are a few basic body language moves that you must master as a twenty-first-century global leader.

Handshakes

The most acceptable form of business greeting is the common handshake, accompanied by a greeting such as, "Hello, William," and a smile. The handshake is thought to have originated as a sign of friendship and peace, represented by an open, weapon-free hand.

The handshake starts relationships and seals deals. Therefore, knowing how to execute a proper handshake is a must. Don't under-shake; a limp handshake signals you as someone who is hesitant, lacking in self-confidence, and can't be trusted. Don't over-shake; an overpowering handshake signals you as a manipulator.

Simple rules for the proper handshake:

- When the web-space between index fingers and thumbs touch, and the other person's palm meets with your palm, firmly close your fingers around their palm.
- Apply a little pressure and look the person in the eye.
- Do not squeeze fingers or cause pain of any type. Pump the person's hand by moving your hand up and down, no more than three times.
- As you shake hands, speak to the person, call their name, and say your name. "Hello, William. My name is Sandra. Nice to meet you/see you again."
- Avoid "extra touches." Don't use your left hand to touch their elbow, arm, or shoulder or clasp it over their hand as you are shaking.
- As you release the other person's hand, pause briefly but purposefully before continuing the conversation.

One of the most important aspects of body language that accompanies the handshake is standing. If you, male or female, are seated and someone, male or female, approaches to shake your hand, rise. If you, male or female, are seated and want to extend your hand to someone, male or female, rise first and then extend your hand for the handshake.

The positive outcome that is desired from an effective handshake occurs when both parties feel respected, equal, and comfortable with each other. Standing such that neither person is looking down on the other signals mutual respect and self-respect. The eye contact made with both parties standing communicates an appreciation and comfortableness with each other as equal human beings. Titles and positions may be at different levels, but at the moment of the greeting, you are equal human beings—showing respect for the other and for themselves.

Gender Gestures

Contemporary business behavior dictates that all people be treated equally in the workplace. Everyone should demonstrate good manners by lending a helping hand when the situation warrants it without regard to gender. Genuine good manners are a show of respect. Displaying good manners gives you instant credibility and provides an immediate point of connection to the person you are interacting with. Always pay attention to the needs of others around you and respond accordingly.

Basic gestures to be observed by both genders for either gender (also called gender-neutral gestures):

- Helping someone with his or her coat.
- Opening and/or holding a door; first person at the door opens the door; lower-ranked person is always first to the door; higher-ranked person says thank you.
- Assisting someone to be seated.
- Giving up your seat to someone older or apparently uncomfortable.
- Standing when someone enters the room, when you are being introduced, and/or when you shake hands.
- Offering to assist in carrying something.
- Intentionally observing others such that, if needed, you can offer a writing instrument, handkerchief, tissue, glass of water, etc.

Behaviors to Avoid

Because humans are creatures of habit, we sometimes unconsciously exhibit behaviors that, unbeknownst to us, are irritating to others in our presence. The person(s) around us may assess the behavior as clownish or crude, which may cause them to label us as rude, impolite, or immature. A few examples of public behaviors that could fall into the clownish category include humming; whistling; chewing hard objects such as pens and pencils; twisting and playing with hair; knuckle popping; snapping fingers to get attention; and ringing/using cell phones and pagers at dinner, in theaters, or in places of worship.

A few examples of public behaviors that could fall into the crude category include belching; farting; spitting; nose picking; scratching private parts or buttocks; gum "games" such as popping or rolling the wad in the mouth; chewing a dead cigar or cigarette; chewing gum; talking with gum in your mouth; talking to people while smoking; eating candy while talking to someone; yawning wide without placing hand over mouth; blowing nose; holding crotch; wearing pants below waist and hips; fingernail chewing; constantly pulling up pants or touching private parts of body.

Here is my list of the top ten toxic behaviors in the workplace. To ensure that your reputation as a professional is not questioned, avoid these items at all cost:

1. Gum chewing
2. Garbled name pronunciation when introducing self
3. Weak, limp, or bone-crushing handshake
4. Arriving late or being late completing any task assigned to you
5. Slouching or sleeping in meetings
6. Gender-suggestive tags on e-mail, home phone, or cell phone message systems
7. Music on home phone or cell phone messaging system
8. Body odor, bad breath, long nails, or dirty nails

9. Drugs, alcohol, cigarettes, or cigars before an interview or before/during work hours
10. Excuses, exemptions, and exceptions

Communication Skills

Being able to make others feel comfortable with you through your words is the third essential component of the ABCs of professional presence. Communicating effectively and easily is crucial for making a good impression. A discussion of communication skills provides a platform to introduce small acts of "being and doing" for personal and professional success: "be engaging, be interested and interesting, and be prepared." These acts of being and doing are of utmost importance in the communication areas discussed below, including the interview, small talk, introductions, and public speaking.

The Interview

One place in which communication skills will definitely mean success or failure is in the interview process. This is not "new news," and the failure possibility may explain why some college students will not engage in career-services offerings even though they have paid for the services through their tuition. As one colleague said, "Education is the only product I know that people are willing to pay for and not get their money's worth." From my twenty-plus years of experience teaching undergraduates, I discovered that the reasons of their lack of engagement is multifaceted, coupling the dislike and distress of rejection and the unknown with their fear of failure.

To help students overcome these anxieties, I created an experiential learning activity in my leadership and professional development course. In the "LPD Interview Combine," I invite ten to twelve corporate representatives from various industries to come to a class and give mock five-minute interviews followed by five-minute critiques. The students participate in the ten-minute interview session in pairs—interviewee and observer, and then they switch roles for another ten-minute session. The students are required to be dressed in strict interview attire and required to complete at least three interviews with three different interviewers over a two-day period. In the last fifteen minutes of the class, the corporate representatives give a one-to-two-minute assessment of their observations of students' strengths and areas of development along with general tips for success based on their firsthand experiences in the workplace.

Students give high ratings to this classroom activity because it forces them to reach beyond their fear of failure, rejection, and the unknown by being required to engage in a no-penalty interview. Also, hearing the corrective comments of corporate representatives directed to the classroom allows the message to be received by individual students without becoming defensive. Students were surprisingly pleased with their interview experiences.

Participating in the fall 2016 LPD Interview Combine were junior- and senior-level professionals in a variety of business functions including human resources, management, sales and marketing, finance, accounting, and consulting. Companies represented were Accenture, Federal Reserve Bank of Atlanta, Boeing, Innovative Marketing, PepsiCo, Radio One, and Trendscend Marketing. The students viewed the corporate representatives' critiques and advice as priceless gems. I have incorporated the major themes and takeaways shared by the corporate representatives in my ten points to effective interviewing that follow.

Point #1: Have a Winner's Mind-Set

When you are being interviewed, you have moved from applicant to candidate. The interviewer has seen your resume and deemed you worthy of thirty minutes or more of his or her valuable time. The interviewer is not the enemy; he or she is there to help you. Your job now is to confirm what he or she already believes is possible: you are a right fit for their organization, you have promise and potential, and you are purposeful and personable. Come prepared and confident, ready to answer the questions, "Why you?" and "What will you do for my company?"

Point #2: The Start

You will be asked to "Tell me about yourself." This question will probably come in the first two minutes of the interview. You must be ready to nail this. After hearing this question, you have two minutes to sell yourself as excellence—a must hire. Respond with your previously well-crafted, succinct elevator speech. The typical elevator speech is a thirty-second pitch that summarizes who you are and what you do that can be shared with anyone, anywhere who is interested in knowing about you. In the interview, you will need to use about two minutes to tell who you are, what you do, and *why* you'd be a perfect fit for the position. Here's an example:

> I'm currently a senior at [name of college], studying [major]. I am a native of [hometown]. I chose to come to [name of college] for three reasons [name them]. Since being here, I have been able to grow strengths in the areas of cognitive skills [accounting, finance, management, marketing] and technical skills [Excel, PowerPoint, KeyNote, statistical packages] as demonstrated through my high academic achievements [give GPA]; as well as intrapersonal, interpersonal, and leadership skills [through my club activities and community service organizations [names with offices held], and internships at [names of companies]. Through these experiences I believe I have gained insights into my emotional intelligence—strengths and areas of improvement—and honed my time-management skills, ability to work on as well as lead a team, and my ability to envision, implement, and see a project through to completion. I am confident that these skills can add value to any organization, however, I am specifically interested in your organization, a leader in the [industry/field] because [tell why you want to a job with this company, i.e., listed

as one of the best companies to work for; strong talent management program; strong rotational program; products that you use and admire; etc.]. My goal is to secure an entry-level role in your organization as a [name the position], adding value as an individual contributor with the long-term goal and aspiration of progression through the company to higher levels of responsibilities and ways to contribute to the achievement of the mission and performance objectives of [name of company].

As you can see, your elevator speech will take time to write and lots of time to practice its effective delivery. It has to be who you are and delivered conversationally (not as a speech). Therefore, you will need to practice, practice, practice until you reach perfection—and then practice your perfect practice. You will interview like you practice. If you want a perfect interview, you must do lots of perfect practices.

Point #3: Your Story

The interviewer will be intrigued, sitting on the edge of his or her seat, and wanting to know more about you and how you became the motivated, high-achieving, service-focused person you are. Be ready to share your story—your journey up to this point in your life. Find it, know it, and make it relevant and consistent with your resume. Tell how you accomplished it. Tell it from different angles. Keep it positive. Be cautious with providing TMI (too much information). Don't over-tell. It is okay to talk about your failures, but you must add how you turned the failure into a learning experience and the resulting competencies.

Your story should express your grit, passion, and purpose for a particular long-term goal coupled with a powerful motivation to achieve it. Be polished in the telling of your story. Use words from the "secret code" of professionalism (add-value, collaboration, teamwork, vision, competencies, skills, and organization/culture fit).

Point #4: The Resume

It must be perfect, accurate, and outcome oriented! Absolutely no mistakes in grammar, spelling, and punctuation—and no lies, misrepresentations, or exaggerations. Your 2.89 GPA cannot be rounded up to 3.0. If you have on your resume that you are fluent in Spanish, be sure that you are. By listing it on your resume, chances are very likely that your interviewer will be fluent and will conduct the interview in Spanish.

Because the interviewer has already seen your resume, use this time to share the backstory of your resume; be able to go in depth on your resume. Fill in the details on the what and the why. Explain how you have grown through the experiences and relate your resume to company needs. Tell the details behind what is on the resume; give examples and be specific. Don't downplay your experiences or embellish them. Focus on the competencies you demonstrated and learned from the experiences.

Point #5: Research the Company

Know something about the company; don't stop researching until you know and can discuss ten facts about the company. Be able to do a deep dive when asking questions about the company, especially if you are interviewing for a sales position. Ask questions based on insights about the company garnered through your research sources, including the Internet, your professors, and your peers who have interned with the company. Seek out alumni from your school who are employed at the company.

Point #6: Control the Interview

Hear the question so you can answer it. Be responsive and conversational. It's your interview; be in control of it. You should be talking more than the interviewer. Your conversation should focus on what *you* can do for the company. Don't be afraid to "not know." When you don't know, say, "I regret I'm not familiar/aware of that item. Can you share a little more about it so that I can take a few notes and do my research on it?" It's okay to ask questions about the question if the interviewer uses language you don't have knowledge of, i.e., company acronyms.

Know when to stop talking. Focus on the interviewer's body language to gauge how your response is being received. The interviewer's perception of you—based upon what you are saying, the pronouns you are using, and your tone of voice—will be the basis of the evaluation of you.

Point #7: Responses to Interviewer's Questions

Give clear answers; slow down when responding; be confident in your responses; use the breath of your experiences in your responses. Connect personal and professional items about your life to show you are a well-rounded and balanced person. Front load your responses. Grab the interviewer's attention by sharing your big results up front and then tell the story using the STAR (situation, task, action, result) behavioral interview method. When asked to discuss your weaknesses, do so confidently as you share how you turned weaknesses into points of growth that are headed toward strengths because you now realize their importance.

Show ways you have demonstrated initiative and shown versatility. Tell what you did, respond with "I" results, and quantify your results. Eliminate filler words: ahs, ums, like, etc. Be concise and organize your responses so that it is easy for the interviewer to remember and relate as positives for you. "My most outstanding traits can be summarized in three words: *dependable, committed*, and a *champion*." Follow with *specific* examples of ways in which you demonstrated each of these traits and how you can add value to the company through these traits.

Every response should include the answer to the interviewer's unspoken question: "So what?" The interviewer asks, "What leadership positions have you held while in college?" Inadequate response: "I was senior class president."

Better response: "I was senior class president and won on a three-point platform that included more open communication between all students and senior administration, 100 percent senior student participation in the senior class gift to the college, and 100 percent senior student participation in a college-wide sustainability project. As seniors, we are the campus leaders. My goal was for us to be seen as leaders by the results of our actions—not just our classification. I was thrilled and humbled by my election to the position. And I am happy to say that our college president has agreed to hold an open-door policy for students for one hour every Thursday between five and six o'clock. As of last week, 45 percent of the senior class had made a donation to the class gift, and I am confident that by senior week, in six months, we will be at 100 percent. The senior class service committee is currently working on the design and implementation plan of the sustainability project that will be presented and voted on at next month's senior class meeting."

Point #8: Body Language

Sit professionally, don't slouch or cross your leg over your knee, and have a strong handshake. It's always an interview—from your entrance into the building (you may be seen by the interviewer getting out of your car and walking into the building), on the elevator, waiting in the lobby, and in the restroom prior to the interview. The interviewer will know you; you will not know the interviewer. Be in interviewee mood at all times—even when you leave the building and return to your car. Execute the ABCs of professional presence at all times!

Point #9: Questions for the Interviewer

Have them! Here's a killer question for the interviewer shared by a recent Morehouse graduate who is now a consulting analyst with Accenture: "What are the three things I can expect to learn from my first year in this position?"

Point #10: The Close

Close the interview by asking for the job and asking for next steps in the interview/hiring process. Take notes, write down the next steps, and follow up. Following up is just as important as the actual interview. Send a thank-you note to the interviewer within twenty-four hours of your interview to express your appreciation for his or her time and to reiterate your interest in the position. After receiving the outcome of the interview, send a second note. If the position was offered, this note will express your gratitude for his or her support and your determination to live up to the interviewer's high opinion of you. If the position was not offered, the note will express your gratitude for the time and consideration given to your application. Regardless of the outcome, stay encouraged.

Internalizing and executing these points will significantly increase your chances of success in the first stage of the interview process, which is also known as round one. Subsequent stages—second and third rounds of the interview process—will require you to engage with additional members of the organization as well as demonstrate skills and competencies in other areas of communication, including small talk, introductions, and public speaking. Here are some tips and techniques for success in these areas.

Small Talk

When engaged in conversations, watch what you say. You don't want to be overheard or quoted in written communication saying any of the following:

- Telling off-color jokes, making off-color remarks (sexist, racist, or vulgar)
- Referring to women in disrespectful ways
- Using a word other than *gay* when referring to homosexual men and *lesbian* when referring to homosexual women
- Using the "n" word

- Cursing
- Referring to women's body parts in slang or derogatory terms
- Comments received as sexual harassment

Being a good conversationalist and at ease when talking to others is learned behavior. Basic steps are as follows:

- Focus on the other person and concentrate on keeping the conversation going. Use the person's name repeatedly in the first two minutes so that you will remember it.
- Be interested in them as well as interesting to them. Be considerate and a good listener.
- Listen with the intent to pick up bits of information and ask questions accordingly.
- Start conversations by sharing a well-placed compliment, discussing the weather, a funny movie, a favorite restaurant, a hobby, a current TV show, a mutual acquaintance, travel, or sports.
- Properly end the conversation by acknowledging the person and bring closure to the talk. "I think I'll go to the bar to get a coke. It was nice speaking with you."

Introductions

A sure sign of professionalism is the ability to make a proper introduction. Simple rules for making introductions in business settings are as follows:

- The lower-status person is introduced to the higher-status person, by saying the higher-status person's name first.

  "Dr. White, may I introduce to you Ronnie Long, my roommate."
  "Ronnie, this is my professor, Dr. White."

(Say something they have in common.) "Dr. White, Ronnie is from Birmingham, your hometown."

"Dr. Jones, please allow me the opportunity to introduce to you Dr. White, my professor."

"Dr. White, this is Dr. Jones, the president of Faith in Action."

(Say something they have in common.) "Dr. Jones, I gave Dr. White a copy of your book, *Leadership in the Twenty-First Century*, as a Christmas gift. She has a special interest in your work because she teaches leadership and professional development."

- When introducing persons of equal rank, it is acceptable to give preference to women, older people, and the person you know least well. Always say the name of the person you which to honor the most, first:

"Mother, may I present Mr. Jenkins, my physics teacher."

"Principal Green, this is my aunt, Mrs. Gladys Day. She is visiting from Birmingham, Alabama."

"Rev. James, have you met Minister Moore, our new youth choir director?"

"Charles, may I introduce to you my office mate, Ryan Green. Ryan, this is our newest salesperson, Charles Jones."

Other considerations:

- Always look at the people you are introducing as you introduce them.
- Always provide more information than the name and title in your introduction (see examples above). This provides a bonding point, puts the parties at ease, and makes their time together more enjoyable and memorable.
- Always let people know when they are being introduced to a member of the media.

Public Speaking

A commonly held belief is that the fear of public speaking, *glossophobia*, is the number one fear for most people—even above the fear of death. This may be true for most people, but for twenty-first-century leaders, this is a fear that must be overcome. How can you give the speech to share your vision with your followers, present your stellar million-dollar marketing campaign to your clients, be the keynote speaker at your church's anniversary banquet, or accept your person of the year community service award from the local YMCA if you have a fear of public speaking? Leaders must learn effective public speaking.

You can significantly decrease your fear of public speaking by doing the following:

- Know what you want to accomplish in the speech.
- Know to whom you are speaking.
- Be well groomed and appropriately dressed.
- Know your material.
- Be convinced that the audience wants to like you.
- Be convinced that the audience wants to hear what you have to say.
- Be natural but appropriate in behavior.
- Use proper grammar—do not use slang or colloquialisms.

If the fear of public speaking is a problem for you, be proactive in finding a solution to address your problem. Join a Toastmasters club; take private lessons from a speech coach; read all you can on your subject; watch tapes of great orators; watch and study webcasted TED (technology, entertainment, and design) Talk videos (short, powerful talks of eighteen minutes or less by subject matter experts from science to business to global issues in more than one hundred languages); observe newscasters; practice, practice, practice; and volunteer to speak at small local functions in your community and at your place of worship. Have your speech coach attend and give you feedback.

Continuously cycle through the preparation, practice, execution, and analysis loop until you are comfortable as a public speaker. Hard work now perfecting your communication skills will pay great dividends in the years to come.

Body Language Skills: Be Engaging!

- Walk purposely and with confidence (shoulders back and looking at eye level).
- Stand straight and attentively. Don't slump shoulders or sway back.
- Think quality not quantity when gesturing; cautiously use waving and pointing.
- Make positive eye contact. Avoid using eyes as weapons of displeasure or destruction.
- Use appropriate facial expressions. Adopt a resting smile on face at all times.
- Master power positions; take up space and widen your stance.
- Shake hands assertively; a soft handshake signals *wimp*, and a hard handshake signals *bully*.
- Accept business cards graciously; treat them as gifts by opening (reading the card) and saying thank you.
- Be aware of proximity; respect others' personal space by staying in the personal zone of 1.5 to 4 feet when in conversation.
- Practice appropriate gender-neutral etiquette; be kind and helpful to all.
- Practice proper dining etiquette; know do's and don'ts; demonstrate when eating.
- Smile; it signals you are approachable and trustworthy.

Listening Skills: Be Interested!

- Stop talking! Enough said.
- Stop walking! Look at the other person; listen with your eyes and your ears.

- Question strategically; probe appropriately and respectfully.
- Repeat what is said occasionally; this helps retain information for later interactions.
- Don't rush the speaker, finish others sentences, or circle with finger for them to finish.
- Be poised and emotionally controlled; don't show disapproval with face, head, or hand gestures.
- Show empathic responsive reactions; share well-placed "really" and "wow."
- Pay close attention; approximately half of what is being said comes through nonverbal behavior, about 40 percent is in tone of voice, and only about 10 percent is in words.
- Don't interrupt; hear the entirety of another's opinion before giving yours.
- Don't argue mentally; keep your mind clear in order to process what is being said.
- Keep your mind on the speaker and the subject; take notes to show interest.

Conversational Skills: Be Interesting!

- Remember people's names; repeat it at least two times in first two minutes of conversation.
- Make proper introductions of others; reintroduce yourself to others.
- Use your voice effectively through tone and pitch; end your greeting with a smile.
- Vary your vocal tone; use voice inflection to emphasize important points and express emotions.
- Use self-humor to your advantage; share stories of lighthearted personal mishaps.
- Don't be condescending; making others the object of jokes deflates them; strive to inflate; a well-placed word of encouragement wins friends.
- Use proper English; avoid slang and colloquialisms— wanna/want to, gonna/going to, y'all/you all.

- Don't use crutches; eliminate filler sounds such as ahs, ums; eliminate filler words such as *okay, you know, so, all right, basically, like,* and *actually.*
- Cultivate a wide vocabulary; learn a new word each day.
- Use a listenable rate of speech; speak slowly, especially when saying your name in an introduction.
- Be clear and concise; get to the point.
- Express praise and encouragement; leave people with favorable impressions of themselves.

Presentation/Public Speaking Skills: Be Prepared!

- Talk about what you know well; know the past, present, and future of your topic.
- Write, practice, and throw away note cards. Own your presentation—and don't read your presentation.
- Mingle with your audience; make an emotional connection.
- Approach lectern enthusiastically, stand erect, and don't hide behind lectern. Swiftly appear on stage, be relaxed, and purposefully move across the stage without pacing back and forth.
- Make eye contact; everyone should feel that you are talking to them.
- Use purposeful hand gestures; stay in the "box," which is the hand-speaking space from the top of your chest to the bottom of your waist; gestures should be expressive and fluid—open hands, palms up, at waist.
- Use non-offensive humor; eliminate anything that is even slightly sexist, sexually suggestive, or racist.
- Tell stories; take your audience on a journey from a personal experience.
- Rehearse with audiovisual equipment; have a backup plan.
- Respond to questions appropriately; start with "Thank you for that question." Not "That was a good question."
- Never lose your audience; have a strong opening, middle, and close.

- Visualize yourself giving a great presentation; be your biggest cheerleader and fan.

The Super Hero Pose

Amy Cuddy, professor and researcher at Harvard Business School, studies how nonverbal behavior and snap judgments affect people. She suggests that engaging in pronounced body stances increases one's self-confidence. She writes in her 2015 book, *Presence*, "When you pretend to be powerful, you are more likely to actually feel powerful." Assuming a power stance with feet apart, elbows out, and hands on hips, such as the Superman or Wonder Woman stance, raises testosterone levels and feelings of invincibility. She suggests engaging in this pose as a warm-up exercise before making a presentation or public appearance.

Deliverables: Your Work Product

The fourth important component of the ABCs of professional presence is your deliverables and your work ethic as evidenced by your work product. A discussion of deliverables that result from your work product provides a platform to add to our small acts of being and doing for personal and professional success: "Be disciplined, be organized, and be punctual."

You will become known by your work product. To become known as a key contender for any position to which you aspire, your response to the following questions must be in the affirmative:

- Do you do what is asked of you in an effective and efficient manner, with little to no supervision or mistakes?
- Do you keep your promises?
- Are you a team player?
- Do you go beyond the call of duty?

All affirmative responses place you in the category of a star performer, a fast-tracker, and possible executive-level material.

Just one negative response places you the category of a good employee—but not leadership material. More than one negative response places you on a three-month improvement plan and headed to the unemployment line.

STAR Performer (Service That Achieves Results)

The STAR performer possesses an owner's mentality. The STAR makes prudent, ethical decisions and takes calculated risks that deliver maximum results, which yield increased revenue and profits for the company and its stakeholders. The STAR performer is viewed as *value-add* to the company by providing exceptional customer service. Company executives see STAR performers as their emerging leaders.

The STAR is unconsciously competent in "career makers," including showing up, being early, keeping their word, and being at the top of the list by doing, executing, and producing. Douglas Cooper, Morehouse College director of career services, uses the acronym FILOGA (first in; last out; good attitude) to describe a STAR performer. Cooper says, "This is the individual who beats the earliest arrival to the office; leaves the office after the latest departure; and does all his or her work with a good attitude."

GOOD Employee (Giving Only What Is on the Document)

The good employee provides customer service as written in the company policy and procedures manual without thinking about and doing what is best for the customer, which often results in unsatisfied customers. The good employee, while trying to follow company rules, may actually subtract value from the company by not being sensitive to the needs of the customer. Good employees make good managers—but not great leaders.

The good employee often engages in "career breakers," including being missing in action, being late, breaking commitments, being at the bottom of the list, trying and giving excuses, and not producing. "It's not part of my job" pervades the mind-set of the good employee.

Good employees may do their job but nothing more, possibly subscribing to LIFOBA (last in; first out; basic attitude). Strive to be a STAR performer—not just a good employee!

In *Strategize to Win*, Harris devotes a significant amount of time to sharing her thoughts on the absolute importance of a STAR performer mentality demonstrated through your deliverables. Harris describes the degree to which you do your job and produce deliverables in and through excellence as "performance currency." She defines performance currency as the "goodwill, reputation, and capital you create by doing your job well and creating stellar deliverables on discrete assignments." She states, "When you consistently complete assignments above expectations, you create performance currency." You may be asking, "What's the value proposition in performance currency?"

According to Harris, the value proposition is huge! "When you have a strong reputation and track record of performance excellence, you can 'exchange' it for a shot at a promotion, a coveted position on an internal task force, a raise, an introduction to more senior people in the company, a respected voice at the decision-making table (where people will listen to you and be influenced by your point of view in important discussions), a spot on the deal team for the next big transaction, an opportunity to present in front of the client, or a chance to recover if you make a really big mistake." Performance currency is the gift you give yourself that keeps on giving!

One's ability to deliver excellent work products, performance currency, does not happen by chance. Being able to deliver efficiently and effectively depends on your ability to execute in three areas: goal setting, planning, and time management. Professionals show exceptional skills in each of these interdependent, tactical areas (Figure 5-1. Work Product Activators).

Having no goals typically results in not having a clear direction as to where you want to go or what you want to accomplish. Setting a goal but not creating a plan to reach the goal typically results in a person not starting the journey toward the goal. Setting a goal and creating a plan but not managing your time so that you can execute your plan typically results in the goal never being reached. Managing your time but not having goals and plans will typically result in wasting your time. As you can see, it takes all three of these elements in order to be an effective and efficient professional. A discussion of each of these areas follows.

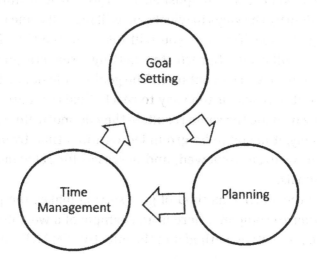

Figure Chapter 5-1. Work Product Activators

Goal Setting

In the 1990s, Edwin A. Locke and Gary P. Latham introduced goal setting as a theory of achieving intentions, expressed as goals. Their research showed a relationship between how difficult and specific a goal was and people's performance of a task. They found that specific and difficult-to-achieve goals, when accepted, led to better task performance than vague or easy goals.

Based on Locke and Latham's research, we know that setting a specific goal such as "increase sales by 25 percent" will result in a higher level of output than a generalized goal of "try hard" or "do your best." Their research along with others in the area of goal setting has resulted in the generally accepted method of creating goals that motivate and lead to goal accomplishment. This method is called creating SMART goals. The acronym stands for the five key elements of the goal-setting process: *specific, measurable, attainable, realistic,* and *timely.*

For a goal to be specific, you must identify the "who, what, where, when, which, and why" of the goal. For a goal to be measurable, you must answer questions related to how much, how many, and how will I know when it is accomplished. For a goal to be attainable, you need to identify the ways in which you will make it come to reality, including the specific steps you will take and the time frame in which you will complete each step. Setting a realistic goal means that you believe you can obtain it. The goal should not be too high, too low, out of reach, or too easy to reach. Goals that are too high or too low provide the same results—they de-motivate. For a goal to be timely, it needs to be grounded within a time frame. Goals should be written, reviewed, and assessed for relevance on an ongoing basis.

Using the SMART method of goal setting makes the planning steps easier to complete. Here is an example of a weight-loss goal using the ineffective method and the effective SMART method.

- *Ineffective Method.* I will try hard to lose weight.
- *Effective Method using the* SMART *Goal-Setting Strategy.* In order to become healthier, I will lose five pounds by August 1 (six weeks from now) by walking one hour, four days a week, joining a health club, hiring a personal trainer, and eliminating nighttime snacks, soft drinks, and desserts.

Planning

"People who fail to plan, plan to fail." This often-heard statement has become a truism of life. It's no surprise that planning is the first of the four functions of management, followed by organizing, leading/directing, and controlling. Planning begins the method for achieving an end through the orderly arrangement of the parts of an overall objective, resulting in a detailed program. Successful management and leadership require the ability to effectively plan.

Without a plan, a logical method that takes into account all aspects of a situation, your chances of achieving a goal are significantly deterred. Inherent in the planning process is the solution to your task at hand. The planning process requires you to methodically move through a series of steps. First, you analyze the current situation with intentionality. Second, you identify the resources you will need to accomplish the goal. Third, you develop the specific strategies and activities to accomplish the goal. Next, you will prioritize the activities in relationship to all of the other things in which you are involved. The last step is to set milestones, targets, and indicators of progress and success.

Plans should be written, reviewed, and assessed for relevance on an ongoing basis. As an example, let's create a plan to achieve the SMART weight-loss goal in the previous section: "In order to become healthier, I will lose five pounds by August 1 (six weeks from now) by walking one hour, four days a week, joining a health club, hiring a personal trainer, and eliminating nighttime snacks, soft drinks, and desserts."

The written plan to accompany this SMART weight-loss goal would include:

- identifying the walking path, health club, and personal trainer
- making contact with the health club and trainer and securing their services
- identifying the days and times for the walks, health club visits, and sessions with the trainer
- identifying a weekly weigh-in day
- creating a log to record the weight-loss progress
- identifying the healthy alternatives to replace junk food

The act of goal setting and planning requires you to FOCUS—*to think it through and write it down.* Your next step is to engage the final element of the deliverables triad—time management. As a result of the synergy produced by these three: goal setting, planning, and time management, you will be prepared for ACTION—*to begin it now and get it done.*

Time Management

How do we incorporate the time-management element to our weight-loss goal and plan scenario? Our time-management activities would center on arranging and adjusting our schedule to accommodate the time it takes to engage in the hour-long walks, trips to the health club, sessions with the trainers, grocery shopping, etc., while still accomplishing the other top priorities on our list, such as work responsibilities, time with family and friends, hobbies, and worship activities.

Specific time-management strategies that could be incorporated include going to bed an hour earlier and getting up an hour earlier; preparing a week's worth of workout clothes to reduce the time to get ready for the workout; weekly stocking the refrigerator, freezer, and pantry with vegetables, fruits, and low-fat snacks; and hiring a personal trainer to come to your home to save the travel time to the gym.

The effective execution of time-management strategies is a direct result of great work habits that allow for the effective and efficient use of our time. Regardless of who you are, there are only twenty-four hours in a day. Effective and efficient professionals are more productive not because they are better at managing time but because they are better at managing themselves within the time-bound twenty-four-hour day. Effective and efficient professionals start with the great use of their time.

In *The 7 Habits of Highly Successful People,* Stephen Covey presents an undeniable argument supporting the personal and professional success gains that can be achieved through the intentional focus on how one uses his or her time, which he details in Habit #3 "Put First Things First." Covey identifies what he considers the essence of the best thinking in the area of time management: organize and execute around priorities, which are defined in your goals and objectives.

According to Covey, effective and efficient professionals stay clear of activities that do not add to the achievement of their goals and objectives, and are not part of their plan—activities Covey defines as *timewasters*. Examples of these time-wasters include Internet surfing; reading Facebook posts; reading endless e-mails and trudging through snail mail; engaging in extreme texting and long personal phone calls; looking for misplaced or lost items because of a lack of organization; and wasting uncontrollable downtime when waiting in lines or at appointments.

Instead, efficient and effective professionals set time limits for routine activities such as answering e-mails and returning phone calls. They have a simple organizational system for important items so that they do not waste time looking for misplaced or lost items.

One such system is the OHIO (only handle it once) rule, which has been around for decades. When coupled with my FRP (final resting place) rule, you can save many hours in a week because you become efficient each day. The OHIO and FRP rules are very effective for preventing piles of paper from cluttering your desk, including mail, company memos, and fliers. Once a piece of paper is picked up the very first time, it should be put down in its FRP—trashed, filed, or passed to the person who is charged with taking care of the item. Use the OHIO and FRP rules when a clothing item is taken off—hang it up or put it in a drawer or the dirty clothes hamper. Once something is used, it is returned to its FRP. Cluttered work and living spaces clutter the mind. Leaders need to develop and practice habits of clarity in all aspects of their lives.

Additional time saver rules are DIN (Do It Now) and DIRTFT (do it right the first time). The extra five minutes spent doing it now, correctly, the first time will save the thirty minutes it will take to explain why it hasn't been done, what went wrong when you finally did it, how you are going to fix it, and then fixing it.

Another technique Covey offers to assist leaders in achieving clarity through effective time management is the idea that all activities can be defined through two dimensions: urgency and importance. Urgent means the activity requires immediate attention, whereas importance has to do with results. Urgent activities put us in react mode. Important activities move us in the direction of accomplishing our goals and life purpose.

Covey demonstrates the usefulness of this concept through his Time Management Matrix (TMM). According to Covey, all activities can be assigned to one of four quadrants. Using Covey's TMM as a framework for the lifestyle of the millennial generation demonstrates the usefulness—or not—of many of the activities that occupy the time of emerging leaders. Here is a sample of those activities and their placement within Covey's TMM:

- ➢ *Quadrant I Activities (Urgent and Important)*
- Paying overdue bills
- Cramming for an exam
- Attending to a medical emergency
- ➢ *Quadrant II Activities (Important but Not Urgent)*
- Paying bills on time
- Studying regularly
- Exercising
- ➢ *Quadrant III Activities (Urgent but Not Important)*
- Rehashing a friend's problems
- Bailing friends and relatives out of problems and situations they refuse to address or handle themselves
- Listening to peers and coworkers' complaints
- ➢ *Quadrant IV Activities (Not Urgent and Not Important)*
- Complaining about your problems
- Watching reality TV shows
- Playing fantasy football and video games

Covey states that effective people "stay out of quadrants III and IV because, urgent or not, they are not important. Effective people also shrink quadrant I down to size by spending more time in quadrant II. *Quadrant II is the heart of effective personal management.* It deals with things that are not urgent, but important." Covey lists quadrant II activities, which include "building relationships, writing a personal mission statement, long-range planning, exercising, preventive maintenance, preparation—all those things we know we need to do, but somehow seldom get around to doing, because they aren't urgent."

To help you put into perspective the interrelationship between goal setting, planning, and time management, here is a case study about two good friends, Paul and David. From this case study, you will be able to see the significant role that Covey's TMM can play in achieving one's goal.

Good Friends, Good Students;
Different Choices, Different Results

Paul and David are good friends with similar goals and interests, including doing well academically (a 3.5 GPA or better each semester) and graduating with a job offer. They both understand that they must consistently go to class, study hard, and complete their assignments. They also agree that balancing their lives through nonacademic activities is also necessary to achieve their goals, referring back to childhood advice— "all work and no play makes Jack a dull boy" (also supported by FOCUS principle 1 "Find Your Power Source").

They created a weekly schedule that included class times, study times, and assignment-completion times. After completing their weekly schedule, which took into account their twenty-hour work-study obligation and personal needs (sleeping, eating, etc.), they were delighted to see that they had about ten hours of free time. Paul rearranged his schedule such that he could attend the weekend parties. David rearranged his schedule to accommodate an hour workout, three days a week; two hours on Sunday to attend worship service; fifteen minutes of daily devotion and meditation, Monday through Friday; and four hours of weekend recreation (attending a party, an athletic event, or a movie; hanging out with friends; visiting with family).

At the beginning of the semester, Paul and David's leadership and professional development instructor gave the class a rather large portfolio assignment. Due at the end of the semester, the thirty-page portfolio would contain a collection of short assignments from throughout the semester and two five-page essays. One week before the portfolio was due, neither Paul nor David had done much work on the portfolio. They both realized it would take a few all-night sessions to complete the assignment.

Being at the end of the semester, Paul's willpower, strength, and stamina had depreciated. His consistent party weekends throughout the semester were taking a toll on him. However, David felt he could take on the physical, mental, and emotional stress and strain of all-night work sessions. His consistent weeks throughout the semester of workouts, spiritual enrichment, weekend recreation, and time with friends and family provided him a source of support upon which to draw (FOCUS principle 1).

Paul was overwhelmed by the situation. David was prepared for the situation. Paul's portfolio was poorly done, earning him sixty of the possible hundred points. David's portfolio was well done, earning him ninety-five of the possible hundred points. Paul's final grade was a B-; he missed his target goal of a 3.5 GPA for the semester. David's final grade was an A; he met his target goal of a 3.5 GPA.

Both Paul and David were good managers of their time in relation to the accomplishment of their goals. Creating their weekly schedule of events allowed them to operate in quadrant II—consistently engaging in activities that are important but not urgent. But as they found out, life happens and you find yourself in quadrant I, faced with a situation that is both urgent and important.

Because David's choice to spend his ten hours of "extra" time each week still in quadrant II—engaging in activities that strengthened his physical, mental, emotional, social, and spiritual dimensions—he was able to complete the assignment and turn in a well-done portfolio. Paul chose to spend his ten hours of "extra" time in quadrant IV—engaging in activities that are pleasant but do not provide support toward the accomplishment of your goals. Same amount of time spent, different results. Paul's ten hours was a cost. David's ten hours was an investment.

I was first introduced to Covey's Habit 3 ("Put First Things First") through a professional development workshop conducted by an associate dean in my PhD program in 1997. I have been richly blessed since that time by incorporating this habit as well as Covey's other six habits into my lifestyle. I strongly believe you will reap great benefits by doing the same. Covey explains the details exceptionally well in his book. I encourage you to buy and read his book; focus on understanding and applying all seven habits as part of your professional growth.

Before closing this section on time management, I would like to provide guidance and advice to emerging leaders around the importance of all choices they face. Sometimes the choice is benign, meaning it is nonthreatening in the overall scheme of your life. Choosing to spend four hours at the Saturday night party instead of studying for the Monday morning final exam may result in a lower course grade, but it won't result in you being kicked out of school, ruining your college experience, or causing negative ramifications for many years down the road.

However, the activities you choose to engage in while at the party—sex, alcohol, and drugs—can have a major negative impact on your life. While immediate gratification may result from time spent in the SAD (sex, alcohol, and drugs) world, the long-term impact can be destructive and sometimes fatal to the achievement of your goals, aspirations, and dreams. The SAD world too often results from the privileged-athlete mind-set; partying lifestyles of some fraternity and sorority members (the Greek life); and unmotivated personalities of unfocused students. My advice to all emerging leaders is to focus on activities that keep you safely in the GLAD world where your "goals lead to achieving your dreams."

Etiquette and Social Skills

> Simply acting like a gentleman is not enough. It
> is *being* a gentleman that is important,
> and that means thinking of others, being there
> when you are needed, and knowing when

> you are not needed. It is what you do and who
> you are—an accumulation of gentlemanly
> behaviors over the course of lifetime.

—John Bridges, *How to Be a Gentleman*

This quote eloquently states the spirit of being a gentle "person." Being a gentleman or a lady is not difficult, but it must be authentic. Gentlemen and ladies know how to make others feel valued, respected, and comfortable in their presence. They make life easier for other people. They do so effortlessly, and they gracefully show their enjoyment and pleasure to be of service to others. This graceful service comes through the art and practice of etiquette. A discussion of etiquette as demonstrated through social skills provides a platform to add even more small acts of being and doing for personal and professional success: "Be helpful, be humble, be nice, be kind."

The fifth and final component of the ABCs of professional presence is etiquette and social skills. The importance of etiquette and social skills is aptly stated by internationally known protocol expert, Letitia Baldridge. According to Baldridge, "As the business world becomes more diverse in race, gender, age, ethnicity, cultures, time zones, use of technology, and formality, leaders must become more sensitive to the ways in which they interface with others. The twenty-first-century leader will be expected to possess impeccable manners that will be appropriate in any diverse, global situation. This etiquette knowledge base is so vast that no one can be expected to know it all." This observation suggests that up-to-date etiquette reference books are a must for the young executive's reference library.

One such book is *The Etiquette Advantage in Business, Third Edition: Personal Skills for Professional Success*, 2014, written by members of the Emily Post family. Emily Post, born in 1872, published her first etiquette book *Etiquette in Society, in Business, in Politics, and at Home* in 1922 at the age of fifty. In the early twentieth century, "etiquette" was not common among America's new immigrants and newly rich, making it difficult for them to fit in with the establishment. Post's book on etiquette immediately became a best seller and helped the unconsciously incompetent acquire social skills and manners by learning the behaviors to avoid and the behaviors to adopt in order to be accepted in professional settings and circles. Her first book is now in its eighteenth edition.

Similar to Emily Post's desire to educate the newly rich in the ways of the establishment social culture in 1922, Karen Grigsby Bates and Karen Elyse Hudson's 1996 book on etiquette, *Basic Black: Home Training for Modern Times,* educates the millennial generation on those topics collectively known in African American culture as "home training." Bates and Hudson define home training as the education, instruction, or discipline of a person in accepted mores or values and possessing behavior that is reflective of proper rearing—in other words, good manners and polite behavior.

Topics found in traditional etiquette books are covered in great detail in *Basic Black* along with the essentials of black American tradition: joining a church, mentoring young people, and family reunions. Bates and Hudson believe that etiquette is about more than just which fork goes where. They are of the opinion that people lose a little piece of themselves when they choose to live their lives without genuine respect for morality, character, kindness, and other people. Those attributes and characteristics reside in "the authentic you."

The thought that knowing which fork to use, how to introduce someone, or how to shake hands could make a difference in your career path may be unsettling to you. My advice is to refer back to chapter 3 "Connect to External Systems" and the work of Dale Carnegie. Carnegie reminds us that human beings are creatures of emotion not logic. Human beings connect emotionally to people they know, like, and trust. Etiquette and social graces will earn you more know, like, and trust dividends than any logic you can present. Great leadership rests on the ability of leaders to get work done with, through, and in service to others. Knowing and demonstrating proper etiquette—the socially acceptable ways of doing and being with others—is a small price to pay to reap the benefits of great leadership.

Business Etiquette Expectations of Twenty-First Century Leaders

Twenty-first-century leaders are expected to know and observe business etiquette concepts and the finest details of professional behaviors. Mastery of these TASKBs will significantly set you apart from the competition:

- attending breakfast, lunch, and dinner business meetings
- avoiding sexual office relationships
- conducting meetings
- dressing appropriately for the occasion
- demonstrating electronic (phone usage) and technology (social media) etiquette
- eliminating use of sexist language
- engaging in small talk
- entertaining business clients
- exhibiting dining etiquette
- giving appropriate business gifts
- giving and receiving invitations
- hosting business clients and visitors
- initiating workplace comfort
- knowing international protocol and etiquette
- making proper introductions
- observing business travel etiquette
- participating in company socials and outings
- putting others at ease
- remembering names
- sending timely business and personal written communications
- shaking hands
- showing deference and gender-neutral chivalry
- using proper forms of titles

Dining Etiquette

There is an expectation in business relationships that a professional will know and exhibit proper dining etiquette. When the expectation is met, professional credibility is quickly established. If you are wondering why dining etiquette is so significant, please allow me to elaborate.

The knowledge and demonstration of dining etiquette protocols signal to others that you possess the professionalism traits of common courtesy, attention to detail, and an openness to learning; care, concern, and respect of others; likeability, trustworthiness, and charm; self-control, self-confidence, and self-respect. You may think that's a lot of value from such a small encounter. It is for this reason that dining etiquette rates so highly as a measure of professionalism. Most people underestimate its worth. For those who master dining etiquette skills, it says, "I'm willing to go the extra mile even when others do not or will not."

To assist you in your desire to be comfortable, make others comfortable, and solidify your reputation as the consummate professional, I've included some basic dining etiquette protocols. For detailed discussions on dining etiquette rules and procedures, please refer to reference materials (websites, videos, and books) by protocol experts such as Karen Grigsby Bates, Karen Elyse Hudson, Nancy Mitchell, Emily Post, and Amy Vanderbilt.

Two common forms of dining styles are the American style of dining and the European (or Continental) style of dining.

American-Style Dining

- *Step One.* When cutting a piece of food, place your fork in your left hand with the handle hidden in the palm of your hand and the fork tines down. Place the knife in your right hand with the handle hidden in the palm of your hand and the serrated edge at a right angle to the plate.
- *Step Two.* After cutting one piece of food, lay your knife across the top of your plate with the serrated edge facing

you. Transfer the fork from your left hand to your right—with the fork handle now showing between your index finger and thumb and the tines facing up. Slightly lower your head and place the food in your mouth.

- *Step Three.* After chewing and swallowing the piece of food, repeat the first two steps.
- *Step Four.* When you choose to lay your utensils down to rest or to listen more intently to the people with whom you're dining, the "rest" position should place the knife across the top of the plate with the serrated edge toward you. Place your fork, tines up, with its handle resting on the lower right side of the plate in the ten o'clock and four o'clock position.
- *Step Five.* When you've completed your meal, place your fork across the center of the plate with the handle to the right and the fork tines down, bring your knife from across the top of the plate and place it next to the fork with serrated blade edge next to fork.

European-Style Dining

- *Step One.* Follow step one of the American style.
- *Step Two.* Rather than transferring the fork to your right hand, leave the knife and fork in the same positions as described in step one. With your knife still in your right hand, lift your fork (containing a bite-sized piece of food) to your mouth, tines down.
- *Step Three.* When you're ready, repeat the first two steps.
- *Step Four.* In European or Continental style, the "rest" position involves placing your knife on the plate first, with its handle to the lower right of the plate. Next place your fork, tines down, on the lower left of the plate so that fork and knife cross.
- *Step Five.* When you've completed your meal, place your utensils in a twelve o'clock and six o'clock position.

The diagram below (Figure Chapter 5-2. Parts of a Formal Dinner Place Setting) is of a formal dinner place setting. The sheer number of different items may cause initial alarm. Don't be intimidated. Mastery of dining etiquette protocol is not intuitive. It comes from instruction and practice. That is why it is important to take time to learn dining etiquette rules and procedures. As already suggested, refer to reference materials (websites, videos, and books) by protocol experts such as Karen Grigsby Bates, Karen Elyse Hudson, Nancy Mitchell, Emily Post, and Amy Vanderbilt. With guidance and practice, you will move from consciously incompetent to consciously competent.

Figure Chapter 5-2. Parts of a Formal Dinner Place Setting

The Etiquette of Dining—Dos

- Respond to invitations (RSVP).
- Arrive promptly, dressed appropriately, five minutes before start of dinner (not earlier and not later).
- Stand behind your chair after entering the dining area.
- Be seated when invited to by the host or hostess.
- Place semi-folded napkin on lap as soon as everyone is seated.
- Sit up straight.
- Use bread plate on your left.
- Use drinking glasses and cups on right.
- Order last when hosting to ensure proper level of service has been delivered for all guests.
- Wait until all guests have been served before starting to eat.
- If host does not provide the grace, discreetly say a short grace to yourself.
- Hold cutlery with fingers, not fists (utilizing either the American or Continental style of dining).
- Start using the outside utensils and work to the inside.
- Break bread with fingers. Use knife to butter bread (never to cut the bread).
- Cut only enough food for the next mouthful.
- Remove unwanted items (small food items) from your mouth the same way they went into your mouth (by discreetly returning the fork to your mouth and placing it on the tip of the fork), return the unwanted item to your plate, hiding it under a bone or other item on your plate.
- Use piece of bread on a fork to soak up sauce or gravy.
- Pass salt and pepper together.
- Gently wipe nose if necessary.
- If unavoidable, burp quietly with hand over mouth and say excuse me.
- Divide private table talk equally between your neighbors.
- Be an appropriate tipper (15–20 percent standard; more for excellent service; never less than 10 percent).

- Remember that "business" is the most important part of a business meal.
- Compliment/thank host and/or hostess upon leaving.
- Send follow-up thank you note to host/hostess.

The Etiquette of Dining—Don'ts

- Tuck napkin in shirt or pants.
- Throw tie over shoulder.
- Take your jacket off to eat.
- Place "other" objects on table, i.e. cell phones and purses.
- Wear hat or cap.
- Begin eating when you are a guest until host begins or indicates you should do so.
- Begin eating when you are the host before everyone at your table is served.
- Chew with mouth open, head in plate, shoveling food in mouth with fork or fingers.
- Overfill mouth; always be able to talk.
- Swap food at the table.
- Dunk your food.
- Remove unwanted food from your mouth with your napkin.
- Draw attention to your diet restrictions or others' eating patterns.
- Crumble crackers in your soup.
- Touch any food with fingers at a formal dinner; exception, your bread.
- Salt or season food before tasting it.
- Slurp or blow liquids.
- Finish meal early or late.
- Smoke at table.
- Perform hygiene or grooming services at table.
- Complain about quality of food or service when you are a guest.
- Push plate away, push chair back from the table, or announce you are finished eating.

- Tilt back in your chair.
- Say anything if you see others doing something on this list.

Reception Savvy: Networking that Works

Being at ease at reception functions is of utmost importance for leaders at every stage of their careers. Receptions are ideal places to meet and greet people who can make a profound difference in your personal, professional, and civic life. We often shy away from these events, especially if we think we will not know anyone or we take a friend and spend one to two hours in a corner, eating finger food, and talking only to our friend. What a waste of time and opportunity. As an emerging leader, you must become comfortable at receptions, mingling and flowing in and out of conversations in order to connect with the people who can make a profound impact on your career. Who knows, if you learn and apply these tips, you may find yourself actually enjoying the process!

Prior to attending the reception, do your homework. Know basic information about the organization sponsoring the event. What is the purpose of the event? Who organized it? Who are the senior people who will be there? Check out the organization's website and google the organizing individuals. Try to find pictures of key people so that you will know who they are when you see them at the event.

Come prepared with at least five conversation starters from current events. For a week prior to the event, read local and national newspapers such as *The Wall Street Journal*, *New York Times*, local and national business magazines, such as *Fortune*, *Forbes*, *BusinessWeek*, and local and national society magazines, such as *The New Yorker*. Watch local and national television news programs, such as CNN and Financial Times; frequent Internet business sites, such as Harvard Business Review and Rockstar Finance; and stay abreast of the latest trends in the financial market by downloading free financial apps such as MarketWatch by Dow Jones and Company, FoxBusiness for iPad, and Bloomberg for iPad.

Use "safe" topics as conversation starters—weather, cultural events, new attractions in the city, major world sporting events—the Masters, Tour de France, Super Bowl, Wimbledon Tennis Championship, World Series, Olympics, etc. You can feel comfortable when the conversation moves into more specific areas of current events in the business world because of your regular review of financial news sources.

Whatever you discuss, *always* approach the topic from the positive angle—and never from a negative angle. Be prepared to talk about your positive personal experiences: summer-abroad travels and studies, internships, hobbies, community service activities, or research and writing on your areas of interest. Never discuss, give your opinion, or answer questions on politics, religion, sex, race, gender, and socioeconomic class issues, or the stereotypes associated with these categories. Your goal is to be seen as an interesting person, not an opinionated person.

At the event, act like you are the host or hostess. Enter with a smile and immediately start greeting, introducing yourself, and shaking hands. Everyone there is apprehensive. As you focus on meeting others' needs, you will soon forget about yourself and appear cool, calm, and collected. By being open and friendly, you will put others at ease, and they will be grateful for your leadership in this area. Once you have met someone and talked to them for a few minutes, introduce them to someone else. Know something about the person so that you can share the information during the introduction. Once you have connected them, you are free to move on to a conversation with others in the room.

Regarding food and beverages—eat before you get there! This event is not to be seen as an opportunity for a free dinner. Although you are not to make a dinner out of the food, you must always *look* as if you are eating and drinking. You must have food and beverage items in your hand. Place just a few, nonmessy items on your plate. You do not have to actually eat them—just have the plate and a beverage glass in your hand.

This is not the time to guzzle down free drinks from the open bar. A glass of wine is always a safe choice. Avoid mixed drinks with hard liquor. One glass of wine should last you for the entire event. If you are not a wine drinker, have the bartender pour you Sprite in a wine glass.

If you are asked to take a picture with someone, put your glass down. You do not want pictures of yourself that look as if you are a heavy drinker floating around when you become the CEO! Keep your plate, glass, and napkin in your left hand; your right hand must always be free and clean for shaking hands.

Reception Savvy: Interactions with Executives

While you are to look like you are eating and drinking, your goal at the reception must be to meet and connect with the major power brokers in business and civic organizations who are in attendance. You can always get something to eat, but you will not always have the opportunity to meet senior executives and civic leaders. Few people who work in an organization get an audience with their senior-level bosses. If you are afforded the opportunity as a student or an intern, be sure you take full advantage of it.

Let me emphasize this point. In my thirteen years (1979–1991) of employment with IBM, I never met Mr. John Akers, IBM president and CEO (1983–1993). In the twelve-year span, (1995–2007) of my employment with Morehouse College under the leadership of President Walter E. Massey, I met a host of CEOs and executives of Fortune 100 companies, including Warren Buffett, chairman, CEO, and largest shareholder of Berkshire Hathaway; Doug Daft, chairman and CEO, The Coca-Cola Company; Ann M. Fudge, group vice president, Kraft Foods; Stanley O'Neal, president, COO, and CEO-designate, Merrill Lynch; Dick Parsons, chairman and CEO, AOL Time Warner; John Thornton, president and co-chief operating officer, Goldman Sachs; and Ted Turner, president, Turner Foundation.

Although exceptionally busy, senior executives will take time to interact with college students (and luckily for me, the professors of the students). Wise college students take advantage of the opportunity to meet and interact with senior executives who visit their campuses and during their internships attend company receptions and networking events. The savvy student recognizes the fact that opportunities to meet CEOs and senior executives once you become an employee and enter the corporate life are rare!

You must be intentional regarding your interaction with the senior-level people at the event. Ask your contact person, the recruiter, professor, etc., to point the key person(s) out to you and introduce you. If need be, introduce yourself. You may think that a CEO is too occupied with other things to have the time or desire to speak with you. In actuality, they are there to meet you and will be impressed with your assertiveness and political acumen in networking.

But please don't introduce yourself to a CEO and ask, "So what do you do?" Again, know who will be there before you get there. Prepare two or three conversation starters specifically for the persons—inquire as to what are their interests outside of the office; reference a positive media citing about them, their spouse, or family member; discuss something you have in common that you are an expert in and can talk about in an interesting manner. Have your elevator speech ready to deliver at all times.

Once you have made the connection, do not leave without an understanding as to how you can be in touch with the person again. Tell the CEO you would like to stay in contact—and *ask* the CEO if this is acceptable to him or her. If it is acceptable, he or she will either offer you a business card or direct you to connect with someone else in the organization.

Have a clean, unwrinkled personal calling card with your name, college, major, e-mail address, and phone number. If you are asked for your resume, say that in consideration of not having them burdened with paper, you will e-mail it immediately. Then go to your computer and do it! On the subject of e-mail addresses, the appropriate professional e-mail address is your firstname. lastname@_____ (common search engine such as gmail.com; yahoo.com; or your school e-mail address). No titles or nicknames (mr, ms, coolguy, prettylady) should be part of an e-mail used for professional contacts.

Be sure to follow up without delay (one to two days) with your communication to the person. Although an e-mail is acceptable, a short handwritten personal note thanking the CEO for his or her time is much more impressive. The CEO met dozens of people at the reception; your goal is to make sure he or she remembers you!

Here is a list of networking questions shared with undergraduate business students by a corporate recruiter. Use this list as is or adapt it to create your own set of conversation starters in preparation for attendance at a corporate information session or career fair. When asking questions, stay focused and engaged with the person to whom you who are speaking. Review chapter 3 for a refresher on effective ways to build relationships.

Reception-Ready Networking Questions to Ask

- Why did you join Superior Management, Inc.?
- How did you land your first job?
- What distinguishes your business area from others at the firm?
- What's your biggest challenge working at Superior?
- What's the best part of your job?
- What was your level of responsibility when you first started at Superior?
- How have your career goals changed since you graduated?
- What's the best career advice you've received?
- Are you part of any mentoring, networking, or affinity groups?
- Does Superior offer any scholarships?
- Does Superior have community-outreach initiatives?
- Does Superior have a global-training program?

Career Development Frameworks: Assessment, Exposure, Promotion!

At the beginning of this chapter, I presented to you the four stages of professional growth: 1) unconsciously incompetent; 2) consciously incompetent; 3) consciously competent; and 4) unconsciously competent. The four stages of competence is a learning model that relates to the psychological states involved in the process of progressing from "don't know what you don't know" (incompetence) to knowledge of and some level of "can do" (competence). Now that you are at the end of chapter 5, your knowledge of the ABCs of professional presence should position you to be at some level of competence in the specific TASKBs (traits, abilities, skills, knowledge, and behaviors) of professional excellence in appropriateness, believability, and credibility through your appearance, body language, communication skills, deliverables, and etiquette/social skills.

In other words, you now know what it takes to add value to an entry-level job and are ready to learn strategies that advance your professional career—how to be perceived as "value-add" in the organization. When you are perceived through assessment and exposure as value-add in the organization, you become a sought-after candidate for promotions through the organizational levels. The three career development frameworks that follow—Career Potential Matrix (CPM), the PIE Theory, and Optimum Career Trajectory (OCT)—will help demystify the process from entry level, add value, to executive level by providing insights into the organizational maze of assessment, exposure, and promotion.

Career Development Framework 1:
The Career Potential Matrix (Assessment)

As professor of the leadership and professional development course in the business program at Morehouse College, I have the opportunity to speak with corporate recruiters from a variety of industries. Engaging in conversations with them helps me stay abreast of the most salient trends in undergraduate recruiting and career advancement. I created the Career Potential Matrix (CPM) based on their descriptions of what it takes to get hired *and* be successful in a corporate organization, how candidates are assessed for company fit, and how new hires are assessed as having the potential for long-term growth with the organization. I organized my findings around two dimensions: substance (technical proficiency and business acumen) and style (presence and professionalism). The CPM is shown in Figure 5-3.

	Style	No Style
Substance	**1** • Strong technical proficiency & business acumen • Sharp presence & professionalism	**2** • Strong technical proficiency & business acumen • Lacking presence & professionalism
Low Substance	**3** • Lacking technical proficiency & business acumen • Sharp presence & professionalism	**4** • Lacking technical proficiency & business acumen • Lacking presence & professionalism

Figure 5-3. Career Potential Matrix (CPM)

Recruiters give the highest grades to those students who exhibit substance and style. They give the lowest grades to those students who have neither style nor substance. Students with substance and no style are preferred to students with style and no substance. The four style-substance sections of the CPM from most desirable to least desirable are: 1) substance and style; 2) substance and no style; 3) low substance and style; and 4) low substance and no style.

Section 1 is the premier section of the CPM. Employees in this section possess substance and style. These employees display excellence in four skill areas: technical, conceptual, intrapersonal, and interpersonal. They demonstrate a strong desire to give their best, add value to the organization, and positively differentiate themselves from their peers. They excel at listening, adapting, and adjusting in implementation and execution. They pride themselves in demonstrating impeccable impression management skills as defined in the ABCs of professional presence. Typically they possess a higher level of maturity than their peers and operate at stage four of professional growth—unconsciously competent.

The career potential in section 1 is unlimited, both inside and outside the organization. These individuals are considered fast-trackers, placed in the high-potential talent-management pool, and given high-profile assignments. Section 1 fast-trackers are invited to breakfast, lunch, and dinner meetings with senior executives and high-profile customers as well as social events with senior-level executives and their spouses. Success and significance are the rewards earned by their high potential for hard work.

Section 2, substance and no-style employees are solid, steady performers. They demonstrate expertise in one or two technical areas but are deficient in interpersonal and/or intrapersonal skills of presence, professionalism, and relationship building. Upper management does not view them as possessing leadership potential since they vacillate in the stages of professional growth from consciously incompetent to consciously competent. The career advancement potential of these employees is limited. While their jobs are secure, their lack of positive impression management skills prevent them from making it to upper management, the president's boardroom or house for dinner, or to be invited to the company's executive suite at the Superdome.

Section 3 of the CPM is the designation of low substance and style. These individuals excel in skills of dress, networking, and engaging in organizational political interchange. However, they lack the solid and transferable technical skills and conceptual skills necessary to perform consistently at an elevated level. Typically, they are consciously incompetent in technical skills but feel that their exceptional interpersonal skills will carry them to the next level of their careers. Their career potential is one to two years of employment per company. Individuals in section 3 can expect to be the second to go in a company downsizing or reorganizing.

Section 4 of the CPM is the designation of low substance and no style. Individuals in this section possess little to no technical, conceptual, intrapersonal, and/or interpersonal skills. They may be unconsciously incompetent of basic professionalism skills or lack a desire to demonstrate effectively the ABCs of professionalism. The career potential for these persons is severely limited. If they beat the odds and get hired, they can expect to last six to eighteen months, depending on the company's industry, position in the industry, number of employees, and strength of competitors. They are the first to be terminated if the company goes through downsizing or reorganizing.

The CPM is an excellent tool to use for self-assessment as to your readiness to be viewed as a viable candidate and/or a high potential in an organization. Be honest with yourself as you conduct the self-assessment; recruiters and human resource professionals in the organization are committed to delivering an accurate assessment of you. If you assess yourself as being in any section other than section 1, possessing style and substance, go back to the beginning of this chapter and invest more time and energy in mastering all of the ABCs of professional presence.

Career Development Framework 2: PIE Theory (Exposure)

Being assessed as belonging in section 1 of the CPM section is the first step in career advancement. The next step is about exposure. Success in the competitive workplace is dependent on the decision makers knowing you, liking you, and trusting you. This idea was explained in chapter 3 "Connect to External Systems." Review the advice of Ms. Carla Harris for a refresher on the importance of "relationship currency." In this discussion of the PIE theory, I share specific strategies that will afford you the opportunity to build relationships that lead to maximum positive exposure. The PIE theory is represented pictorially in Figure 5-4.

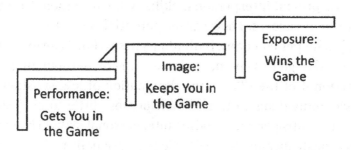

Figure 5-4. The PIE Theory

The acronym PIE stands for performance, image, and exposure. If compared to the CPM, performance would be synonymous with substance and image would be synonymous with style. The PIE theory states that while each of the three elements is vital and necessary for success at a current job level, your ability to move up to the next level or levels in your career will be dependent upon your amount of exposure. If they don't know you, they can't promote you. Considering that most people at your level are doing well in performance and image, the deciding factor for promotions will be relationships rather than performance and image.

Regardless of how well you can do something or how good you look, only through exposure will others know who you are. There are millions of great singers in the world, but the limited few get the big-exposure breaks that allow them to make it to the top— just ask Kelly Clarkson, Ruben Studdard, Fantasia Barrino, Carrie Underwood, Taylor Hicks, Jordin Sparks, and Jennifer Hudson. Unlike the millions of wanna-be professional singers in the world, these men and women have the television show *American Idol* to thank for providing a platform for exposure and resulting stardom.

Use the following executable strategies and tactics for each of the three components of the PIE theory to reach professional excellence. See each component of the PIE theory as a step toward your ultimate goal of success and significance.

The first component of the PIE theory is *Performance Gets You in the Game.* Think of nine to five as the first shift. (In actuality, it will probably be more like seven to seven.) Focus on executing your performance plan. Become an expert; develop and perfect your craft/area of expertise. Be seen at the right place, at the right time, doing the right thing. Keep your name in the top 25 percent of every performance-measurement list. Your goal is to be one of the top three performers.

Observe protocol and boundaries; always be respectful. Never be late to work, for meetings, or when turning in work assignments. Always reply to an RSVP. Use good judgment when returning phone calls and responding to e-mails—immediate responses to bosses and within twenty-four hours for all others.

Acknowledge other's help with a timely e-mail, acknowledge gifts via thank-you cards, and give/send gifts when appropriate. Be courteous to administrative support, and never be unreachable. Provide your contact information and notify them of your whereabouts daily so that you can be readily located if necessary. Avoid absenteeism.

The second component of the PIE theory is *Image Keeps You in the Game*. You must present yourself as a self-confident and competent professional at all times. Consistently execute the ABCs of professional presence. Always be "appropriate, believable, and credible in appearance, body language, communication skills, deliverables, and etiquette/social skills" (refer to earlier section of this chapter for details).

A social skill mastery that often gets overlooked is judiciously managing one's presence in social media and the technological space. Be diligent in regard to protecting your online image and reputation. Think before you post, text, snap, tweet, call, e-mail, etc. There is no wall that separates your social life from your professional life in the world of technology. Any communication you make via technology lives for eternity and will sooner or later find its way into the hands of a potential employer or business partner.

The third component of the PIE theory is *Exposure Wins the Game*. It's your ace card; but don't play it without impeccable image and top performance—style and substance! Think of five to nine o'clock after the traditional workday as a second shift that allows you to focus on executing your exposure plan: *It's all about relationship currency.*

Who you know is important in your quest for professional success. Strive to build a network of acquaintances. Meet and greet every day, everywhere—elevator, company cafeteria, division meeting, etc. Seek out, attend, and participate in CEO and senior executives' pet projects. Participate in after-hours company events. Attend receptions, dinners, picnics, outings, special events, and your boss's social events. Do lunch and happy hours with peers; take your spouse, not your friend. Word of caution—bringing multiple "friends" (a different one each week) to work-related events is not a positive career move.

Seek visibility for you and your company by attending and speaking at conferences. Write positive opinion letters to newspaper and magazine editors. Participate in citywide cultural events, visit museums, and attend theaters, concerts, and sporting events. Volunteer in community-service projects. Support and grow your personal network; attend events given by your alma mater, fraternity/sorority, and social organizations. Honor your friends' invitations.

Astute individuals recognize the fact that "who you know" is not the only criteria to professional success. I make the case that what is equally—and often more—important is *who knows you, what who knows about you, and what who says about you.* You are constantly watched by others, including many people you don't know. Your accomplishments and your setbacks can easily spread throughout the organization and into the general public. People you don't know will know you. Some will know the good about you, and some will know the not so good. Some will say the good about you, and some will say the not so good.

Therefore, you must always deliver excellence and sell yourself as excellence. Utilize your expertise in venues outside your organization. Demonstrate your knowledge by publishing and speaking in your area of expertise so that those you don't know but know you can speak about you in a positive manner. Your goal is to have others sell you. When other people with winning brands recommend your services and introduce you to their networks, you have successfully put the PIE theory into action.

The two previous career development frameworks, CPM and PIE theory, succinctly summarized the factors that determine career success—substance, also referred to as performance, technical proficiency, and business acumen; style, also referred to as image, presence, and professionalism; and exposure—if they don't know you, they can't promote you. The final career development framework will shed light on the typical corporate organizational promotion pathway.

Career Development Framework 3:
Optimum Career Trajectory (Promotion)

The final career-development framework I present is the Optimum Career Trajectory (OCT). The OCT (see Figure 5-5) will give you a summary perspective on what it takes and how long it takes for the "top-talent" performers in CPM section 1—substance and style who have mastered the PIE theory, to get to the top executive level—the "sweet spot" in the company.

The OCT provides an overview of the job levels that exist in most organizational settings along with time frames and responsibilities. The career progression described is "typical" but can be different based on the needs of the company, industry, environmental factors, the TASKBs you bring to the job, your relationships in and out of the company, timing, and pure luck.

Becoming familiar with the standard organizational "top-talent" movement will take some of the guesswork out of the career-movement pathway. All time frames are hypothetical, but they are based on the typical progression of top-performing individuals who ascend to higher levels in the organization in which they began as entry-level new hires.

In accepting your first job after earning your undergraduate degree, you will be placed in an entry-level position. You will be considered an *individual contributor (IC)* as you will have no responsibility to lead others. Typical titles include management trainee, analyst, and consultant. Your focus should be on developing and demonstrating technical expertise and interpersonal skills; delivering your performance objectives; building business acumen and horizontal relationships; and exhibiting goodwill. Your time in the entry-level position will be three to five years from your initial hiring by the company.

Your first management promotion will place you in *first-level management*. ICs will report to you. Your title will include the word "manager." You will have the responsibility to motivate your team to achieve product and/or profit goals and objectives set by your superiors. Your focus should be on developing your operational knowledge of the business, developing your direct reports, ensuring customer satisfaction, delivering your team-performance objectives, and building vertical relationships and goodwill. Your time in the first-level management position will be six to ten years from your start with the company.

The next management level will place you in *middle management*. Reporting to you will be first-level managers. Typical job titles include director and vice president. You will have the responsibility to lead and direct multiple managers within a business unit to achieve product/profit goals and objectives set by your superiors. Your focus will be on perfecting your operational knowledge of the business, the industry, and your competitors and ensuring your direct reports are developing their teams, satisfying their customers, and delivering their team-performance objectives. Relationship building will be focused on verticals in other areas of the company. Your time in the second-level management position will be eleven to fifteen years from your start with the company.

After middle management, you will enter into the *first level of executive management*. Reporting to you will be middle managers. You will have profit and loss responsibilities for entire divisions of the company. According to BlueSteps.com,

> Profit and loss (P & L) responsibility is one of the most important responsibilities of any executive position. Having P & L responsibility involves monitoring the net income after expenses for a department or entire organization, with direct influence on how company resources are allocated. Those with P & L responsibility often give final approval for new projects and are required to find ways to cut budget expenditure and ensure every program is generating a positive ROI.

In *first level of executive management*, you will be expected to set the goals and objectives for your division that will allow the company to meet the strategic goals and objectives set by the senior executives. Titles at this level include division president, executive director, and general consul. You will report into the C-suite officers of the company. Your focus will be on mastering organizational leadership skills, driving performance, and achieving high profit margins. Building strong, favorable relationships with C-suite officers is non-negotiable at the executive level. Time in your third management position will be sixteen or more years from your start with the company.

The top level in executive management is *senior executive management*. These highest-level executives usually have titles beginning with "chief" and are therefore usually called "C-level" executives or part of the "C-suite." The traditional three such officers are chief executive officer (CEO), chief operations officer (COO), and chief financial officer (CFO). The CEO must own the vision, allocate resources, build the company culture, make good decisions, and oversee and deliver company performance. The COO and CFO, along with other C-suite officers (see chapter 6), report to the CEO; the CEO reports to the board of directors. As a C-suite officer, your focus will be on preserving the profitability and image of the company. You will be positioned to reach the C-suite in twenty or more years from your start with the company. Upon reaching this level, your expertise and status will be sought by other organizations who will ask you to serve as a member of their boards of directors.

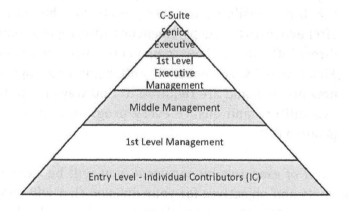

Figure 5-5. Optimum Career Trajectory (OCT)

From *FOCUS* to *ACTION*

To the young leaders who have been coddled throughout the K-12 educational socialization process under the impression that performance in and of itself will get you to the top—be forewarned! While the class valedictorian is the person with the highest GPA, and being the most popular will get you the most votes and elected homecoming and prom king or queen, getting to the top in the organizational setting requires more. It requires focus—intentional intensity on achieving your goals through the keen alignment of your thoughts, plans, and actions while excelling in all aspects of the ABCs of professional presence.

The final principle of the FOCUS intrapersonal skills module, *Sell Yourself As Excellence*, presents a set of simple acts of "being and doing" for personal and professional success: "Be engaging; be interested and interesting; be prepared; be disciplined; be organized; be punctual; be helpful; be humble; be nice; be kind." These small acts enable the big acts of being and doing discussed in chapter 3: "Be the authentic you, be likeable, and be strategic."

In order to maximize your career potential, you have to present yourself strategically as a well-balanced package of style and substance, high potential and high performance—an emerging leader who wants to add value to the organization and to society. Just as elite professional athletes have invested years and years in the practice and play of their sport to reach the performance level of unconscious competence in all areas of their craft, so will you.

With the five principles of the FOCUS module of intrapersonal skills as part of your toolbox, you are now prepared to transition to the ACTION interpersonal skills module. The first competency level, *Awesome Professionalism*, begins our ACTION journey toward great leadership with a look into the executive lifestyle, including the C-suite, corporate culture, corporate power, and corporate politics. An introduction to the dynamic atmosphere of executive-level professionalism will shed light on the need for emerging leaders to deliver awesome professionalism, grounded in a mindset of excellence.

Chapter Summary

Excellence in the workplace is a worthy goal. Scripture says to pay careful attention to our own work, getting satisfaction from a job well done and not having the need to compare ourselves to anyone else, as we are each responsible for our own work. Internalizing and operationalizing this goal at the beginning of one's career is the heart of the message found in this chapter.

The objective of this chapter is to demonstrate how emerging leaders start their careers by adding value to an organization and strategically position themselves to be viewed as "value-add" in an organization, leading to higher levels of responsibility within their organizations. Employees who possess a value-add mind-set and are grounded in excellence are noticed by upper-level management because they are more likely to deliver a high level of workplace competency.

Entry-level employees enter the organization with the goal to "add value," i.e., to "fit in." They must learn the "secret code" of the workplace in regards to expectations and requirements in the area of professionalism. The *"secret code"* being the *ABCs of professional presence*—being able to demonstrate the specific TASKBs (traits, abilities, skills, knowledge, and behaviors) of professional excellence in *appropriateness, believability, and credibility through appearance, body language, communication skills, deliverables, and etiquette/social skills.*

The chapter provides details on the what, how, dos, and don'ts, for each of the ABCs of professional presence. After mastering the ability to "add value" through impeccable delivery of the ABCs of professional presence, the emerging leader transitions to the "value-add" mind-set.

Value-add employees quickly earn a reputation for being respected professionals and indispensable team players, consistently delivering exceptional performance in technical prowess and relationship management, horizontally and vertically, inside and outside the organization. The value-add mind-set is based on Andrews's criteria on how to evaluate the professional quality of an occupation and McGuigan's professionalism attributes of the individual working in an occupation.

The chapter presents three career-development frameworks that enable the move to a value-add mind-set. The Career Potential Matrix (CPM) gives detailed descriptions of four employee types in the workplace based on substance (performance) and style (image). Possessing style and substance is the most desirable of the four employee types and sets the stage to engage the PIE theory. The PIE theory is defined as performance, image, and exposure. All three elements are significant for a professional with exposure serving as the ace card for advancement in career levels.

The final career development framework is the Optimum Career Trajectory (OPT) that shows the "exemplary" career movement of a STAR employee. Rated as a high potential (hi-po) in the company, the STAR, fast-track employee may move through five levels of job responsibilities that will take him or her from an entry-level position to the C-suite in fifteen years.

Just as you have become unconsciously competent in knowing the ABCs of the English language, with practice, you can become unconsciously competent in the ABCs of professional presence. It is at this level that the employee characteristically exhibits professional behaviors higher than the norm. Some may see these traits and behaviors as simple and easy and of no importance. The true professional operating with a value-add mind-set, grounded in excellence, knows these traits and behaviors are significant and essential.

I close the chapter by sharing my aspiration for you. The fundamental aspiration is not that you add value by simply "fitting in" but that you become value-add by "standing up and standing out," exhibiting both substance *and* style through exceptional performance, impeccable image, tactical exposure, and strategic significance to the organization. Adding value is where you will start—learning and performing your ABCs of professional presence. Being value-add is where you should be headed as you *sell yourself as excellence.*

Leadership and Professional Development Exercises

Key Terms

- ABCs of professional presence
- altruistic versus egoistic
- Business Etiquette Expectations of Twenty-First Century Leaders
- Career Potential Matrix (CPM)
- Covey's Habit 3
- Covey's Quadrant II
- five attributes of professionalism
- four stages of professional growth
- four types of business attire
- gender-neutral etiquette
- governing professional organization
- impression management
- Optimum Career Trajectory (OCT)
- PIE theory
- profession
- professional
- professionalism
- small acts of being and doing in communication, deliverables, and etiquette
- SMART goals
- STAR versus good performer
- Toxic workplace behaviors

Questions to Discuss

1. What is the fifth principle of the FOCUS module?
2. What are the four stages in growth of professional skills? Why are they important to know?
3. What are the ABCs of professional presence? Why is each component important for impression management?

4. How do the three career-development strategies (the PIE theory, the CPM, and the OCT) complement one another to deliver career success?

5. What are the five criteria to evaluate the professional quality of an occupation? What are the five attributes of professionalism?

Questions to Consider

1. Which of the four stages of professional growth do you currently reside? Are you pleased with your current stage? If yes, why? If no, why not?

2. Honestly assess your level of style and substance according to the CPM. At what level of the CPM would an employer rate you? Will that level and rating support you in the accomplishment of your personal and professional goals and objectives?

3. Which of the ABCs of professional presence will you commit to improving *today*? Set an improvement goal using the SMART system. Share it with your mentor or coach. Ask him or her to hold you accountable for reaching your goal.

4. Do you believe that selling yourself as excellence honors your faith as well as other components of your winning support system? Why or why not?

5. What will you stop doing *today* because it hinders your ability to sell yourself as excellence? What will you intentionally start doing *today* so that you can focus on selling yourself as excellence?

Books to Stimulate Your Mind

- *Basic Black: Home Training for Modern Times* by Karen Grigsby Bates and Karen Elyse Hudson (1996)
- *The 7 Habits of Highly Effective People* by Stephen Covey (1989)
- *They Don't Teach Corporate in College: A Twenty-Something's Guide to the Business World* by Alexandra Levit (2009)

The Johnson White Leadership Model

Module 2 ACTION

Introduction

Leadership is often confused with other things, specifically
management. But management requires an entirely different
set of skills. As I see it, leadership revolves around vision,
ideas, direction, and has more to do with inspiring people as
to direction and goals than with day-to-day implementation ...
One can't lead unless he can leverage more than his own
capabilities ... You have to be capable of inspiring other
people to do things without actually sitting on top of them
with a checklist—which is management, not leadership.

—John Sculley in Bennis, *On Becoming A Leader*

The second module of the JWLM identifies the interpersonal
skills needed for effective twenty-first-century leadership
(Figure Module 2. JWLM Summary). These skills are presented as
ACTION—a mnemonic that serves a dual purpose. First, ACTION
aids in the memory retrieval of the multiplicity of information
that comprises interpersonal TASKBs. Secondly, the meaning of
the word action—*the fact or process of doing something, typically
to achieve an aim*— succinctly defines the desired outcome of
interpersonal skills for effective leadership and professionalism.
In the case of the JWLM, the aim of ACTION is to achieve great
leadership with and through others.

Figure Module 2. JWLM Summary

Building Interpersonal Skills: ACTION

Being able to participate effectively in the influence process of leadership does not happen overnight. It is a *growth* process resulting from the accumulation of knowledge over time garnered through education, experience, and personal examination.

Growth is often represented via a hierarchical approach. One of the most recognizable hierarchical models is Maslow's 1947 hierarchy of needs. Maslow's theory has two distinct characteristics: it is predetermined in order of importance and lower-level needs must be met before the higher needs can be reached. Maslow identified five general levels of motivating needs: physiological (basic survival needs), safety (absence of danger), belonging (acceptance by others), esteem (valued by others), and self-actualization (life achievements).

The ACTION module of the JWLM is also described via five levels. Similar to Maslow's hierarchy of needs theory, each level of the ACTION module has a predetermined order of importance, and the lower levels must be met before the higher levels can be achieved. Each level represents one of the *competency domains* associated with being an effective twenty-first-century leader.

Competency domains are defined as the collective TASKBs (traits, abilities, skills, knowledge, and behaviors) that one must possess within that area in order to produce at a level of high proficiency and excellence.

The five competency domains or tenets of the ACTION module are:

#1. Awesome Professionalism. (A Leader's Commitment to Personal Best)

This is the ability to execute the ABCs of professional presence while adhering to the cultural norms in the organizational setting; delivering consistently exceptional results with special attention to details in small or large tasks; phenomenal conscientiousness that demonstrates readiness for senior-level leadership.

#2. Courageous Character. (A Leader's Commitment to Do Good and Not Harm)

This is the ability to consistently demonstrate ethical behaviors including integrity, trustworthiness, sound judgment, courage, conviction, and personal accountability; possessing an unquestionable personal brand; wise and judicious use of power and influence.

#3. Tenacious Inclusion. (A Leader's Commitment to Respect in the Workplace)

This is the ability to embrace, appreciate, develop, and serve all people—diversity and social awareness. Leaders who operate from a position of cultural inclusion are open to using the gifts and talents of all people in the organization such that they can contribute, add value, and possess a feeling of belonging in the organization. These leaders purposely strive to be personally free from stereotypes, prejudices, and biases, and accept none of these attitudes from employees or customers.

#4. Optimal Service. (A Leader's Commitment to Enhancing Others' Self-Worth)

This is the ability to give back to others demonstrated through a personal commitment to improving the community in which you live and work and assisting the organization in which you work to address social needs in the communities they affect. Stewardship of the planet, which lays the foundation for prosperity and well-being for generations to come—through the protection of natural resources—is an expectation of leaders and their organizations as they deliver optimal service in the twenty-first century.

#5. Noble Leadership. (A Leader's Commitment to Ethical Goal Achievement)

This is the ability to guide, direct, steer, and navigate the twenty-first-century leadership process effectively through the ethical and prudent use of power and influence. Noble leadership is a process that is described in four components—partnership, relationship, companionship, and championship—resulting in the attainment of shared goals and positive outcomes.

In summary, the ACTION module asserts that once leaders have established themselves as consummate professionals with moral character and unwavering ethics who openly seek to embrace others and are dedicated to serving them, they are ready to step into positions of leadership, using their power of influence to help their organization be its best while achieving its mission, goals, and objectives. Leaders grow into a state of full potential by empowering others to reach theirs. It is at this point that noble leadership exists.

Because effective leaders can and do get things done, make ACTION—literally and figuratively—a habit in your life. Chapters 6–10 provides the details on the TASKBs that constitute each of the five competency domains in the ACTION module.

CHAPTER 6

Awesome Professionalism

Now more than ever you are the architect of your
own growth—and increasing your organizational
influence is an ongoing process that requires:

- Job mastery
- Political acuity
- Meticulous relationship management
- Visibility to the right people
- A willingness to take a well-gauged risk or two

—Judith Ross, "Building a New Ladder to
the Top," *Harvard Business Review*

At the very top of a company, a subtle sorting process reveals
who might become CEO and who won't. The irony is, what
makes you a contender isn't enough to make you a winner.

—Dan Ciampa, "Almost Ready: How Leaders
Move Up," *Harvard Business Review*

Your education and exposure to the five principles of the FOCUS
module of intrapersonal development have enabled you to grow
to a sufficient level of personal development. You are now ready
to begin working on the skills you will need to master in order

to make your mark in the public arena. In other words, you are now ready to begin your developmental journey to the top by learning the interpersonal and leadership competencies needed to be the leader of others at the highest organizational levels. The aim of this chapter is to start you on that journey with executive-level professionalism, the first of the five competency domains of executive leadership as defined in the ACTION module of the JWLM.

This is a critical entry point into the public arena of leadership. Awesome professionalism is synonymous with Maslow's first level of human needs in the organizational setting (physiological). The most basic human physiological needs include food, water, shelter, and oxygen. In the organization, such basic needs are for adequate heat, air, and base salary to ensure workers can get the job done. These needs are supplied by the organization to all of its employees. On the other hand, the emerging leader has to take on the personal responsibility of being able to survive the fierce competitive (dog-eat-dog) aspect of the workplace, the political battles inherent in all organizations, and people relationships. Awesome professionalism is a strategic tool emerging leaders will need to employ to safeguard their survival and provide a safety net in times of uncertainty and organizational change.

Expectations for success at entry-level jobs include dressing appropriately, proper handshaking, dining skills, small-talk savvy, error-free work, *and* relationship building. These topics were covered in the FOCUS module of intrapersonal skills development. In principle 3, Harris's concept of relationship currency was discussed. In principle 5, the ABCs of professional presence summarized the critical professionalism TASKBs needed for career success.

These professional skills are foundational, fundamental, and essential, but they are not sufficient to take you to the top of an organization. The purpose of the ACTION module is to demonstrate how your interpersonal skills build on your intrapersonal foundation in order to ascend to higher levels of the organization. FOCUS shared ways and means of adding value to an organization. ACTION is about *being* value-add.

Professionalism in the Corporate Setting: Play to Win!

Before this discussion, let us cover an important observation. When some individuals hear the word "corporate," they immediately shut down. Their minds bring up the negative images they see on TV and in the movies of working in corporate America—endless rows of cubicles and desks with no privacy and employees dressed in uncomfortable, unfashionable suits and neck-choking ties. Visions of bosses who don't know their employees' names, clients who can't be satisfied, and endless in-boxes of paperwork. They see unfair political games being played; promotions and recognition given to those who least deserve it; and hard-to-deal-with coworkers, bosses' favorites, and bosses' targets. The list of undesirable images is endless.

Individuals with these booby-traps as images in their minds think, *This only happens in corporate America. If I go to work somewhere else, like in education, sports, religion, nonprofit, philanthropy, or health-care areas—or I become an entrepreneur—I will avoid the negative aspects of work found in corporate America.* Unfortunately, this mind-set is wrong!

The parts of corporate America just described are not indigenous to corporate America; they are present in all places where you find people working together. While the task side of work life differs from setting to setting and industry to industry, the human side does not. All organizations are made of people. Therefore, all organizations small and large, including hospitals and churches; schools, colleges, and universities; local, state, and national governments; and those in the nonprofit industry, will have their share of political maneuvering. Navigating organizational life is unavoidable.

Since it is everywhere, do not spend time trying to elude it. Your time is best spent learning how to master the challenge of organizational life and create the opportunity to excel. Think of it as a game. All games have rules, and if you don't know the rules or don't play by the rules, you lose. If you learn the rules and master the rules, you position yourself to win.

This discussion is designed to help you win the corporate game! Again, don't let the terminology be a stumbling block to your understanding of the material. Corporate is just another word for organization—any place where a group of people comes together to achieve a goal.

Let me repeat the game metaphor; it's that important! Game denotes that there are rules that govern how people act in the organization: those who study, learn, and apply the rules "win," and those who argue, complain, or ignore them "lose." Winning means that you have added value to the organization, its stakeholders, your peers, and yourself. Losing means you have missed an opportunity to grow, develop, and make a contribution to something bigger than yourself. Losing is no fun. Winning is all fun. Take heed to the discussions that follow so that you can enjoy playing and winning the Super Bowl of professional life!

Insights into Corporate Culture, Power, and Politics

The corporate world is a fascinating, dynamic place. It lays claim to many of the movers and shakers, the powerful and influential people of our world. Being a part of the corporate world can be a very rewarding experience or a not-so-pleasant one. What makes it pleasant for some and not for others is understanding that business is conducted in the corporate world as a game. To move ahead and win means understanding the game and its rules.

So you will be aware of what is happening on the playing field around you, this chapter explains the controlling forces of the corporate world—corporate culture, corporate power, executive lifestyle, abuse of power, moving to the top, and the relationship of corporate politics and diversity. To help you move ahead and win, a few winning strategies are provided. These proven strategies are based on research as well as my personal experiences and observations gathered from working and winning in corporate and educational organizations for more than thirty years.

Life in the Organization: Corporate Culture

Corporate or organizational culture refers to a system of shared meaning held by members that distinguishes the organization from other organizations. The concept of corporate culture became a hot management topic in the 1980s and has since been determined to have far-reaching ramifications for all members of the organizations—even those outside their boundaries. Organizational culture outlines the appropriate behavior for employees. It is the way things are done in an organization. With a clearly defined culture, members of the organization know what is expected of them and what to expect from the organization.

Culture conveys a sense of who the company is and must be communicated to all stakeholders. It is the glue that holds the organization together by giving employees a sense of identity with the company. Culture provides a unifying theme for the organization, giving focus and direction to the firm. Culture can be weak or strong, depending on the age, traditions, and successes of the company. Culture is often based on the founder's or company heroes' beliefs; the the older a company is, the more time it has to settle into a tradition, perpetuated through rites and rituals, and therefore harder to change. Longevity also implies success, another fortifier of corporate culture.

It is the role of those in power to preserve, safeguard, and protect the organization's culture. The evidence of one's acceptance into a company's culture is determined by how much he or she is perceived to be a team player and will have a direct effect on one's ability to succeed and move ahead in the company. When your personality matches the organization's culture, you are positioned to move up in the organization. Any conflicts are minor and manageable and can be accepted by both parties. Others in the organization are talking about you positively, asking for your input, assigning you special projects, and accepting you as a team member.

As a team player, you have immersed yourself in the culture and effectively demonstrated the ABCs of professional presence.

You have dressed the part, attended company picnics, Christmas parties, secretaries' appreciation celebrations, and peers' social events. You have made your bosses look good by producing work that is important to them and not just to you. You have showed respect for authority and become indispensable by going the extra mile. You have clearly demonstrated that you can be trusted with the small and are ready for the big. Your professionalism from an entry-level position through multiple management positions has demonstrated that you understand how to present yourself as a professional worthy of serving in an executive-level position. You are now seen as "value-add" and positioned for the top—the corporate executive C-suite.

Life at the Top: Corporate Power

The authority to get things done—the clout to make decisions with the stroke of a pen—lies with the top management decision makers. Because the traditional titles for the top management decision makers include the word *chief,* their collective office is labeled the C-suite. Specific titles include chief executive officer (CEO), chief operating officer (COO), chief financial officer (CFO), chief marketing officer (CMO), chief information officer (CIO), and chief diversity officer (CDO). Other executive-level titles, which may or may not be considered senior level or C-suite, include presidents, executive vice presidents (EVP), divisional presidents, and senior vice presidents (SVP).

The C-suite is considered the most important and influential group of individuals at a company. Being a member of this group comes with high-stakes decision making, a more demanding workload, and high compensation. In addition to defining, perpetuating, and safeguarding the corporate culture, this level sets the strategic direction of the company and makes policy decisions based on this direction. These decisions determine the way the company conducts business. Rarely, if ever, are these decisions challenged or changed by those outside the C-suite.

Persons who hold senior-level positions have historically risen through line positions—jobs with direct contact with the customer and/or product, i.e., sales, marketing, and manufacturing. Senior-level executives have successfully managed bottom-line responsibilities that include profit and loss (P&L). It is virtually impossible to get a senior position running a business if you don't know how the business runs. Depending on its culture, senior-level managers may come from inside or outside the organization.

Organizations whose history goes back to the nineteenth and early twentieth centuries—oil, transportation, finance, consumer goods, technology/telephone companies—have a very traditional, established, conventional approach to the visual demonstration of the power held by members of the C-suite. In these companies, the silent language of material possessions is strongly felt at the senior executive level.

Even the most casual observer would be able to discern that these individuals are in power because they occupy extremely large corner offices. Located on the top floor of a multistory building, the offices have panoramic views overlooking the landmarks of the city. The office décor is exquisite with wood-paneled rooms, high ceilings, and marble floors. The offices are decorated with fine mahogany wood furniture, large desks, leather chairs, and carved credenzas, six-to-twelve-person conference tables, plush sofas and chairs, sitting areas for visitors, and no paper clutter.

Strategically placed throughout the room are icons depicting the company's history and traditions; artifacts depicting the executive's sporting interests; personal performance awards; and photos of family members, especially children. There is plush greenery in the office, giving you the feeling that everything is calm and under control. A significant number of gatekeepers—executive assistants, administrative assistants, and secretaries—will be located immediately outside C-suite members' doors.

Corporate organizations with a more recent history—founded in 1980s to 2000s—are opting for a different visual image. Internet-based companies such as Google, Facebook, and YouTube—and some more traditional companies who desire to brand themselves as the company of choice for the best and brightest of the millennial generation—have adopted a more relaxed workplace style. In these companies, top executives and managers at all levels are forgoing the opulence of the traditional executive office. These executives may even have desks and no-wall offices on the floors with lower-level employees.

Executive Lifestyle

Because of the recent abuses of executive power that some feel contributed to America's economic collapse in 2007, the plush executive lifestyle has lost some of its glamour. Nevertheless, it still exists. According to *Forbes* contributor Scott DeCarlo, in 2011, the chief executives of the five hundred biggest companies in the United States (as measured by a composite ranking of sales, profits, assets, and market value) earned $5.2 billion, averaging out to $10.5 million apiece.

Compensation packages include stock options and million-dollar bonuses. In addition, executives receive perks such as housing allowances, cars/limos/drivers, entertainment budgets, unlimited travel in corporate jets, memberships in private country clubs and city clubs. Chances are, however, these lavish lifestyles will continue to come under scrutiny. As a demonstration of leadership and professionalism, executives in the twenty-first century would be wise to diminish excess and the appearance of greed in the executive lifestyle.

A mainstay leisure activity at the executive level is golf. There are numerous reasons why golf is the leisure activity of CEOs, namely secluded exposure. Golf is a bonding ritual among leaders across all organizations. It provides an opportunity to conduct "quasi-business" in a private and often neutral setting; an opportunity to study potential business partners or subordinates outside the work setting; and it's couched in an aura of gentility and elitism. Golf gets the executive outdoors, away from ringing telephones and demanding subordinates, while simultaneously satisfying the competitive nature of the corporate power players and their need to conduct business.

A possible downside to corporate power and the pampered corporate lifestyle it affords is the time commitment. Senior-level executives have a commitment to the job that goes well beyond that of any other member of the organization. Senior-level executives are always on—twenty-four hours, seven days a week. In addition to the work of running the organization, they also are the public relations face of the organization and are expected to represent their organization at civic, nonprofit, and charitable events. This type of commitment unavoidably requires sacrifices, especially in the area of family time. The degree of sacrifice made depends upon the personality and style of the executive.

Abuse of Power

A far-reaching problem regarding corporate power is its abuse. The abuse of power can occur at any level in the organization, and it is extremely detrimental when it occurs at the executive level. Negative behaviors such as sexual misconduct, harassment, racial or lifestyle faux pas, unethical business practices, and greed for personal gain are often found at the executive levels. Organizations that tolerate these detrimental behaviors expose themselves to the potential weakening of their corporate culture, a negative public image, and possible severe financial penalties brought on through litigation by affected parties. You must *never* be involved in any questionable behaviors and immediately report observed abuse of company resources to the organization's ethics hotline, legal counsel, or other appropriate entity.

Corporate Politics and Diversity

Corporate politics consists of the informal, unwritten procedures for making things happen or not happen in an organization. Corporate politics are often viewed as the ugly side of the corporate game because they have been credited with causing the exclusion of diversity in corporate America, especially at the power levels.

The demographic makeup of the power level shows that power in corporate America is held in the hands of white males.

The term *glass ceiling* is used to describe the invisible barrier that separates women and minorities from top leadership positions. They can look up through the ceiling, but prevailing attitudes are invisible obstacles to the advancement of diverse groups. According to researcher Richard Daft, the glass ceiling persists because top-level corporate culture in most organizations still revolves around traditional management thinking, a vertical hierarchy populated by white, American-born males who often hire and promote people who look, act, and think like them. Daft also reports on research that suggests the existence of "glass walls" that serve as invisible barriers to important lateral movement within the organization.

Since the 1970s, three different initiatives have attempted to break the glass ceiling: quotas, affirmative action, and diversity initiatives. The first two, quotas and affirmation action, were government-mandated programs. The quota program of the 1970s, which attempted to dictate the number of minorities a company must hire, gave way to the affirmation action programs of the 1980s, which set a minimum number of positions that must be held by minorities. As a result of these two programs, the representation of minorities in corporate America did increase from the pre-1970s era. Although the majority population has challenged the legality of these programs in the courts, they were effective methods of increasing the presence of women and minorities in corporate America in the second half of the twentieth century.

In the 1990s, as the business focus shifted to a global marketplace, corporate America took the lead in bringing minorities into the inner circle. Corporate America responded to the changing demographics of the workforce with a variety of diversity-management programs. In order to increase the bottom line, corporate America began to view diversity as an asset that brings a broad range of viewpoints and problem-solving skills to the decision-making process. Daft states that one goal for twenty-first-century global organizations is to ensure that all employees— women, ethnic and racial minorities, gay people, the disabled, the elderly, as well as white males—are given equal opportunities in the workplace.

Research conducted by IMD International Search and Consulting finds the number of women and minorities who hold C-suite positions worldwide is significantly low. Approximately 20 percent of C-Suite executives are a different nationality than the country in which their headquarters are based. However, less than 10 percent (9.2 percent of CEOs, 9.9 percent of CFOs, and 8.1 percent of COOs) are of an ethnic minority.

According to a 2016 *Fortune* magazine special report on race and culture in the C-Suite, executive-level advancement for black men is one of the lowest of all groups. In "Leading While Black: An Inside Look at What's Keeping Black Men Out of the Executive Suite," Ellen McGirt reports on the hard-numbered reality of corporate America stating that racial diversity continues to be a challenge and is practically nonexistent in the executive ranks. McGirt writes, "There have been only fifteen black CEOs in the history of the *Fortune* 500, of whom five are currently in the role."

C-suite statistics for women suggest they have "slightly cracked" rather than broken the glass ceiling. Recent survey numbers show that only 6.8 percent of CEOs are women, while 9.9 percent and 10.9 percent have risen to CFO and COO respectively—numbers that do not bode well for the advancement of women into the C-Suite.

An expanded discussion of diversity and inclusion in the organizational setting is provided in chapter 8.

Moving to the Top

In "Building a Ladder to the Top," Judith Ross states that today's corporate environment is a maze of constant flux because of mergers and acquisitions and leaves emerging leaders asking, "What is the best way to move up in this volatile environment?" Ross proposes that executive hopefuls in the twenty-first century will have to build their own ladders to the top. Skills proposed by Ross include developing deep competence in your job, perfecting social and political skills, convincing other people of your own ideas, and collaborating and compromising in order to implement your agenda and move your organization forward. Ross also notes that moving up within an organization means building a good relationship with every single person you interact with—from mailroom workers to the CEO. Visibility through volunteering for high-stakes projects and strategic use of the word "no" can also be very effective ways to increase your influence in an organization.

In "Almost Ready: How Leaders Move Up," Dan Ciampa writes that would-be CEOs too often fail to recognize that the qualities and skills they relied on to get to the number two position are different from those they will need to become CEO. Individuals for the top positions in organizations are not just known as "good" candidates; they are considered "elite" candidates. Elite candidates demonstrate an edge over their competition in three areas of executive leadership and professionalism: management savvy, political intelligence, and personal style.

The good candidate demonstrates management-savvy skills by knowing what is required operationally for short-term results and motivates others to do it. The candidate prioritizes and uses his or her time well. Delegation of tasks and development of the talent of the work team are also mastered. Additional skills honed by the elite candidate include the ability to resist jumping in personally to solve problems others can handle and making the right judgments about what to expend energy on. The elite candidate is careful to maintain control of key decisions and strategies of the organization while retaining the loyalty of all people in the organization by making them feel appreciated.

In the area of political intelligence, Ciampa identifies skills of the good candidate as being sensitive to the accuracy of organizational political currents; being able to build relationships horizontally and vertically and to quickly adapt to relationship patterns in unfamiliar environments; does not become involved in office politics—the office grapevine, gossip, and territorial feuds; and having his or her capabilities known by the CEO and board members. The elite candidate is able to demonstrate these skills without giving the air of being self-serving or being labeled "political." Relationship management is handled by the elite candidate in such a way that peers and subordinates go out of their way to help.

The personal style of the good candidate demonstrates all the TASKBs of a STAR performer—intensity and drive to excel, hardworking, going beyond the call of duty in time and effort, showing enthusiasm toward company initiatives, and being a leader among peers. The elite candidate positions himself or herself for the CEO job by doing these things exceptionally well while making the success look effortless. The elite candidate stays cool, calm, and collected regardless of the tension in the workplace, knowing when to hold back and when to let go. Championing the recognition of others' performances and being a role model to improve their performances are also skills that have been honed by the elite candidate.

Many of the good and elite candidate capabilities identified by Ciampa are part of FOCUS, such as uses time well, prioritizes, delegates, builds relationships, ensures exposure to CEO, STAR performer, driven to excel, hardworking, doesn't seem self-serving, makes success look effortless (unconsciously competent), and manages energy to avoid burnout. These capabilities are classified as intrapersonal skills.

Other capabilities listed by Ciampa that good and elite candidates must possess fall in the category of interpersonal and leadership skills, including motivating others, organizing others, and pushing them to achieve more than they think they can; reading political currents; making people feel appreciated and loyal, allowing others' performances to be recognized, and enabling peers to improve their performances. ACTION addresses these capabilities and additional ones through the five competency domains of awesome professionalism, courageous character, tenacious inclusion, optimal service, and noble leadership.

Please note! FOCUS precedes ACTION in the JWLM. Always remember that you must have your intrapersonal skills in order before you can effectively engage your interpersonal and leadership skills. The combination of the three skill sets—intrapersonal, interpersonal, and leadership—that will allow you to reach the top and stay at the top!

Winning the Corporate Game

Your goal must be to win the corporate game of whatever organization you choose to join. I adamantly encourage emerging leaders to consciously hold "winning" as a personal career goal. It is at this point in your career—holding a senior title and sitting at the table where decisions are being made—that you have the potential to influence policy resulting in change. At the senior level, you can positively affect the lives and families of the people in the organization, your customers, your stockholders, society as a whole, *and* leave a legacy of goodwill.

Winning means you are part of the organization's "in group." As such, you are viewed as a valuable asset, a contributing member of the team, assisting and leading the charge to achieve the corporate goals and objectives. Winning strategies to place in your executive professionalism toolbox include

- a powerful mentor—someone to guide you through the corporate political structure and murky waters;
- a powerful sponsor—someone who can move you up the corporate ladder with one phone call;
- a network of influential decision makers in your company and other companies;
- memberships in professional groups;
- impeccable performance and image;
- assertive ways to be included in the activities of the power network of your company and industry;
- active participation in company affinity groups;
- active participation in the social, cultural, and community life of your surrounding area; and
- assertive (collaborative not combative) responses to "ism" remarks/jokes with facts, not anger or aggression; assume

comments are from a lack of understanding, not racism, sexism, ageism, or look-ism.

If you are having difficulty getting into the executive pipeline, do not presume your absence from the fast track is due to racism or sexism. Do a personal inventory of your intrapersonal, interpersonal, leadership, and technical skills along with performance results. Be sure your performance is in line with or exceeds the fast-trackers. Expand your skills. Discuss your situation with your mentor and ask for assistance in creating a personal development plan.

If you find yourself in a staff position, stay no more than one to two years. Do not take two or three different staff jobs in a row; alternate between line and staff. Also be sure to mend any broken relationships you may have in the organization.

If you are certain that you have effectively executed all the winning strategies outlined above and find yourself playing in the wrong position—one that does not afford you the opportunity to use your best skills and abilities, here are additional strategies you can try that might assist you in obtaining your desired position on the team.

- Ask for the job(s) you want. If not given the job, ask for specifics of what you need to do to get the job the next time.
- Keep detailed documentation of performance, including thank-you letters from customers and peers.
- Apprise your manager on your performance progress and inform him or her whenever you accomplish one of the items.
- Ask your manager how he or she perceives your performance and progress.

If you come to the conclusion that there is not a fit between your skills, talents, and personality and the organizational culture and decide to leave, *do not* burn your bridges. Leave as a respected professional with an appropriate letter of recommendation in hand. Be sure your resume is up to date and results driven. Contact a professional executive placement firm and advise them of your possible availability.

Beyond Corporate America

Expertise in executive professionalism demonstrates capability in the first level of the ACTION hierarchy of needs to ascend to the highest positions in an organization. While I used corporate America as the framework for the discussion on executive-level professionalism, know that top positions in all fields require unconscious competence in the competency domain of awesome professionalism.

The significant contributions that can be made by occupying executive-level positions cuts across all professions. What is needed in the twenty-first century are policy makers in industry, education, politics, religion, public services, military, science, technology, and health care who are sensitive to the needs of all demographics of the United States.

Chapter Summary

This chapter covers the professionalism competencies a twenty-first-century emerging leader must possess in order to reach the top levels of an organization—competencies that go far and beyond the ABCs of professional presence. These competencies show your aptitude and qualifications for high-level responsibilities and service. Referred to in this chapter as executive-level professionalism, this set of competencies enables you to earn an executive-level position in the C-suite—the most powerful positions in the organization. At this level, you are not just adding value—you are known and perceived as "value-add." This chapter gives you a look into the inner workings of the C-suite, including corporate culture, corporate power and lifestyle, and corporate politics.

Qualities and characteristics needed to obtain a power position or be placed in the pipeline for one are presented. Top-level positions require skills that go past being a good candidate to that of being an elite candidate. Characteristics of candidates who are contenders to reach the top of the organization include uses time well, prioritizes, delegates, builds relationships, ensures personal exposure to CEO, STAR performance, driven to excel, hardworking, and accurately reads political currents. In addition, the elite candidate doesn't seem self-serving, makes success look effortless, isn't labeled "political," and manages energy to avoid burnout.

Emerging leaders who are seen as possible contenders for the top positions in an organization have a reputation for consistently exceeding performance expectations. They are known as educated risk takers who are willing to make personal sacrifices. The dominant power structure is comfortable with their personal style. These young leaders seek out challenging assignments, resulting in multifunctional and multicultural experiences. They are involved in and lead community-service projects. They emulate those who are in power positions in dress and hobbies, which allows them to connect to the power players outside the office through golf or other mutual interests. Emerging leaders consciously guard career assignments and spend minimal to no time in staff jobs focused on administration, communications, or community outreach.

Understanding the competencies associated with executive professionalism as you begin your organizational career can shave years off your trajectory to becoming a top leader (see chapter 5). Instead of haphazardly meandering through your first two years in the organization, not even knowing a game is being played, intentionally chart your path to success and significance.

You can start on day one by learning the right skills, asking the right questions, and asking for the right assignments that will position you in the pipeline to senior management. Living, working, and enjoying the perks and benefits of being a member of the C-suite is the position from which you can serve others in a greater capacity through policy decision making. Never underestimate the power of *awesome professionalism!*

Leadership and Professional Development Exercises

Key Terms

- C-suite
- corporate culture
- corporate politics
- corporate power
- executive-level professionalism
- office politics
- the elite candidate
- the good candidate

Questions to Discuss

1. What is the first competency domain of the ACTION module?
2. How does awesome professionalism differ from sell yourself as excellence?
3. What are the differences in qualities and characteristics of the good candidate and the elite candidate for executive-level positions? Of what significance is senior/executive-level leadership?
4. How does "executive life" differ from other parts of organizational life in a company? Where does the C-suite get its name?
5. How are corporate culture, corporate power, and corporate politics defined? What are some strategies to survive and thrive in an organizational setting in order to reach the top?

Questions to Consider

1. How comfortable are you with the concept of organizational culture, power, and politics? Explain.
2. Do you see yourself thriving in a corporate setting? Why or why not?

3. Do you see yourself in senior leadership at the company (organization, entertainment field, etc.) of your choice, whether an established company or one that you started as an entrepreneur?
4. Do you believe that striving for a senior-level position in an organization honors your faith as well as other components of your winning support system?
5. What action will you commit to engaging in today that would set you on the trajectory for a senior-level leadership position in an organization?

Books to Stimulate Your Mind

- *32 Ways to Be a Champion in Business* by Earvin "Magic" Johnson, entrepreneur and community leader (2008)
- *Why Should White Guys Have All the Fun? How Reginald Lewis Created a Billion-Dollar Business Empire* by Reginald F. Lewis and Blair S. Walker (1995)
- *Breaking Through: The Making of Minority Executives in Corporate America* by David A. Thomas and John J. Gabarro (1999)

CHAPTER 7

Courageous Character

Our studies validate that character is critically important in leadership development and may result in longer-term benefits than other attributes associated with leadership—competence for example. Individuals perceived as low in character were seen as fostering environments where others either make or accept unethical decisions that can negatively influence job performance. An individual's leadership and character are critical to an organization financially, but perhaps even more important, they are absolutely crucial to its long-term health, esprit de corps, and reputation.

—Dana Born, US Air Force, retired brigadier general, "Character Counts," *Harvard Kennedy School* magazine

Madoff sentenced to 150 years in prison—Disgraced investor gets maximum sentence for massive Ponzi scheme. www.msnbc.msn.com, June 29, 2009

Lay and Skilling's day of reckoning—Enron ex-CEO and founder convicted on fraud and conspiracy charges; sentencing slated for September. www.money.cnn.com, May 25, 2006

Nixon Resigns. www.washingtonpost.com, August 9, 1974

These three chilling headlines tell the story of fallen leaders. How did these leaders come to such a place in their lives? What were they thinking? How could they do it? While we may never know the answers to these questions, their behaviors call into question their ethics, morals, core values, integrity, motivation orientation, and use or abuse of power—concepts collectively called *character*. Character is the second competency domain of the ACTION module of the JWLM.

As the second competency domain of ACTION, courageous character is synonymous with Maslow's second level of human needs (safety). The safety level of human needs entails a safe and secure physical and emotional environment and freedom from threats such as violence and for an orderly society.

In the organizational workplace, safety needs reflect the need for safe workplaces, fringe benefits, job security, and financial stability such that job benefits and job security remain intact. The responsibility to ensure these needs are met in the organization falls on the shoulders of company executives. Without unshakeable character grounded in ethics, morals, and values, executive leaders will not be able to meet the safety level of human needs, especially those requiring the financial solvency of the organizations they lead. Followers first and foremost want leaders they can trust.

It is incumbent upon emerging leaders to build their careers on the courageous character competency domain of skills in order to steer clear of the personal and professional ruins portrayed in the headlines opening this chapter. Small character-based acts of "being and doing" result in big acts of personal and professional success: "Be truthful, be honest, and be trustworthy."

Defining Character

And Dr. King learned as he went along. He came
to see that leadership is more inspiration
than administration, that change is more evolution than
revolution. He learned what the great leaders learned—that they
must persuade their adversaries and inspire their followers.

And he understood that character is the foundation upon which
all other elements rest. Accordingly, he made decisions based
on the dictates of his conscience—choosing good over evil,
justice over injustice, and acting "because it is right to do it."

—Donald Phillips, *Martin Luther King Jr. on Leadership*

Within *Merriam Webster's* definition of character, you find words
and phrases that relate to leadership and professionalism:
one of the attributes or features that make up and distinguish
an individual; the complex of mental and ethical traits marking
and often individualizing a person, group, or nation; main or
essential nature especially as strongly marked and serving to
distinguish; reputation; moral excellence and firmness; literary
sketch of the qualities of a social type. In addition, values are also
essential components of a person's character as well as a person's
fundamental beliefs and public reputation.

From the ancient Greek philosophers Aristotle, Plato, and
Socrates, society has come to believe that character and ethics
are synonymous. The Greek word for "ethics" is ethos and can be
translated as "character." Ethos also means "customs, manners,
habits." The ethos or ethics that one operates from is how character
is expressed in the world.

Character includes more than behavior, encompassing one's way
of both doing and being in the world. It pertains to the question, "What
do I do?" and also to the equally important question, "Who am I?" It
is about moral self-examination. "Who do you think you are?" That is
the essence of the character question. *Who* we are is our character.

We do not arrive in the world with character. Rather than being
born with character, it develops from our birth. The composition of
our being is created through the various ways we look at our world
and how we understand our place in the world. These inputs come
from a variety of sources, including family, friends, and foes. Our
character "comes to be" as we become who we are.

Kolp and Rea go back to the works of the great philosophers to
identify the salient components of character. The authors write,

"Aristotle summarized character formation in his opening words on ethics: 'Every art and every inquiry, and similarly every action and pursuit, is thought to aim at some good.' Simply put, character formation is the making of good people. When we are taught character, we learn about our ethos, our ethics."

Character Components

The seven marks of character are the seven classical virtues— *courage, faith, justice, prudence, temperance, love,* and *hope.* The seven classical virtues provide focus for our personal lives and our professional lives because they intensely describe a way of life that strives for unquestionable character.

Character begins with *courage.* Without it, nothing would be done—and no risks would be taken. *Faith,* another word for trust, always transcends the individual. It invests leaders in something or someone outside of themselves. *Justice* has as its core meaning "fair" and "equal." It does not mean that every person has to have the same portion, but the decision process that guides the dividing of the portions has to be done with fairness. *Prudence* is synonymous with wisdom, meaning sensible, reasonable, foresight, and common sense. As the desired end to leadership includes justice and compassion, prudence is the means to the ends, especially when the end relates to matters of future survival and growth.

Temperance means moderation, balance, discipline, and self-control. When life is balanced in work and play, there is less likelihood that self-indulgence will become an issue through overworking or laziness, which are both forms of unhealthy self-indulgence. The question of how we spend our time is also a matter of the virtue temperance.

In the business world, the virtue *love* is best expressed as care, compassion, and mercy. Leaders can demonstrate these character qualities as they make decisions in regard to how they treat employees in tough times such as during loss of jobs through no fault of their own, including mergers and acquisitions, downsizings, layoffs, and plant closings. Leaders are to couple the virtue of love with courage, which allows them to act boldly with justice in good faith.

The final virtue, *hope*, points us confidently to the future, just beyond what is presently true. Hope is a critical component of strategic leadership because strategy involves being intentional in setting a future. Hope connects us back to the starting point, courage, the first of the seven virtues.

The link between hope and courage is best stated by Kolp and Rea: "The fundamental knowledge and feeling that there is a way out of difficulty, that things can work out, that we as humans can somehow handle and manage internal and external reality, that there are 'solutions.'" Hope is the switch that turns courage into action. Collectively, the seven classical virtues are the beginning point for teaching character.

Teaching Character

Character is taught everywhere. Every encounter and experience has the potential to form character positively or negatively. Character is taught before kindergarten and preschool through the teaching and modeling influence of parents, grandparents, neighbors, churches, synagogues, or mosques, and it continues through our encounters with friends, peers, and bosses who model behavior (good and bad). Character is taught more formally as an ethics component of a class, such as in a philosophy class, a business ethics class, or an executive seminar.

The effectiveness of college-level programs specifically designed to improve character has been questioned. One example of concern is the work of military academies—institutions with some of the most intensive character-development training, including honor codes and requiring students to take classes in ethics, law, sexual harassment, and substance abuse prevention. Considering military academies experience incidents of cheating on exams, sexual harassment, and alcohol abuse, the argument can be made that core values and personality traits are mostly set by the time a person enters college.

Character development may be better achieved via situational factors than character-development programs. For any institution, having an environment with constant reminders to its students on the ethical expectations and punishments whenever they are caught deviating from the standards may have greater effect on character development. Ultimately, character development comes through a formation process that begins early in life and continues throughout life based on situational factors that may include character-development programs.

Character and Moral Maturity

Effective leadership requires one's character development to include moral development. Daft states, "All leadership practices can be used for good or evil and thus have a moral dimension. Moral leadership is about distinguishing right from wrong and doing right; seeking the just, the honest, the good, and the right conduct in its practice. Moral leadership gives life to others and enhances the lives of others. Immoral leadership takes away from others in order to enhance oneself." Because leaders have great influence over others, moral maturity is a goal of character development.

The capacity to make moral choices is related to a person's level of moral development, which comes through maturation and education. Kohlberg's three levels of moral development is an example of the maturation process. The first level, pre-conventional, is a state where the person is focused on rewards and punishments in pursuit of self-interest. The second level, conventional, is where a person uses cultural norms as moral guidance, defining moral reasoning largely by others' expectations. The third level, post-conventional, is based on a personal code that is in line with a universal code of ethics, such as the seven classical virtues or Kidder's eight universal values.

Level 1: Pre-Conventional. Self-interest motivates behavior to meet ones' own needs to gain rewards while following rules and being obedient to authority to avoid punishment.

- Student: "I cheat on tests to get a good grade so I can pass the class and graduate."
- Employee: "I lie to customers to sell more products and get higher commission checks."

Level 2: Conventional. Living up to expectations of acceptable behavior defined by others, which motivates behavior to fulfill duties and obligations.

- Student: "I cheat on tests because other students do it too."
- Employee: "I lie to customers because the other sales reps do it too."

Level 3: Post-Conventional. Behavior is motivated by universal principles of right and wrong, regardless of the leader or group.

- Student: "I do not cheat on tests because it is wrong."
- Employee: "I do not lie to customers because it is wrong."

Justifying Unethical Behavior

People believe most people, including themselves, are good people; people who understand right and wrong behavior and have a conscience. However, many people, including themselves, will still engage in unethical behavior. Because most people work hard at seeing themselves in a positive manner, they often justify unethical behavior to protect their self-concept to avoid a guilty conscience or feelings of remorse. The process of reinterpreting immoral behavior is called *moral justification.*

Moral justification can be used by people at each of Kohlberg's three levels of moral development. At the pre-conventional and conventional levels, individuals commonly use one or more of the following six justifications.

Advantageous Comparison. Comparing self to others who are worse.

- "I took one, but Joe took four."

Attribution of blame. Unethical behavior was caused by another.

- "He looked at me, so I hit him."

Diffusion of Responsibility. Entire group participating in unethical behavior.

- "We all took bribes."

Displacement of Responsibility. Individual blames others for unethical behavior.

- "I was just following orders."

Disregard or Distortion of Consequences. Minimizing harm of unethical behavior.

- "Wal-Mart is a big chain. I'm just taking one. They won't miss it."

Euphemistic Labeling. Using "cosmetic" words to make behavior sound acceptable.

- Terrorist group sounds bad while freedom fighters sounds good.

An example at the post-conventional level of reinterpreting immoral behavior in terms of a higher purpose is that of the work of Dr. Martin Luther King Jr. To fight for the civil rights of African Americans in the 1960s, Dr. King used civil disobedience tactics such as riding in the front of the bus and lunch-counter sit-ins, all of which were illegal, to successfully achieve his goal of ending segregation. Persons may take exception to the classification of civil disobedience as immoral behavior. Agreeing with Dr. King's thinking that "injustice anywhere is a threat to justice everywhere," persons may believe that when human rights are being violated, moral behavior compels the fight for justice through civil disobedience.

In the organizational setting, situational causes of unethical behaviors at the pre-conventional and conventional levels include highly competitive circumstances, unsupervised situations, absence of formal ethics policy or code of ethics, absence of punishment of unethical behavior, and rewarding unethical behavior. Unethical behaviors tend not to be reported by observers when the perception is that the violation is not serious or when the offenders are the observer's friends. The term "whistleblower" is given to a person who reports unethical or illegal activities in a private or public organization. Whistleblower activities may be classified as post-conventional organizational behaviors.

Testing Character: Power, Influence, and Leadership

Nearly all men can stand adversity, but if you want
to test a man's character, give him power.

—Abraham Lincoln

Power may be one of the most important concepts in the study of leadership; some may even say power is synonymous with leadership. In the organizational setting, power is defined as "the *ability* of one person in an organization to *influence* other people to bring about desired outcomes." This definition of power reflects the goal of leadership, which can be simply stated as "getting things done through others." Therefore, power is an important tool for leaders because it is a means to an end—an ability. However, the actual change comes as a result of influence and not from the power.

Influence is the *effect* a person's "power" has on the attitudes, values, beliefs, or actions of others. Power and influence are often used interchangeably, but there are distinctions in the two. Power is the *capacity to cause* a change in a person, and influence may be thought of as the *degree of actual change*. Leadership can be viewed as synergy resulting from the judicious use of *power* in an *influential* relationship among leaders and followers who intend real changes and outcomes that reflect shared purposes.

Therefore power, influence, and leadership are intrinsically mixed and can result in great good or great harm to the organization or society, depending on the character (virtues and values) of the leader. For this reason, we examine all three in relationship to character.

Sources of Power

There are two sources of power: *position power* and *personal power*. Position power is afforded a person by the organization based on the assigned role and title in the organization. Personal power is awarded by others in the organization based on the *attributes of the person* and the relationship the person has with others. Top management has position power and gives it to others in the organization by appointing leaders of the team, department, division, or company. Followers bestow personal power on leaders based on the leader's behavior. Charismatic leaders are examples of having leadership through personal power. The two power sources are not mutually exclusive.

Types of Power

One of the most widely used categorization methods of the types of power was created by French and Raven in the late 1950s. The researchers developed a taxonomy comprised of five different types of power: 1) legitimate—authority based on the user's position in the organization given by the organization, i.e., formal titles; 2) reward—the ability to influence others with something of value to them; 3) coercive—involves punishment and withholding of rewards to influence compliance; 4) referent—based on the user's personal relationships with others; and 5) expert—based on the user's skill and knowledge. Legitimate, reward, and coercive power bases are associated with a leader's position. Referent and expert power bases are sourced by the person.

More recently, two additional power bases have been identified: *connection power* and *information power.* Connection power is created by the user's relationship with influential people. Information power is having access to vital information *and* control over its distribution to others. These two power bases are especially relevant in the twenty-first-century global workplace and can result from the leader's position or person.

Responses to Power

One way leaders can gauge their effectiveness is to examine the success of their attempts to influence their followers—the response of followers to their requests. Three distinct outcomes that may result from the use of power: compliance, resistance, or commitment.

When leaders successfully use their position power (legitimate, reward, or coercive), followers respond through compliance. Followers comply with the directions of the leader, obey orders, and carry out instructions whether they agree with the leader or not. In this case, the followers typically do just enough to get by and may not contribute to their full potential.

If the followers feel that the leader's use of legitimate power is excessive, the followers may resist the attempt to influence. Resistance is seen in the actions of followers who deliberately try to avoid carrying out instructions or attempt to disobey orders altogether. The two responses to positional power, compliance and resistance, demonstrate that leaders who rely solely on positional power will find their effectiveness limited.

The leader's use of personal power results in a more desired follower response. Followers are more likely to respond with commitment when a leader uses personal power bases—expert or referent. Commitment means that followers adopt the leader's viewpoint and enthusiastically carry out instructions. Effective leaders seek follower commitment rather than compliance or resistance in that compliance may work in routine matters but in the promotion of organizational change, follower commitment is the end goal. Successful leaders wisely exercise both personal and position power.

Leader Motives for Power

What motivates a person to want to have influence, power, or control over others? Individuals with a high need for power derive psychological satisfaction from influencing others. Individuals with this personality type seek positions where they can influence others and often concurrently hold positions of influence in different organizations. High-power-need individuals readily offer ideas, suggestions, and opinions, and they seek information they can use to influence others. They are often good at building relationships and assessing power networks, and they can be outspoken and forceful.

The need for power can be expressed in two ways: personalized and socialized. Individuals with a high need for personalized power may also exhibit personality traits of being selfish, impulsive, uninhibited, and lacking self-control. These individuals will exercise power for their own self-centered needs and not for the good of the group or organization.

In contrast, socialized power is exercised in the service of higher goals to others or organizations and often involves self-sacrifice toward those goals. Socialized power implies a more emotionally and morally mature person who utilizes an empowering rather than an autocratic style of management and leadership.

How Much Power Should Leaders Have?

While leaders need power to be effective, the amount of power necessary will depend on what needs to be accomplished and the leader's skill in using what power is available.

When major changes are taking place in the organization and strong opposition is likely, the leader will need more power. A leader in this situation will want to use personal power *and* positional power. Strong personal power, expert and referent, is needed to persuade people that change is necessary and desirable. Strong positional power will be needed to overcome the opposition and buy time for the acceptance of the proposed changes.

The belief that power corrupts is especially relevant for position power. Throughout history, many political leaders with strong position power have used it to dominate and exploit subordinates. Reliance solely on position power is dangerous as it may block the formation of loyal organizational relationships needed to ferry the leader in times of tumult and uncertainty.

Influence Tactics

Influence refers to the actual change in behavior that results from power being exercised through a leadership relationship. When a leader is making a simple request that is clearly legitimate because it is relevant to the follower's work and something he or she knows how to do, the follower will typically agree and proceed to complete the request.

However, if the requested action is unpleasant, difficult, beyond the normal workday, or requires the upgrade of the follower's skills, the follower may be reluctant to complete the task. At that point, what does a leader do?

Gary Yukl lists the following eleven proactive influence tactics that leaders can employ to move their followers into action:

1) *Apprising.* Leader shows the follower the personal benefit or potential to advancement of career for completing the request/task.
2) *Coalition Tactics.* Leader enlists the aid of others or references the support of others to persuade followers to carry out the request/task.

3) *Collaboration.* Leader offers to provide follower-relevant resources and assistance if the follower carries out the request/task.

4) *Consultation.* Leader encourages participation of follower in creating or improving the activity proposal or plan for which the follower's support and assistance is needed.

5) *Exchange.* Leader offers follower an incentive such as an exchange of favors now or later if the follower will support or complete the request/task.

6) *Ingratiation.* Leader uses praise and flattery to express confidence in the follower's ability to carry out the request/task.

7) *Inspirational Appeals.* Leader gains commitment to request/task by appealing to the values, ideals, or emotions of follower.

8) *Legitimating Tactics.* Leader references rules, formal policies, or official documents to establish the legitimacy of the request/task.

9) *Personal Appeals.* Leader asks the follower to carry out request/task based on friendship or personal favor.

10) *Pressure.* Leader uses demands, threats, frequent checking, or persistent reminders to the follower regarding the request/task.

11) *Rational Persuasion.* Leader uses logical arguments and factual evidence to show feasibility and relevance of the request/task to the follower.

Leading with Character

> When wealth is lost, nothing is lost;
> when health is lost, something is lost;
> when character is lost, all is lost.
>
> —Billy Graham

Awesome professionalism was discussed in chapter 6 as a way to identify to decision makers that you are ready to ascend to an executive-level position. However, your character will determine whether you can courageously handle the power, pressure, prestige, and privilege that is inherent to an executive-level position.

How do the decision makers determine your character? By the name you make for yourself on "Main Street." Main Street is the term used by David D'Alessandro to describe the place where the people who make up your organization, including bosses, clients, vendors, peers, subordinates, and these people's significant others watch and evaluate you and from which they form an opinion of you. These opinions spread like wildfire through what is in reality, a very small professional world in which everybody talks. "Your bosses talk, your clients talk, your vendors talk, your peers talk, and your subordinates talk. And the significant others *really* talk," reiterates D'Alessandro.

As a result of these thousands of opinions created by thousands of transactions, a kind of consensus about who you are is generated. The consensus goes by many names, including your reputation, public image, legend, character, and personal brand. See your personal brand as an advertisement for your character. One's personal brand is a commercial that plays in the minds of the decision makers when your name is discussed on Main Street. The facts presented by your personal brand will affect your professional and personal success. Work hard to ensure your personal brand is a *positive* spokesperson for your character.

In *Career Warfare: 10 Rules for Building a Successful Personal Brand and Fighting to Keep It,* D'Alessandro suggests a variety of ways to build, protect, and enhance your personal brand. He says to first accept the fact that your behavior defines you; you are going to be judged not on what you perceive to be your internal traits, intentions, and desires, but rather your external actions. With that being true, be uniquely useful. Acquire a reputation for honesty and excellent judgment. Develop a reputation for leadership—getting things done fairly and with excellence through others. Develop focus, fearlessness, a willingness to think boldly, and a gift for making work fun for the people you manage.

Carson Dye, author of *Leadership in Health Care*, shares his perspective on key ways leaders operationalize (put into practice) their ethics. Dye states, "Unlike any other activities by leaders, the ethical decisions of leaders, especially senior leaders, are observed more closely—and are likely to be more critiqued—by everyone in the organization." Dye's guidelines for leaders to follow in order to demonstrate their commitment to character excellence start with weighing the cost of not being ethical. Ask yourself, "What is the downside risk if I get caught exhibiting unethical behavior? Is the payoff worth my career, my reputation, my livelihood?"

He resolutely expresses to leaders to tell the truth; don't exaggerate; do as you say and honor any promise made; use power appropriately and cautiously; admit mistakes; be trustworthy; manage expense accounts prudently; and minimize—or eliminate—excessive perks and benefits.

Chapter Summary

If an analogy were made between the interpersonal module ACTION and the body, character would play the role of ACTION's heart. Just as a heart pumps the life-sustaining blood throughout the human body, character drives the thoughts, motives, and actions that give life to a leader's vision. Therefore, it is imperative that twenty-first-century global leaders consistently examine their character to ensure their ethics, values, morals, and principles line up with the seven classical virtues of courage, faith, justice, prudence, temperance, love, and hope. Effective leaders are to operate from Kohlberg's highest stage of moral reasoning—level three post-conventional. At this level, the leader is doing what is right because it is the right thing to do. He or she is committed to the character-based small acts of being and doing: "Be truthful, be honest, and be trustworthy."

Effective leadership tools for the twenty-first century include power and influence. Leaders are to know and use the types of power (personal and positional); sources of power (legitimate, reward, coercive, expert, and referent; connection and information); and the eleven associated proactive influencing tactics.

Leaders must anticipate follower response options to the use of power (resistance, compliance, and commitment) and adjust their leadership styles accordingly. Leaders should strive not to abuse their power. At all times, leaders must critically examine their motives for having and using power (personalized or socialized) and decide how much and what type of power they need in order to accomplish the organizational goals for which they are responsible.

Character is the competency domain that will ensure the longevity and protect the legacy of your contribution as a twenty-first-century global leader. The road that effective twenty-first-century leaders travel to reach the end goal of being known as a leader with a personal brand of success and significance is paved by *courageous character.*

Above all else, guard your heart, for
everything you do flows from it.
—Proverbs 4:23 (NIV)

A good name is more desirable than great riches;
to be esteemed is better than silver or gold.
—Proverbs 22:1 (NIV)

Leadership and Professional Development Exercises

Key Terms

- character
- character-based small acts of being and doing

- commitment
- compliance
- connection power
- eleven proactive influencing tactics
- five power bases
- influence
- information power
- Kohlberg's three stages of moral development
- leadership
- personal branding
- personal power
- personalized need for power
- position power
- power
- resistance
- seven classical virtues
- six justifications for unethical behavior
- socialized need for power
- whistleblower

Questions to Discuss

1. What is the second competency domain of the ACTION module?
2. What are the seven classical virtues? Define each.
3. Which level of Kohlberg's three stages of moral development should great leaders strive to operate? Why?
4. What is the interrelationship between power, influence, and leadership?
5. What does it mean to have power? What are the sources of power, types of power and associated influencing tactics, responses to the use of power, and leader motives for having and using power?

Questions to Consider

1. What role does character play in your life? Do you feel the seven classical virtues are relevant in a twenty-first-century society?
2. What role does moral maturity play in your life? Do you feel moral maturity is critical for effective twenty-first-century leadership?
3. Which do you prefer to have—power or influence? Why?
4. Do you believe that having courageous character honors your faith as well as other components of your winning support system?
5. What personality trait or behavior will you stop doing *today* because it hinders your ability to have a personal brand built on courageous character? What personality trait or behavior will you intentionally start doing *today* because it will support your desire to have a personal brand built on courageous character?

Books to Stimulate Your Mind

- *As A Man Thinketh* by James Allen (1903)
- *Career Warfare: 10 Rules for Building a Successful Personal Brand and Fighting to Keep It* by David D'Alessandro (2004)
- *Rosa Parks: My Story* by Rosa Parks with Jim Haskins *(1992)*

CHAPTER 8

Tenacious Inclusion

> But I have asserted a firm conviction—a conviction rooted
> in my faith in God and my faith in the American people—
> that working together we can move beyond some of our
> old racial wounds, and that in fact we have no choice if we
> are to continue on the path of a more perfect union.
>
> —Barack Obama, "A More Perfect Union"

This chapter begins with a quote from a speech given by Senator Barack Obama in March 2008 while on the campaign trail to become the forty-fourth president of the United States. Eight months later, he won! Barack Obama's election in November 2008 to the highest position in America, and undoubtedly the most powerful position in the world, was an historic event on many levels—most notably because of his race, ethnicity, and cultural heritage. In the same speech, "A More Perfect Union," Senator Obama provided the details of his heritage and his upbringing.

> I am the son of a black man from Kenya and a white woman from Kansas. I was raised with the help of a white grandfather who survived a depression to serve in Patton's Army during World War II and a white grandmother who worked on a bomber assembly line at Fort Leavenworth while he was overseas. I've gone to some of the best schools

in America and lived in one of the world's poorest nations. I am married to a black American who carries within her the blood of slaves and slave-owners—an inheritance we pass on to our two precious daughters. I have brothers, sisters, nieces, nephews, uncles, and cousins, of every race and every hue, scattered across three continents, and for as long as I live, I will never forget that in no other country on earth is my story even possible.

In February 2007, when Obama announced his candidacy for the White House, most people doubted his chances of winning. The general skepticism weighed on his race, ethnicity, and cultural heritage. While many saw it as a liability, Obama, the quintessential twenty-first-century global leader, saw it as an asset. Obama never doubted that "diversity" could and should be used as a strategic force for the benefit of all. He assembled a diverse team of supporters, representing a multitude of age, race, and ethnicity groups, as well as social, economic, and educational levels, and accomplished the impossible: an African American man became president of the United States. Senator Obama's decision to seek and ability to run successfully for the presidency of the United States of America can be used as a textbook example of putting "theory into practice" based on the intrapersonal, interpersonal, and leadership skills identified via the JWLM.

Let's do a quick recap of Obama's intrapersonal skills, using the FOCUS module as a framework. Beginning with FOCUS principle 1, the physically fit Obama stepped out in faith strengthened by the support of his family and friends. Secondly, Obama's self-confidence, self-awareness, and comfortableness with his own identity, undergirded by principled values, demonstrates his mastery of FOCUS principle 2. Thirdly, his exemplary charismatic ability to build relationships validates his mastery of FOCUS principle 3. Next, Obama demonstrated keen knowledge and concern for national and international issues, the essence of FOCUS principle 4. And lastly, at all times being the best at who he is and what he does demonstrated his commitment to FOCUS principle 5.

With strong intrapersonal skills as a foundation, Senator Obama handily expressed mastery of impeccable interpersonal skills through flawless execution of the five competency domains or tenets of the ACTION module of the JWLM. Senator Obama demonstrated awesome professionalism, distinguishing himself as an elite candidate ready and able to fulfill the duties of the highest office in America. His personal and professional life exhibited the beliefs, virtues, and values on which our country was founded, showing him to be a man of courageous character. His commitment to tenacious inclusion and optimal service was demonstrated through his sensitivity to addressing the needs of diverse others. As a result of these competencies, Obama was propelled to his calling by earning the trust of the people of the United States who elected him to occupy the noble leadership position of president.

History books will provide evidence of Obama's mastery of leadership skills and competencies defined in the JWLM. All indications in the present point to an Obama legacy of leadership greatness. Without a doubt, I believe Obama is and will be a classic example of how "FOCUS in ACTION Is Great Leadership."

Just as Senator Obama became President Obama, you too can achieve the seemingly impossible through acquiring and delivering flawless principles (intrapersonal skills) and competencies (interpersonal skills). To assist you in mastering another level of twenty-first-century interpersonal competencies, this chapter will explore the competency domain of tenacious inclusion. In this domain, I identify the diversity and inclusion skills that will propel you to the heights of your calling.

Understanding Culture

Culture can aptly be described as the glue that holds a group together. The group could be collections of like people based on race, gender, age, ethnicity, or physical characteristics; public entities such as for-profit and not-for-profit businesses and organizations; places of worship, schools, colleges, and universities; fraternities and sororities; professional sports teams; or private entities such as families, friends, and social networks. From a historical and anthropological perspective, culture is defined as a shared pattern of beliefs, values, norms, attitudes, and behaviors that are transferred from generations to generations. From a socio-political perspective, culture is defined in the context of the dimensions of race, gender, ethnicity, sexuality, gender, religion, etc.

In the United States, attributes that form the dominant culture are white skin, Christianity, physical and economic ability, heterosexuality, and English as a primary language. The population that has one or more of the dominant characteristics also enjoys privilege and access, which means, among other things, that they do not have to acknowledge their culture as the norm and that they have access to resources, connections, and status. Privilege for the dominant group obviously creates a potential for dynamics of domination.

This domination potential (positional power) obtained through access and privilege creates a cultural environment for a leader to excel or derail. The focus of this chapter is on building twenty-first-century leaders of all races, genders, and ethnicities with the skills and competencies to excel in multicultural organizations and the world.

Diversity and Inclusion

We are a global organization. The September 11 [2001] event demonstrates to us that our employees must be multicultural and multifunctional. Global organizations need friends and must act responsibly to all; just embrace diversity in order to be successful in the twenty-first-century world we are entering into.

—John Thornton, president, Goldman Sachs,
remarks to Morehouse College students, November 16, 2001

I am often asked about the difference between diversity and inclusion. One of the best answers I have heard is given by Vernã

Myers, a nationally recognized expert on diversity and inclusion within the legal field: "Diversity is being invited to the party; inclusion is being asked to dance."

The distinction is valid and worth noting since it is necessary to have a focus on both diversity and inclusion. To go to the party and not dance is certainly no fun. And you certainly can't enjoy the fun of dancing at the party if you have not been invited to the party. Another way of differentiating the two terms is to say diversity is about counting the numbers to see that women and minorities are progressing to leadership posts while inclusiveness is about making the numbers count—about all individuals feeling cherished and equal.

Business success in the twenty-first-century global economy dictates a change in the face of the country's workforce as well as its leadership to reflect the face of America's population. Success at diversity and inclusion is as much an individual's professional responsibility as it is an organization's. Leaders have the added responsibility of ensuring that their organizations satisfy the third level of Maslow's hierarchy of human needs (belongingness) within the context of their organizational settings.

Acceptance by peers, friendships, being part of a group, and being loved are natural desires of human beings. In the organization, these needs influence the desire for good relationships with coworkers, participation in a work team, and a positive relationship with supervisors. The third competency domain of the ACTION module addresses the human need for belongingness in the organizational setting, providing frameworks to assist you in becoming the leader who demonstrates and champions excellence in diversity and inclusion at both the individual and organizational level.

Terms and Concepts

A variety of terms and concepts fall into the category of *diversity* and *inclusion*. Diversity includes everyone, referring to the differences among people in terms of dimensions such as age, ethnicity, gender, and race. When a workforce includes people with different human qualities or from different cultural groups, *workforce diversity* is present. *Global diversity* or globalization happens when hiring employees in many countries with varying social value systems, language, religion, attitudes, and education. *Biculturalism* or "double-consciousness" describes the sociocultural skills and attitudes used by racial minorities as they move back and forth between the dominant culture and their own ethnic or racial culture.

The *glass ceiling* refers to an invisible barrier that separates women and minorities from top leadership positions. "At the highest levels of business, there is indeed a barrier only rarely penetrated by women or persons of color," was the conclusion published in the 1995 report by the Glass Ceiling Commission. The federal report stated, "97 percent of the senior managers of Fortune 1000 industrial and Fortune 500 companies are white and 95 to 97 percent are male." Comparing these percentages to America in which two-thirds of the population, and 57 percent of the working population, is female, or minorities, or both, it was highlighted that the race and gender composition at the top of the corporate hierarchy "does not yet look anything like America." Research in this phenomenon continues as decades of findings consistently remain the same—very little diversity is seen at the senior levels of organizations.

A 2015 article in the *Huffington Post* notes that little has changed in the demographic makeup of senior executives in corporate organizations since this seminal report done by the federal government in 1995. In 2014, just over 4 percent of Fortune 500 CEOs were minorities, a classification including African Americans, Asians, and Latin Americans. In the article, Jillian Berman quotes Ronald C. Parker, CEO of the Executive Leadership Council, an organization representing top black executives in the Fortune 500: "At one time there were as many as 12 black CEOs in the Fortune 500." Parker attributes the decline in recent years partly due to the push toward globalization. "As America's top companies placed more value on leaders with international experience, they focused less on women and minorities," states Parker.

The 2015 *Fortune* 50 Most Powerful Women (MPW) in Business list provides slightly better news for women. The list features twenty-seven CEOs—with nineteen of them leading Fortune 500 companies. The article by Patricia Sellers noted this was a vast improvement since the MPW list was first published in 1998 with just two Fortune 500 CEOs among the fifty women.

In contrast to the glass ceiling, which refers to barriers in vertical movement to top leadership positions for women and minorities, the term *glass walls* refers to invisible barriers to important horizontal (lateral) movement within the organization. The glass wall effect is often the result of prejudice, preventing someone to do a different job or do their job more effectively.

Opportunity gap describes the lack of opportunities for many minorities to obtain the same level of education as white, American-born individuals. The belief that one's own group or subculture is inherently superior to other groups and cultures is called *ethnocentrism*. The *white male club* is a term used to describe executive-level positions from which women and minorities are heavily outnumbered by white men, many of whom treat the few women and minorities differently from the way they treat their white male colleagues.

White privilege, also referred to as racial privilege, is the notion that white subjects accrue advantages by virtue of being constructed as white. Peggy McIntosh, author of "White Privilege and Male Privilege," identified the following as examples of privileges enjoyed by whites:

- I can be reasonably sure that if I ask to talk to "the person in charge," I will be facing a person of my race.
- I can be late to a meeting without having the lateness reflect on my race.
- If I have low credibility as a leader, I can be sure that my race is not the problem.

Warren Buffett, chairman, CEO, and largest shareholder of Berkshire Hathaway, and one of the richest men in the world, provided an example of white privilege to fifty Morehouse and Spelman students during an executive lecture in February 1998. When asked by a student how he became so successful, Buffett replied, "I won the ovarian lottery. I was born white, male, and in America."

The challenge facing efforts to move diversity and inclusion from special attention initiatives to the fabric of the business cycle is hindered by the reality of human existence. In general, people feel more comfortable and satisfied dealing with others who are like themselves demographically, socially, and culturally. This is known as the *paradox of diversity*. While the workplace is aggressively working toward diversity and inclusion, ethnic groups still do not interact socially in our communities.

For many of us, the intrapersonal and interpersonal skills necessary to be a champion at cultural inclusion fully and comfortably do not come naturally. Based on the culture in which you were raised (also known as your subculture), you may hold views and opinions of others that are not positive. This could be the result of a multitude of reasons, including misguided teachings from role models and peers, personal experiences, and a fear of the unknown.

Regardless of the source of our aversion to diversity and inclusion, the result is the same. We resort to labels, *stereotypes, prejudice, and discrimination*. Stedman Graham in *Diversity: Leaders not Labels*, provides us with working definitions for these terms.

> Labels and stereotypes are exaggerated images or distorted "truths" about a person or group allowing for little or no social variation or individual difference, usually passed along by peers, family members or the media. Such labels are often used in an attempt to arouse prejudice in an audience by targeting or reinforcing its fears or biases. Labels can be negative or positive but are more often negative.

Prejudice or "prejudging," is an attitude, opinion, or judgment about a group or an individual and is often accompanied by fear, hatred, or ignorance. It is learned usually from a close circle of friends, acquaintances, family members, or peer groups, is directed outward to another group or individual, and can be passed along to the next generation. Prejudice is largely negative and often acquired with other biases early in life, surfacing in ethnic jokes, slurs, and discrimination.

Discrimination is an act of prejudice against a person or group, ranging from insults to hate crimes, to predatory or exclusionary policies or legislation. It often begins with prejudices, negative stereotypes, or negative events that involve a person or many persons of a group and are thus falsely held to be representative of an entire group.

One obvious way to bring people together and show that they are valued is to see and address them as they see themselves—not with stereotypical labels. Graham cautions against the use of labels on people. "Labels placed on individuals by other people seldom reflect what's on the inside. But they often do dictate how we view people and ultimately how they view us."

Groups and individuals who often experience the negative repercussions of labels, stereotypes, prejudices, and discrimination include African Americans, Muslims, Jews, Arab Americans, Asian Americans, Pacific Islanders, Gays, lesbians, bisexuals, and transgendered people, Latinos and Hispanic Americans, Native Americans, people with disabilities, and women.

Recognition of, respect for, and usage of the appropriate terms for people of all ethnicities, cultural backgrounds, lifestyle choices, physical and mental abilities, and genders is nonnegotiable for the twenty-first-century leader. Demanding the same behavior of others in your four circles of influence (home, place of worship, community, and workplace) should also be nonnegotiable.

Recent events in America between law enforcement and African Americans, both males and females, has introduced the need for an understanding of a new form of stereotyping named *unconscious bias* or *implicit association*. Unconscious bias refers to social stereotypes about certain groups of people that individuals form outside their own conscious awareness, which are often incompatible with their conscious values. The caveat surrounding this type of bias is that it happens automatically and is outside of a person's control. It is triggered by the person's brain making quick judgments and assessments of people and situations, and it is influenced by the person's background, cultural environment, and personal experiences. Harsh and deadly encounters between police and people of color are a frequent result of unconscious bias.

Excelling at Cultural Inclusion

The twenty-first-century leader must be intentional about acquiring the intrapersonal and interpersonal skills necessary to eliminate attitudes and behaviors that are informed by or result from labels, stereotypes, prejudices, and discrimination. Effective leadership will require both leaders and followers to adopt progressive, inclusionary ideas in their personal and professional lives in order to overcome the paradox of diversity.

Individuals who judge the difference in others as undesirable, wrong, or immoral are said to possess an ethnocentric view of life. *Ethnocentrism* is the belief that one's race or culture is better than others and is characterized by intolerant behavior or hostility toward cultures different from their own. These feelings typically originate from stereotypes that have festered into prejudices, discrimination, and blatant forms of racism, sexism, and classism. Unfortunately, "isms" is a chronic disease that plagues our global society.

For some people, the discomfort with different others results from a lack of exposure to different cultures and ways of life. These individuals must become aware and acknowledge that cultures different from their own exist—with a goal of seeking a level of understanding about different cultures in terms of the values, customs, and beliefs of the differing cultures. Understanding other cultures is the first step toward a culturally inclusive mind-set. Through concerted efforts on their part, individuals can begin to accept and respect the validity of other cultures without any comparison to their own.

It is the role and responsibility of twenty-first-century leaders to operate at an even higher level of cultural inclusion—going beyond merely accepting and respecting other cultures. The leader must appreciate and value others, knowing that strengths and weaknesses exist in all cultures, including their own. The culturally inclusive leader will seek to adopt and integrate the strengths of other cultures into the culture of the organization. Ultimately, the leader will lead from a *multicultural mind-set*, seeking to constantly learn and grow from new experiences shared with new people.

Excelling at cultural inclusion means that you are fully comfortable with people who are different from you in any form or fashion, including race, gender, sexual lifestyle, family lifestyle, ethnicity, culture, background, socioeconomic level, educational level, religion, abilities and disabilities, size, and shape. In this mind-set, a person is *culture blind* and seeks connection with people based on shared principles and values.

"Tenacious" Cultural Inclusion as a Leader Competency

The message sent by the leader through words and actions about the role of minorities and the importance of multiculturalism in an organization is one of the most important parts of leadership work. Leaders who can build an organizational culture that embraces and promotes the positive cultural differences of all employees and customers will reap the benefits of success and significance for themselves, their organizations, and their societies. Leaders with a multicultural mind-set ensure that the culture of their organization promotes inclusiveness, social justice, affirmation, mutual respect, and harmony for women, minority groups, and all who are different.

In order to lead from a multicultural mind-set, the leader must understand that diversity means more than race and gender. Diversity in the workplace today encompasses race, ethnicity, gender, sexual orientation, religious affiliation, generation, disability, personality type, and thinking style. Merely having the faces of individuals from these groups in your organization does not equate to an inclusive environment. Business leaders must strive to create an atmosphere where multiple voices are heard and their opinions are valued and considered. Efforts should include recruiting plans and retention programs in order to employ and keep a diverse workforce.

Success in diversity and inclusion (D&I) does not happen by chance. Multiple practices and measures must be employed to ensure that a multicultural mind-set is being employed in all levels of the organization. In addition to monitoring and implementing changes based on employee responses on D&I surveys and consistent feedback about policies, organizations should institute mentoring programs, employee resource (affinity) groups, and multicultural talent management. At the executive level, D&I training programs must become part of senior executive leadership development, along with accountability expectations as part of senior leadership performance plans for achieving D&I goals and objectives.

A leader with a truly developed multicultural mind-set recognizes the connection between innovation and D&I: diversity and inclusion sparks innovation. Cognitive diversity breeds high performance while completing complex tasks. Workforces powered by diverse thinkers hold the ability to foster innovation by 1) resolving issues in different ways, proving there are multiple ways to arrive at a conclusion; 2) providing multiple perspectives and diverse interpretations to representing a problem, enabling teams to discover multiple resolutions and solutions; 3) and allowing the use of multiple predictive models.

The job of the twenty-first-century leader will be to send the message throughout the organization that all people, whether part of the majority or minority (including racial and ethnic minorities, gender and sexual minorities, religious minorities, age minorities, and disabled minorities) will be fully valued members of the organization and not subjected to discrimination or marginalization within the organization or by clients outside the organizations.

While the leadership process is comprised of the leader, followers, and situation, the leader influences the culture and organizational processes that determine how decisions are made, how others behave, and what is accepted and tolerated (and what is not). Therefore, developing the competency of a multicultural mind-set is indisputable for the effective twenty-first-century leader.

The Workplace and Islamic Religious Practices

Demographers say that Islam is one of the fastest growing religions in the United States. The growing Muslim population adds new elements for employers to consider in regard to issues regarding multiculturalism and diversity.

In *An Employer's Guide to Islamic Religious Practices*, Dr. Mohamed Nimer, director of research for the Council on American-Islamic Relations Center, states that Muslims' actions and behaviors, based on adherence to their religious laws and customs as well as following the Quran teaching, should not be viewed as an insult or an unwillingness to communicate. This may include Muslim men wearing of beards or a small head covering *(kufi)*. In public, many Muslim women wear loose-fitting, non-revealing clothing, known as *hijab*.

Dr. Nimer says that other Muslim customs, such as a reluctance to shake the hand of an unrelated person of the opposite sex and avoiding sustained eye contact between men and women, are a sign of personal modesty. Many Muslims are reluctant to take part in social gatherings celebrating religious holidays or other faiths or where alcohol is served.

These examples of cultural differences may find themselves in your workplace. The twenty-first-century leader will not allow the professional success of any employee to be hindered by religious customs and traditions.

The Other Side of a Multicultural Mindset

The premise that a multicultural mind-set is advantageous to the success of an organization lends itself to examination from another viewpoint. The question must be asked, "Are there culture-based values and attitudes at the follower level and the leadership level that do not support organizational success?"

In reality, there are actual cultural differences that influence our attitudes toward time, physical space, and authority. At the follower level, those differences that result in poor work habits, such as tardiness and absenteeism simply because an employee's time orientation is culturally different from mainstream, will not be accepted by organizations.

At the leadership level, there are actual cultural differences that influence attitudes and values toward people that affect leadership style. GLOBE (Global Leadership and Organizational Behavior Effectiveness) investigated whether different attributes of leadership are valued more in some cultures than in others. The GLOBE program began in 1991 as the brainchild of Robert J. House of the Wharton School of the University of Pennsylvania. It has collected data from more than seventeen thousand middle managers from ninety-two countries.

The research identified leader attributes and behaviors in three categories: 1) universally viewed as positive; 2) universally viewed as negative; and 3) culturally contingent.

Included in the category of universally viewed as positive are trustworthy, just, honest, plans ahead, excellence oriented, confidence builder, win-win problem solver, administratively skilled, encouraging, informed, positive, dynamic, communicative, team builder, motivational, intelligent, and decisive.

Attributes and behaviors universally viewed as negative include loner, asocial, non-cooperative, irritable, non-explicit, egocentric, ruthless, and dictatorial. Examples of culturally contingent attributes and behaviors are ambitious, cautious, compassionate, domineering, independent, individualistic, logical, orderly, sincere, worldly, formal, and sensitive.

Becoming a Twenty-First Century Multicultural Leader

There is much agreement in the leadership literature on the competencies (skills and abilities) of twenty-first-century multicultural leaders. However, the heavy work to become a multicultural leader can only be done by the leader. Multicultural leaders must—through intent, awareness, knowledge, perseverance, and commitment—engage their hearts, minds, and will to act in the process of becoming a multicultural leader.

As a start, leaders desiring a multicultural mind-set can use twenty-first-century technology to become better acquainted with the cultures, values, and assumptions of diverse groups. Through the public domain of the World Wide Web, access to a wealth of information on different countries and their cultures, values, and business etiquette is offered. Books, videos of cultural customs, current news stories, and firsthand accounts of life in other countries can be assessed at no financial expense. Astute twenty-first-century leaders will proactively access this information and use it to learn and understand values, attitudes, and behaviors of cultures beyond their own.

The heavy lifting associated with developing a multicultural mind-set requires leaders to begin with themselves by increasing recognition of their own cultural influences and biases. Acknowledging the customs, attitudes, and values in one's own culture makes it easier to accept different cultures' central characteristics. Multicultural leaders will need to be sensitive to the internal organizational culture and external community culture. They are to hold their organizations accountable to a core value of inclusion and develop strategic community relationships that provide visible proof of the organization's commitment to D&I.

Through authentic engagements and messaging, multicultural leaders ultimately serve as the champions of their organizations' diversity efforts. They guide their organizations' moral compass such that it moves from merely meeting legal requirements for diversity to the realization that diversity is a competitive weapon and moral imperative for their organizations.

Successful multicultural leaders possess a strong foundational base of intrapersonal skills developed through a commitment to self-understanding, personal growth, and continuous learning. They also possess perceptive interpersonal skills such that their social interactions with others from diverse backgrounds and experiences are engaging and meaningful. As a result, these leaders operate from a multicultural mind-set that allows them to acquire knowledge about other cultures and leverage cultural differences in order to strengthen their organizations' competitive advantage.

Chapter Summary

Diversity is a way of life in the twenty-first century. Diversity brings differences in thoughts, values, perspectives, and ways of knowing, being, and doing. Differences must be viewed as positive, not negative. However, the differences will undoubtedly lead to leadership challenges—challenges in how to achieve organizational goals while mitigating the internal and external demands generated by diversity.

Your job as a twenty-first-century global leader is to overcome the challenges through the understanding and practice of *cultural inclusion*—a term used to describe the intrapersonal, interpersonal, and intercultural skill sets needed to cross cultural lines to bring diverse others together. It goes beyond embracing diversity as a business initiative that positively affects the bottom line. Cultural inclusion must be viewed as a critical leadership skill set because it is ultimately necessary for the benefit/survival of all mankind.

Success at cultural inclusion requires knowledge of the terms and concepts associated with diversity and inclusion. The chapter includes definitions of culture, diversity, inclusion, workforce diversity, global diversity, biculturalism, glass ceiling, opportunity gap, white privilege, paradox of diversity, stereotypes, prejudice, discrimination, unconscious bias, implicit association, and ethnocentrism.

This chapter presents findings to assist you in understanding and mastering diversity and inclusion. Commitment and perseverance in learning and applying the cultural inclusion competencies that lead to a multicultural mind-set will result in great personal and professional success and satisfaction—just as it did for President Obama. As a twenty-first-century leader, you too are called to use your position, influence, and power to eliminate divisions among the people of your organization, your community, and society as a whole. Your moral responsibility is to promote *tenacious inclusion!*

Leadership and Professional Development Exercises

Key Terms

- biculturalism
- culture
- culture blind
- discrimination
- diversity
- ethnocentrism
- glass ceiling
- glass walls
- global diversity
- implicit association
- inclusion
- multicultural mind-set
- opportunity gap
- paradox of diversity
- prejudice
- stereotypes
- unconscious bias
- white male club
- white privilege
- workforce diversity

Questions to Discuss

1. What is the third competency domain of the ACTION module? Define and explain.
2. What is meant by the term *culture*? How does it impact the lens through which persons see themselves, others, and the world?

3. What is the difference between diversity and inclusion? How does the paradox of diversity impact the realization of diversity and inclusion?
4. Define stereotypes, prejudice, and discrimination. What role do they play in unconscious bias and implicit association?
5. Identify ways in which a person moves from an ethnocentrism mind-set to a multicultural mind-set.

Questions to Consider

1. How would you respond to someone who was of the opinion that inclusion is an illusion? Do you agree or disagree? Why?
2. How important is it to you that diversity and inclusion remain at the forefront of organizational initiatives? Explain your response.
3. Do you have friends in your inner circle who are different from you in regard to ethnicity/race, religious beliefs, lifestyle, sexual orientation, or socioeconomic class? If yes or no, is it by choice? Do you hold feelings of phobia or disdain toward diverse people? Why or why not?
4. Do you believe that subscribing to tenacious inclusion honors your faith as well as other components of your winning support system? Why or why not?
5. What behavior will you stop doing *today* because it hinders your ability to be a person who shows respect to all peoples? What behavior will you intentionally start doing *today* because it will show others that you respect all peoples?

Books to Stimulate Your Mind

- *Dreams from My Father* by Barack Obama (1995)
- *How the Poor Can Save Capitalism* by John Hope Bryant (2014)
- *Under Our Skin: Getting Real about Race and Getting Free from the Fears and Frustrations that Divide Us* by Benjamin Watson (2015)

CHAPTER 9

Optimal Service

As the year 2000 approached, I was invited to
speak at a major forum and asked to address
this question: "What is the world's greatest challenge in the
new millennium?" It was an interesting assignment, and I
replied, with little doubt, that the greatest challenge we
face is the growing chasm between the
rich and poor people on earth.

—Jimmy Carter, *Our Endangered Values: America's Moral Crisis*

The call to service has continuously been at the forefront of societal issues. Jimmy Carter, thirty-ninth president of the United States writes, "All major religious faiths are shaped by prophetic mandates to do justice, love mercy, protect and care for widows and orphans, and exemplify God's compassion for the poor and victimized." Robert M. Franklin, tenth president of Morehouse College, echoes this mandate in his 2007 book, *Crisis in the Village: Restoring Hope in African American Communities.* In the introduction he shares his reason for writing the book.

This is a contribution to the conversation about what can and must be done to do a better job of "people making," especially "child-making." And ultimately, we must discover and implement the science and art of making better

211

families, communities, and we hope a better nation and global community. This is the work that Dr. King referred to as building the "beloved community." It is work that will require the collective efforts, cooperation, and investment of the entire nation.

Caring for the poor and victimized and building the beloved community is the work of service. Service provides a means by which humans fulfill the need to feel a sense of self-worth and self-esteem through the giving of their resources—time, talent, and treasures—to the betterment of society. These desires for a positive self-image and for attention, recognition, and appreciation from others is defined as the esteem level of human needs—the fourth of Maslow's five levels of human needs.

In the 1960s, hundreds of college students answered the call to service as foot soldiers in the civil rights movement. Franklin states, "Thanks to the sacrifices and courage of college students during the civil rights movement, America is a better nation." Luckily for society, today's college students and new entrants to the workforce are once again finding positive self-image, attention, recognition, and self-esteem in service to others.

Signs point to a movement within the millennial generation that one way they are seeking to fulfill their needs in the area of esteem is through giving and not getting. In *The Trophy Kids Grow Up*, Ron Alsop notes as a contradictory attitude and behavior the millennial generation's affinity for service. He writes, "'It's all about me' might seem to be the mantra of these self-absorbed young people who aspire to be financially successful so they can pay off college loans and afford their digital toys, international travels, and other pleasures. But many millennials ... also demonstrate strong concern about social and environmental issues and tend to be active in community service."

Ryan Scott writes in a January 2015 article in *Forbes* magazine on findings that those under age thirty are likely to say citizens have a "very important obligation" to volunteer. Unlike older generations, millennials have been exposed to volunteering in many areas of their lives—each one reinforcing the message that giving back should be a natural way of life, including in their workplaces. He reports data that found that an organization's volunteer policies affected millennials' decisions in the job-application process, the decision to interview, and the decision to accept an offer.

These are positive signs for our communities and workplaces as emerging leaders are poised to excel in the Optimal Service competency domain of skills. This chapter will cover the concepts and TASKBs associated with the service component of ACTION.

Service throughout Society

Service is defined in very simple terms—giving of your time, talents, and gifts, to uplift, support, and develop the less fortunate and the needy. In the twenty-first century, the service model encompasses three concepts. The first is the intentional, proactive actions by corporations and organizations to prevent harm to consumers, communities, and the environment through ethical business practices, commonly referred to as corporate social responsibility. The second is the idea of servant-leadership, which includes the acts of individuals and organizations helping others help themselves. The third service model concept is civic engagement through acts of volunteerism, community service, and service-learning. A discussion of the three service model concepts follows.

Corporate Social Responsibility

Corporate social responsibility (CSR) can be viewed as a twentieth-century response to the consumer outrage with the many examples of fraud by executives and harmful products produced by companies. ASQ (American Society for Quality), the world's leading professional membership organization devoted to quality and the ISO (International Organization for Standardization), which writes international standards for business, government, and society, have weighed in on the need for better citizenship actions and behaviors by corporations.

The ASQ website displays the following:

> ASQ believes that being "socially responsible" means that people and organizations must behave ethically and with sensitivity toward social, cultural, economic and environmental issues. Striving for social responsibility helps individuals, organizations and governments have a positive impact on development, business and society with a positive contribution to bottom-line results.

Likewise, ISO states:

> In the wake of increasing globalization, we have become increasingly conscious not only of what we buy, but also how the goods and services we buy have been produced. Environmentally harmful production, child labor, dangerous working environments and other inhumane conditions are examples of issues being brought into the open. All companies and organizations aiming at long-term profitability and credibility are starting to realize that they must act in accordance with norms of right and wrong.

The Journal for Quality and Participation says, "Although there is no commonly accepted definition of social responsibility, the expectation that organizations apply socially responsible practices is increasing rapidly across the globe." The *Journal* says, "Social responsibility refers to an organization's commitment to conduct business in a consistent manner that meets or surpasses the ethical, legal, commercial/operations, and public expectations society has of it."

Proponents of social responsibility believe that it goes beyond this level, involving long-term planetary stewardship and sustainability—and even, if necessary, investing funds and other resources that actually may reduce profits or expend resources without directly fulfilling the organization's mission. There are also opponents to this idea who feel that investing in altruistic programs undermines shareholder earnings. While existing methods of assessing organizational performance to determine the long-term value of social responsibility are limited, the *Journal* writes that there does appear to be an implicit relationship between an organization's social responsibility reputation and its effect on the bottom line (positive or negative).

At the close of the twentieth century, sustainability came to the forefront of corporate responsibility discussions by way of a concept called the *triple bottom line*. The triple bottom line concept calls for companies to prepare for three different and distinguishable bottom lines. The first is profit, being financially responsible in the "bottom line" of the profit and loss account. Second is being socially responsible in its operations to employees and customers. The final area is being environmentally responsible to the planet through sustainability practices. Awareness, sensitivity, and responsiveness to profit, people, and planet has become a corporate responsibility expectation.

Servant-Leadership

Servant-leadership is a term coined by Robert Greenleaf in his 1970 essay, "The Servant as Leader." Greenleaf noted in his essay that servant-leadership begins with the "natural feeling that one wants to serve."

A *servant-leader* is a leader who is focused on serving others. Servant-leadership is a model of leadership that puts serving others—employees, customers, and community—as the number one priority. The servant-leader is characterized first and foremost as a person who serves others, rather than directing or controlling others. The servant-leader puts others' needs and interests above his or her own.

Servant-leaders can be anyone—government officials, business executives, academic administrators, nonprofit leaders, military commanders, coaches, friends, or neighbors. They do most of the things that other leaders do, including providing a vision, motivating followers, managing, communicating, and achieving the bottom-line results of the organization. What distinguishes servant-leaders from other leaders is that they are focused on others—not just themselves—and they are motivated to make life better for others and not just for themselves.

Servant-leaders are distinguished by their focus and motivation for others, regardless of their titles, roles, or positions. In *The Case for Servant Leadership,* Kent Keith lists the four basic precepts of Greenleaf's servant-leadership model: to put service before self-interest, listen first to confirm others, inspire trust by being trustworthy, and nourish others and help them become whole. The key characteristics of servant-leaders include self-awareness, listening, empathy, healing, persuasion, conceptualization, foresight, stewardship, commitment to others' growth, and building community.

Civic Engagement

One of the most recognizable and repeated lines of any presidential inaugural address is that of President John F. Kennedy. In his 1961 speech, he said, "Ask not what your country can do for you, but what you can do for your country." This charge came after his statement that reads, "The energy, the faith, the devotion which we bring to this endeavor will light our country and all who serve it—and the glow from that fire can truly light the world." President Kennedy was speaking to what we still hold as true today: it is our responsibility to be world leaders by simply being local leaders who serve. This act of service at the local level is often referred to as *civic engagement.*

A definition of civic engagement is given to us by Thomas Ehrlich, editor of *Excerpts from Civic Responsibility and Higher Education*:

> Civic engagement means working to make a difference in the civic life of our communities and developing the combination of knowledge, skills, values and motivation to make that difference. It means promoting the quality of life

in a community, through both political and non-political processes.

Ehrlich goes on to provide what he believes to be the duties of the civically responsible individual:

A morally and civically responsible individual recognizes himself or herself as a member of a larger social fabric and therefore considers social problems to be at least partly his or her own; such an individual is willing to see the moral and civic dimensions of issues, to make and justify informed moral and civic judgments, and to take action when appropriate.

Civic engagement can take on a variety of forms. The usual forms are volunteerism, community service, and service-learning, which are all terms used in educational settings.

Volunteerism is undoubtedly the most common form of civic engagement. It is the act of one or more people for a short time period, usually a few hours to a full day, accomplishing a specific goal. A great example of volunteerism happens across the country on the Martin Luther King Jr. Day. Through tireless efforts by the late Mrs. Coretta Scott King, widow of the slain leader, President Ronald Reagan signed legislation proclaiming the third Monday in January as the annual federal holiday. The first official celebration took place on January 20, 1986.

In commemoration of the life and legacy of Dr. Martin Luther King Jr., a national call to service through volunteerism is made on the holiday. In fact, the King holiday is referred to as "celebrating a day on and not a day off." Businesses such as the architectural firm, Perkins+Will, which states "a deep dedication to sustainability and social responsibility" on its website will have significant numbers of its employees volunteering on the King holiday. A January 2016 story in the *Atlanta Journal-Constitution* reported, "Roughly 200 employees of the Atlanta office of Perkins+Will will be out in the community on Martin Luther King Jr. Day, repairing homes, feeding the hungry, cleaning up a cemetery, or working with young environmentalists."

Volunteerism becomes a form of experiential education when instructors require students to engage in an activity outside of the classroom where some service or good work is performed. The activity, which typically occurs over a few hours for just one day, is not designed to result in reciprocity between those doing the service and those being served—and neither is there an intentional reflection assignment for the students. The focus of the engagement is service with motivation based on civic duty, religious conviction, or altruism (concern for the welfare of others). Examples include collecting canned goods to feed the homeless, stocking a food bank, serving at a soup kitchen, cleaning a community park, or participating in a Habitat for Humanity home-building project.

The second form of civic engagement, *community service*, is often used synonymously with volunteerism. When used as an instructional strategy by teachers, it also serves as a form of experiential education. Community service distinguishes itself from volunteerism in the educational setting when the engagement takes on a longer time frame—two or three hours per week—for several weeks. During this time, students are engaged in activities where some service or good work is performed. Due to their repeated contact with the service recipients, students also have an opportunity to learn how their service makes a difference in the lives of the service recipients.

When engaged in community service as an educational activity, the focus, like volunteerism, is service with motivation based on civic duty, religious conviction, or altruism. Typically there is no expectation of an exchange between those doing the service and those being served, and no structured reflection is required for the assignment.

Student organizations such as clubs, honor societies, and Greek organizations often have service as part of their mission. These groups frequently achieve this part of their mission through a community service project in which their members will spend two or three hours per week over a six-to-eight-week period mentoring at elementary schools and community after-school programs.

The last form of civic engagement, *service-learning*, is distinctly different from more traditional forms of civic engagement, including volunteerism and community service. Service-learning is most commonly thought of as "a form of experiential learning where students apply academic knowledge and critical thinking skills to address genuine community needs."

The Wisconsin Department of Public Instruction website provides the following definition of service-learning:

> Service-learning is a teaching and learning methodology which fosters civic responsibility and applies classroom learning through meaningful service to the community. The strongest service-learning experiences occur when the service is meaningfully immersed in ongoing learning and is a natural part of the curriculum that extends into the community. Service-learning is an essential strategy in providing a rigorous and relevant curriculum which will prepare students to succeed in the twenty-first century.

Service-learning separates itself from volunteerism and community service in two important ways: students learn how their service makes a difference in themselves and the lives of the service recipients and learning is intentionally linked to academics. These two learning outcomes result from the inclusion of formative and summative reflection assignments as part of the service-learning experience.

The goal of service-learning is to engage students in activities designed to address or meet a community need coupled with intentional mutual benefit between those doing the service and those being served. The motivation is based on addressing or meeting a community need by emphasizing both learning and service.

Service-learning has been a critical component of the pedagogy of my Leadership and Professional Development (LPD) course since the class began in 1996. In the past two decades, more than three thousand Morehouse College business students have completed the course and the service-learning assignment. Students are required to give twenty hours of service through a team-based service-learning project (SLP) to a local community site over a ten-week period outside of the class meeting hours. Service sites are in the urban areas of Atlanta and have included elementary, middle, and high schools as well as after-school programs, community centers, and senior citizen residential homes.

Responses to an end-of-course survey taken by more than four hundred LPD students resulted in overwhelming support of the assignment. The end-of-course survey asked students to answer the following question based on their SLP experience: "If you had a choice between taking a section of this course that did not require a twenty-hour service project and one that did, which would you choose?" More than 90 percent (364 students) responded that they would choose the section with the required SLP assignment (see chapter 11 for a full description of the SLP assignment.)

CSR, Servant Leadership, and Civic Engagement in ACTION

How awesome it would be for an entity to achieve a level of optimal service through the integration of all three service concepts: corporate social responsibility, servant-leadership, and civic engagement. This would be an innovative twenty-first-century service model that responds to Dr. King's call for a "revolution in our values" to address the ills and shortcomings of our society in addressing the needs of all peoples. Your first response might be doubtful. However, while it may seem difficult and improbable, it is doable and possible. One such model is that of the nonprofit organization Operation HOPE.

Founded by John Hope Bryant, Operation HOPE is dedicated to helping low-wealth communities attain financial literacy empowerment. Bryant was running a successful financial-services firm when the 1992 Los Angeles riots, sparked by the police beating of Rodney King, broke out in which fifty-five people were killed and more than two thousand were injured. Bryant says, "I created Operation Hope in 1992, immediately following the Rodney King Riots of 1992, to change the world."

Operation HOPE is now a global organization that has served more than two million people. It has directed more than $2 billion of private and public capital into urban, inner-city and under-served communities, with more than twenty-three thousand HOPE Corps volunteers (a form of civic engagement), and more than four thousand public schools engaged around the Operation HOPE mission and movement, which is "silver rights empowerment, making free enterprise work for everyone." Bryant used his gift of charismatic servant-leadership and indefatigable energy to transform the minds of business leaders across the globe from a "profit-only" mind-set to a "profit-*and*-people" mind-set.

In his best-seller, *Love Leadership*, Bryant outlines his five laws of love-based leadership. Bryant challenges business leaders to rethink their purpose. "The third law of love leadership, love makes money, involves your purpose in business. As I learned from my days of hustling as an entrepreneur, that purpose must be to do good if you want sustainable prosperity and yes, money, to be a measurable by-product of your business."

Sharing Bryant's commitment to his third law of love leadership as a business philosophy is Crown Prince Haakon, heir apparent to the throne of Norway. Prince Haakon helps us see the spiritual connection between doing good and getting good in return.

It's deeply human to want to do good. If we're separated from that deep need to do good for other people, something essential is lost. I would say the same thing [is true] for companies. If a company separates doing good for people and making a profit, and then cuts out the doing good part, something essential is lost. Gandhi said that if you look at all leaders doing bad things, with time, they all fall. Only good things persist over time (Quoted in *Love Leadership*).

Leaders like John Hope Bryant and Crown Prince Haakon—champions for optimal service through CSR, servant-leadership, and civic engagement in their workplaces, communities, places of worship, and homes—are doing their part to ensure that "good things persist over time."

Chapter Summary

The goal of this chapter on service is twofold: to inspire students to become committed to living lives of service because it is just the right thing to do (post-conventional moral maturity) and to help students understand that service is a key component of being an effective twenty-first-century leader.

Chapter topics include a discussion of three concepts and competencies associated with service: corporate social responsibility (CSR), servant-leadership, and civic engagement through volunteerism, community service, and service-learning.

CSR "refers to an organization's commitment to conduct business in a consistent manner that meets or surpasses the ethical, legal, commercial/operations, and public expectations society has of it." Added to the definition is the duty of companies to engage in sustainability practices via attention to the "triple bottom line" comprised of profit, people, and planet.

Greenleaf's servant-leadership model is introduced, which includes four basic precepts: 1) put service before self-interest; 2) listen first to confirm others; 3) inspire trust by being trustworthy; and 4) nourish others and help them become whole. Greenleaf's ten key servant-leader characteristics are presented: self-awareness, listening, empathy, healing, persuasion, conceptualization, foresight, stewardship, commitment to others' growth, and building community.

Civic engagement, which is based on the idea that morally and civically responsible individuals recognize they are members of a larger social fabric and therefore have a duty to recognize and address social problems and own a commitment to the resolution of the problem. This chapter presented ways in which social problems are being addressed, including volunteerism, community service, and service-learning. These forms of civic engagement are widely used in the educational setting.

The chapter includes a brief discussion of a service-learning project (SLP) assignment in my leadership and professional development class, a required course for all business majors at Morehouse College. Responses to an end-of-course survey taken by more than four hundred of the business students resulted in overwhelming support of the assignment. The end-of-course survey asked students to answer the following question based on their SLP experience: "If you had a choice between taking a section of this course that did not require a twenty-hour service project and one that did, which would you choose?" More than 90 percent responded that they would choose the section with the required SLP assignment. When asked why they would select to do the SLP, responses included:

- Community service is key in becoming a leader. Leadership is not only an influential process but also a service.
- The SLP shows how much professional exposure of black men is needed in the community, especially at a young age.
- It was more rewarding than I ever thought it would be.

This data reflects positive teaching and learning outcomes resulting from a level of personal joy and pleasure gained from giving *optimal service!*

Leadership and Professional Development Exercises

Key Terms

- civic engagement
- community service
- corporate social responsibility (CSR)
- servant-leader
- servant-leadership
- service

- service-learning
- triple bottom line (TBL)
- volunteerism

Questions to Discuss

1. What is the fourth competency domain of the ACTION module? Explain.
2. What is corporate social responsibility (CSR)? What are its pros and cons?
3. What is the triple bottom line (TBL)? Discuss its importance.
4. What are the key characteristics of servant-leaders?
5. What is civic engagement? Explain. How do volunteerism, community service, and service-learning differ?

Questions to Consider

1. What role does service play in achieving success in your personal and professional life?
2. How do you feel about civic engagement? Are you involved in service activities? Why or why not?
3. Do you believe that it makes "business sense" for a company to contribute to the betterment of society? Why or why not?
4. Do you believe that service to humanity honors your faith as well as other components of your winning support system? Why or why not?
5. What action will you take *today* to start or increase your level of involvement in civic engagement activities?

Books to Stimulate Your Mind

- *Love Leadership* by John Hope Bryant (2009)
- *Crisis in the Village: Restoring Hope in African-American Communities* by Robert Franklin (2007)
- *Doing Business by the Good Book: 52 Lessons on Success Straight from the Bible* by David Steward (2004)

CHAPTER 10

Noble Leadership

We are faced with immensely threatening problems—terrorism,
AIDS, drugs, depletion of the ozone layer, the threat of nuclear
conflict, toxic waste, the real possibility of economic disaster ...
I do not find the problems themselves as frightening as the
questions they raise concerning our capacity to gather our
forces and act. No doubt many of the grave problems
that beset us have discoverable, though difficult, solutions.
But to mobilize the required resources and to bear what
sacrifices are necessary calls for a capacity to focus our
energies, a capacity for sustained commitment.

—John W. Gardner, "The Cry for Leadership"

The opening quote by Gardner reminds us that, though difficult,
the solutions to our problems are discoverable. The question is
whether we have the "capacity to focus our energies and sustain
our commitment" to finding the solutions. In the final competency
domain of the ACTION module of interpersonal skills—*noble
leadership*—we will discuss the ways and means by which leaders
can marshal the resources to build capacity and commitment to
finding solutions.

   Noble leadership is synonymous with Maslow's fifth and highest
level of human needs— self-actualization. The self-actualization
level represents "the need for self-fulfillment; developing one's

full potential, increasing one's competence, and becoming a better person." Self-actualization needs can be met in the organization by providing people with opportunities to grow, be empowered and creative, and acquire training for challenging assignments and advancements.

The domain of noble leadership provides a platform from which emerging leaders reach their highest potential. Noble leadership requires the blend of the previous competencies of awesome professionalism, courageous character, tenacious inclusion, and optimal service. Together, these competencies enable emerging leaders to grow into empowered leaders of integrity who use their creative cognitive, affective, and behavioral skills to address twenty-first-century issues and challenges.

Leadership development must view the desire to become a better person as an innate characteristic of human beings. Better people result in better homes, better communities, better organizations, and better societies. That is the ultimate goal of noble leadership—developing emerging leaders who will put their *focus in action* for the betterment of all mankind.

James MacGregor Burns, a founding researcher in leadership theory, says, "Leadership is one of the most observed and least understood phenomena on earth." His assessment echoes throughout the field of leadership. After decades of work by leadership researchers and theorists, there is agreement on the statement, "Clearly, no one best way to lead exists," and that leadership is both an art and science.

Colonel Mark Homig states in his 2001 article on transformational leadership, "After reading Burns, Kotter, Tichy, Jung, Einstein, Humphreys, and the biographies of military leaders from throughout the ages, the conclusion seems quite clear. Leadership principles are timeless, while the models that examine those principles may change." Ageless leadership principles are based on classical virtues and universal values that cross cultures and bring joy and meaning to human life. These ageless principles have resulted in the theoretical or scientific aspects of leadership. From theory, models of leadership are created.

However, leadership models change because the *way* work gets done changes—not the universal values and principles—based on technological advances, innovation, and new ideas that result from the practice of leadership. The fluidity of models that results from practice represents the art of leadership. Therefore, knowing both the art and science of leadership by studying both the practice and theory of leadership is critically important for emerging leaders who are called to create progressive solutions to twenty-first-century challenges.

The quote below from John Sculley, former CEO of Apple Computer, highlights the need for the energy, ideas, and enthusiasm of a new breed of leaders in the twenty-first century.

> If you look at the post-World War II era when we were at the center of the world's economy during the industrial age, the emphasis was on self-sufficiency in every sort of enterprise ... Organizations were very hierarchal. That model is no longer appropriate. The new model is global in scale, an interdependent network ... How do you lead in this idea-intensive, interdependent-network environment? It requires a wholly different set of skills, based on ideas, people, and values ... The new generation of leaders is going to be more intellectually aware ... so the people who're going to surface, to rise to the top, are going to be people who are comfortable with and excited by ideas and information.
>
> —John Sculley, quoted in Bennis, *On Becoming a Leader*

Thus the JWLM presents *noble leadership* as a construct that blends the art and science of leadership into a framework that incorporates the needs of the people of the organization and the work of the organization. The model is one of a whole-brain approach to leadership, consisting of four actionable parts: partnership, relationship, companionship, and championship. This chapter will help you to understand the importance of the final act of "being and doing" that results in a *big* act of personal and professional success: "Be whole."

The Art and Science of Leadership in the Twenty-First Century

As proven in the vast amounts of leadership research over the past hundred years, central to the realization of a positive outcome of the leadership process is the leader's ability to influence (inspire, guide, direct, steer, and navigate) the people in an organization. Leaders must also possess a definitive understanding of the nature of the technical work of the organization—the tasks. Leadership success requires both the people skills and the task-related skills (trait and behavior theories of leadership). Ned Herrmann, a twentieth-century American creativity researcher and author, presents these differing skill sets as originating from how the human brain is constructed, a concept he calls "whole brain."

Noble Leadership Requires Whole-Brain Leaders

Herrmann's depiction of the brain centers on the idea of a person's preference for right-brained versus left-brained thinking. According to Herrmann, the two quadrants that make up the left side of the brain (quadrants A and B) are associated with logical thinking, analysis of facts, and processing numbers, and with planning, organizing facts, and careful, detailed review. The thinking style dominated by the left side of the brain is rational and realistic, with a propensity for critical thinking, dealing with numbers and technical matters.

The two quadrants that make up the right side of the brain (quadrants C and D) are associated with interpersonal relationships and affect intuitive and emotional thought processes. The right side of the brain allows for conceptualizing, synthesizing, and integrating facts and patterns—seeing the big picture rather than the details. The values-based style dominated by the right side of the brain is sensitive to others and enjoys interacting with and teaching others.

In *The Leadership Experience*, Daft explained the science of the brain stating "in the 1960s and 1970s, scientists also discovered that the distinct hemispheres influence thinking, which led to an interest in what has been called left-brained-versus-right-brained thinking patterns. The left hemisphere is associated with logical, analytical thinking and a linear approach to problem solving, whereas the right hemisphere is associated with creative, intuitive, values-based thought processes." This discovery served as an excellent metaphor for understanding different thinking styles and resulting leader behaviors.

Using Herrmann's neurological conceptualization depicting the human brain as two hemispheres each with two quadrants, and each quadrant controlling different thinking styles, Daft crafted a "whole-brain" approach to effective leadership. Daft suggests leaders with predominately quadrant-A (upper-left) thinking style tend to be directive and authoritative; focus on tasks and activities; like to deal with concrete information and facts. Quadrant-B (lower-left) leaders are typically conservative and highly traditional; avoid risks and strive for stability; may insist on following rules and procedures, no matter the circumstances; well-organized, reliable, and neat; like to establish plans and procedures and get things done on time.

Leaders with a predominantly quadrant-C (lower-right) style are friendly, trusting, and empathetic; concerned with people's feelings more than tasks and procedures, and may put emphasis on employee development and training. A leader with a quadrant-D (upper-right) preference is visionary and imaginative, likes to speculate, to break the rules, and to take risks. The quadrant-D leader is holistic, imaginative, and adventurous; enjoys change, experimentation, and taking risks, and generally allows followers a great deal of freedom and flexibility.

In *On Becoming a Leader,* Bennis contends that effective leaders are whole-brain people; capable of using both the logical left side of the brain and conceptual right side of the brain.

Noting that the American organizational life is a left-brain culture, highly logical, analytical, technical, controlled, conservative, and administrative, and has resulted in people who are its products ... dominated and shaped by those same characteristics. What organizations are in dire need of, according to Bennis, are people with more right-brain qualities ... more intuitive, conceptual, synthesizing, and artistic. The most effective leaders, as noted by Bennis, whatever their occupations, rely as much on their intuitive and conceptual skills as in their logical and analytical talents. "They are whole-brained people, capable of using both sides of their brain."

The noble leadership competency domain of the JWLM is based on the concept of a whole-brain leadership style. Through a leadership process I refer to as PRCC, the JWLM presents noble leadership as a non-hierarchal combination of excellence in leading people and completing tasks.

The PRCC Process

The whole-brain concept as described by Herrmann, Daft, and Bennis provides a framework to present the process that summarizes the roles and functions of the JWLM definition of the effective twenty-first-century global leader. The process is comprised of four components: partnership, relationship, companionship, and championship (PRCC). A leader utilizing the whole-brain leadership style would be in mastery of both the people side of business and the task side of business.

Mastery in the people side calls for adeptness in the human factor—the ability to understand and deal sensitively with the human elements of an organization. This calls for the abilities to inspire action through shared visioning; communicating with passion; navigating complex and ambiguous relationships; as well as building, maintaining, and motivating teams. Whole-brain leaders understand and appreciate the people side of business because it is through the people of the organization that the work gets done and organizational goals are met. They also understand the importance of getting the work done and have a meticulous interest in ensuring tasks are completed and goals are met.

Mastery in the task side calls for exceptional business skills, which include analyzing issues, making decisions, having financial savvy, thinking strategically, and executing the tasks that lead to the realization of organizational goals and objectives. Whole-brain leaders are effective because they use the whole-brain leadership style—mastery of *both* the people side and the task side.

The first component of the PRCC leadership process, located in the upper-right quadrant, is partnership and describes the agreement between the leader and the followers to come together in response to a call to action communicated by a visionary, courageous, hopeful leader. It is a mutually agreed upon *want* for something bigger, better, and different than the current status quo. Below in the bottom-right quadrant is relationship, which entails the "rules of engagement" between the leader and followers that determine how they treat each other. It is the *will* or resolve of the partners (leader and followers) in the process to respect each others' similarities and value each others' differences.

The third component, companionship, located in the bottom-left quadrant, represents the commitment of both the leader and the followers to the jobs they are assigned to do in order to accomplish the vision. It is the *work* that each partner must perform in order to accomplish the vision. Since the work will be different for each partner, all work is valued and seen as integral to the success of the leadership process.

Championship, located in the upper-left quadrant, is the final component. It represents the tough mind-set and in many ways channeled mentality that must be possessed by both the leader and the followers in order to see the vision through to reality. It is the *win* of the leadership process that signifies the achievement of the goal and the realization of the vision.

Figure Chapter 10-1 provides a depiction of the PRCC leadership process—a whole-brain leadership style.

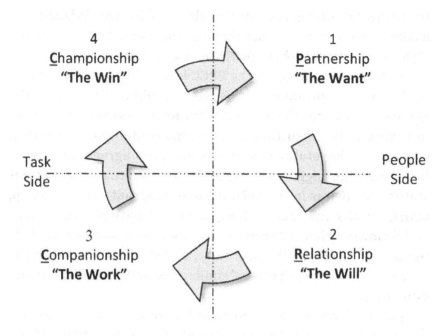

Figure Chapter 10-1. The PRCC Whole-Brain Leadership Process

In order for the PRCC leadership process to be successful, it takes unrelenting focus, energy, and initiative, from all actors in the process—the leader, the followers, and the organization. Hughes, Ginnett, and Curphy refer to this triad as the interactional framework for analyzing leadership. They suggest that while each of these actors should be examined on the individual level, their interaction plays a significant role in understanding leadership success. How leaders and followers affect each other, how the organization or situation can constrain or facilitate a leader's actions, and how the leader can change different aspects of the situation in order to be more effective are all important scenarios to be studied.

The interactional framework of analyzing leadership demonstrates the acute role of the leader in the leadership process. The leader's connection to the followers and to the situation critically affects the outcome of the leadership process. The PRCC process proposes that the leader is the *most* important actor because it is the leader's shoulders on which the success or failure of the PRCC process will fall. Success via the PRCC process is driven by the leader who possesses a whole-brain leadership style.

Note that the practice of whole-brain leadership is depicted in a circular format, which recognizes that as a strategy, the leadership process must be in continuous movement from one component to the next in order to be effective. Due to situational factors, such as changes in organizational leadership, team members, competitive forces, and environmental factors, tactics may require the movement in reverse as well as forward. The overarching goal of the circular framework suggests that as the actors in the process—the leader(s), the followers, and the organization—find mutually beneficial success, they view themselves as an effective team and become willing to continue in the process, positioning them to set and achieve larger visions and higher goals.

Whole-Brain Leadership in Action via the PRCC Process

The work of the leader in each of the four components of the PRCC is different. The leader who effectively progresses through the PRCC leadership process will need to demonstrate mastery of varying TASKBs at each stage of the process.

At stage one of PRCC, the leader is called to be the visionary, to establish a *partnership* with followers based on the need for a change. Challenging the status quo comes easy to courageous leaders who own and embrace their role of being the visionary in the leadership process. Whole-brain leaders see themselves as the *spark* in the leadership process: ethical, hopeful, and able to see beyond "what is" and envision a better "what if." They not only dream big dreams, but through imagery, storytelling, and astute command of language, they clearly and continuously articulate their vision, both verbally and in written communication. These leaders are able to convince their followers that the vision is a worthy pursuit for all.

Robert Dockson, former CalFed president, CEO, and chairman, says,

> I think the first thing one has to do [in setting out to change a culture] is get people on one's side and show them where you want to take the company. Trust is vital. People trust you when you don't play games with them, when you put everything on the table and speak honestly to them. I think you have trust in a man who has vision and can make you see his vision is the right thing to do.

As a result, the vision grows to become a living and breathing entity that defines the organization's culture and represents the heart and soul of the partnership that is established between the leader, followers, and the organization.

The second stage of PRCC requires the leader to be a master *relationship* builder. The quickest way to fail in the leadership process is to have a leader who is incapable of building and sustaining a positive rapport with his or her followers. Effective leaders build alliances with their followers by being trustworthy, empathetic, accountable, transparent, emotionally intelligent, understanding, approachable, open, and fun to be with. Effective leaders establish strong bonds with their followers by listening with their eyes as well as ears, having a sense of humor, laughing at themselves, and being a good example by demonstrating the interpersonal skills they expect from their followers.

Effective leaders are the gatekeepers of the relationship culture of the organization, which will come and go based on the example set by the leader. The leader's disposition of goodwill dictates the level of goodwill present in an organization among the members as well as toward the leader. Whole-brain leaders serve as the *spirit* that moves followers from the destructive mentality of independence to a constructive position of interdependence within the team and the organization.

Barbara Corday, president of Columbia Pictures Television, says

> I have always been very pleased and happy and proud of the fact that I not only know all the people who work for me, but I know their husbands' and wives' names, and I know their children's names, and I know who's been sick, and I know what to ask. That's what's special to me in a work atmosphere. I think that's what people appreciate, and that's why they want to be there, and that's why they're loyal, and that's why they care about what they're doing ... Getting people on your side has a lot to do with spirit, a lot to do with team atmosphere.

Success at establishing partnership and building relationship enables the leader to begin the third stage of the PRCC leadership process: sustaining *companionship*. At the third stage, the leadership process moves to the task side of the whole-brain leader model and the heavy lifting begins for the followers. Seeing a task through from start to finish can become an insurmountable burden for some. While the initial intentions are good, the reality of the scope of work may become overwhelming to followers. Missed deadlines, boredom, apathy, absenteeism, physical illnesses, emotional wounds, and mental scars begin to rob followers of the ability to stay the course and get the job done. What do leaders do in these situations?

Effective, whole-brain leaders become the energizing force that says and demonstrates to their followers, "You are not alone. *We* can do this." Bennis says, "Leaders are there when it counts; they are ready to support their coworkers in the moments that matter." Effective leaders seek and act on input from their people on how to make the environment whole again; they listen, and they respond. They identify personal development opportunities for others and allow time for them to participate—a time of rejuvenation similar to the R & R breaks in the armed services.

During this stage, effective leaders become visible doers, working alongside their followers to get the task done.

Effective leaders encourage and empower people to develop an entrepreneurial attitude and mind-set toward their work, focusing on resilience, excellence, teamwork, and customer satisfaction. Effective leaders make the tough decisions, blame softly, and hold their people accountable.

To be an effective leader, the companionship actions outlined here cannot be a one-time happening. Effective leaders work tirelessly with their followers. They are the wheel, the *spiral* that continuously stimulates, supports, and sustains their efforts.

The final stage of PRCC is to create *championship.* Effective leaders are "in it to win it." The win is not for themselves, but for the entities that matter the most: the followers, the organization, and the society the leader has been called to serve. Whole-brain leaders, through their sincere, unwavering belief in their vision and their followers, are steadfast in their commitment to leave a legacy of achievement and excellence to which the followers and the organization can say with pride, "Look at what *we* did." At this point, whole-brain leaders experience the *splendor* of leadership, rejoicing in the knowledge that their followers along with themselves have reached a point of self-fulfillment—mutual self-actualization.

Leaders intentionally celebrate the achievements of their teams and organizations. Through these celebrations, leaders express pride in their followers' success, show appreciation for their hard work and dedication, and inspire the followers to join with them again in the PRCC leadership process, setting new visions and reaching new heights.

Carson Dye states,

> People enjoy celebration. Effective leaders understand the need to occasionally pause and reflect upon progress that has been made. A celebration not only embodies the joy, relief, and pride of the accomplishment, it also resounds the gratitude leaders have for staff who were instrumental in the progress. People who are able to see that their efforts have made a difference and are appreciated are likely to repeat their performance in the future and feel empowered.

Empowerment is a strong motivation because it makes people feel in control and valued.

The championship stage can also be called the leader's paradox: while leaders are the most important element of making the PRCC leadership process work, they view themselves as the least important element of why it worked. It is *not* about the leader; it's about the people!

The PRCC Process in Summary

- Stage 1. The leader establishes a *partnership* with followers; ignited by communicating a visionary *spark* that results in a mutual *want* for a change to better.
- Stage 2. The leader builds a *relationship* with followers; embodied through a *spirit* of trust and respect that results in a mutual *will* for a change to better.
- Stage 3. The leader sustains *companionship* with followers, functioning as a *spiral* alongside followers, continuously reenergizing followers in response to fatigue; resilient and resolute in ensuring the *work* gets done for a change to better.
- Stage 4. The leader creates *championship* through followers; celebrating the *splendor* of the *win* that results from empowered followers who have met their goal for the betterment of the group, the organization, and/or society as a whole.

A Whole-Brain Leader in Action

One of the greatest examples of noble leadership through the PRCC process is the work of Dr. Martin Luther King Jr., in the Montgomery bus boycott. The Montgomery bus boycott campaign lasted 374 days from December 1, 1955—when Rosa Parks, an African American woman, was arrested for refusing to surrender her seat to a white person—to December 20, 1956. Dr. King, who in 1954 at the age of twenty-five had been appointed as pastor of Montgomery's Dexter Avenue Baptist Church, was asked to lead the boycott. Through his poetic communication skills and charismatic interpersonal skills, this very young man quickly established a partnership and built a relationship with the African American community of Montgomery. As a result, he was able to engage blacks in Montgomery to rise up against the segregated bus transportation system.

At one point in the yearlong battle, Dr. King visited his parents in Atlanta. He received word that a Montgomery grand jury had indicted him along with eighty-eight fellow boycotters. He was told he would be arrested if he returned to Montgomery. His father asked some of his trusted advisors and counselors to meet with Martin and join him in urging Martin not to return to Montgomery. The young King, entering into the companionship phase of the PRCC leadership process, announced to the assembled group that he had decided to go back to Montgomery.

According to Orville Vernon Burton in Dr. Benjamin E. Mays's autobiography, *Born to Rebel*, King described what happened next:

> In the moment of silence that followed I heard my father break into tears. I looked at Dr. Mays, one of the great influences in my life. Perhaps he had heard my unspoken plea. At any rate, he was soon defending my position strongly. Then others joined in supporting me.

Upon his return to Montgomery, Dr. King and the eighty-eight others were arrested, booked, and entered into the jail cells as companions.

Beginning in June 1956, a series of United States district court rulings and Supreme Court affirmations declared that racial segregation on city bus lines was unconstitutional. Dr. King's efforts along with thousands of others, resulted in a win—a championship—the final phase of the PRCC leadership process. On December 20, 1956, the boycott ended and buses in Montgomery were integrated.

In *Stride Toward Freedom: The Montgomery Story*, King chronicles the yearlong bus strike, which was ended by the Supreme Court decision.

> I had decided that after many months of struggling with my people for the goal of justice I should not sit back and watch, but should lead them back to the buses myself. I asked Ralph Abernathy, E. D. Nixon, and Glenn Smiley to join me in riding on the first integrated bus ... Glenn Smiley sat next to me. So I rode the first integrated bus in Montgomery with a white minister, and a native Southerner, as my seatmate.

Dr. King had led his followers to a win!

Whole-Brain Leadership: Process and Position

Leadership can be viewed as a two-sided coin with process on one side and position on the other. PRCC, as previously demonstrated, presents a logical framework for understanding the process side of leadership. However, the other side of the coin, position, must also be addressed.

The phrase "leadership is not a position" is often heard in leadership development settings as well as the general public. The phrase "leadership is not a position" is a warning to people with titles that, in and of itself, the title does not make you a leader. What makes you a leader is having people follow you. People do not follow titles; they follow courage. The courage of a leader transforms a walk (leading without followers) to a movement (leading with followers). The value of PRCC is that it presents leaders with identified TASKBs that, when adopted, collectively demonstrate leader courage. And leader courage is an expectation that comes along with the title.

Emerging leaders take note. Leader courage starts with owning one's *responsibility* to the followers—to step up to the challenge and be *the* leader. People with the *title* of leader must lead. As a result, they are able to gain and sustain the followers' *response* of commitment to the shared vision, goals, and objectives espoused by the leader and therein a commitment to engage in the PRCC process.

The person with the title must call the shots, make the hard decisions, and live with the consequences. It is a tough job, and the person with the title must take action because it is his or her responsibility. Doing the job with courage and character is one of the critical attributes that distinguish whole-brain leaders from position-only, "half-brain leaders." To drive the PRCC leadership process of noble leadership, the person with the positional title of leader must have "courageous character."

"Leadership is not a position" gives us a catchy phrase to utilize when we talk about leadership, but it also opens a dangerous window of escape for leaders. We have seen too many companies, organizations, institutions, cities, states, and countries fall because their *titled* leaders abandoned their responsibility to be *the* leader. When you are the person with the title, you own the problem and have the ethical responsibility to demonstrate courage and character in order to fix the problem.

Everybody can be *a* leader in the situation, but *the* leader—the *person with the title*—has the responsibility to be out front in the PRCC process, leading the charge to the solution through courage and character in partnership with inspired, committed followers. When the people despair, Dr. Martin Luther King Jr. said, "[*the*] leader has the responsibility of trying to find an answer."

Whole-Brain Leadership and Teams

The PRCC process is not a one-person endeavor. As the person whose responsibility it is to drive the PRCC process, the leader holds the precarious position of being the most important actor in the equation. However, the work of the PRCC process moves from vision (partnership) to reality (championship) only through the committed efforts of the followers in the equation (the "field hands.") Followers have the dubious dual role of being individual contributors *and* team members. As team members, their role in the

PRCC process is to bring complementary skills to the process and commit to a common purpose and a set of performance goals and common expectations to which they hold themselves accountable to achieve. Due to the crucial role of the team in the PRCC leadership process, an examination of team effectiveness is warranted.

Daft defines team as "a unit of two or more people who interact and coordinate their work to accomplish a shared goal of purpose." An important aspect of team effectiveness is membership size. In the work environment, it is two or more people, typically on the lower side of fifteen. Secondly, the members of the team have complementary skills. Thirdly, the people on a team share common goals.

A team and a group are not the same. All teams are groups, but not all groups are teams. The term *group* describes a collection of people who work together in the same physical or virtual space. They typically have individual performance objectives and goals and work individually and independently to achieve them. Leadership in a group tends to be very hierarchical.

Team members possess a collective mentality that shares information, insights, and perspectives. Teams make decisions that support each individual to do his or her own job better and/or reinforce each other's individual performance standards and may have shared responsibilities. Leadership in a team is more likely to be participative or empowerment-oriented.

There are advantages and disadvantages to teamwork. The advantages to teamwork include synergy in that the team's total output exceeds the sum of the various members' contributions. Also, team members typically evaluate one another's thinking, which tends to prevent major errors and generates continuous improvement and innovation.

One disadvantage to teamwork is the problem members face with the pressure to conform to group standards of performance and conduct. Another challenge is the resistance to team effort because of perceived intrusion on a member's autonomy. Social loafing, shirking of individuality responsibility, and groupthink (the tendency of team members to go along with a decision not on the basis of its merit but because they do not want to go against the majority view) are other disadvantages of teams. Research concludes that the advantages of teamwork far outweigh the disadvantages.

Effective leaders know that effective, smooth-functioning teams don't happen by accident. Successful, capable teams are built by effective leaders who take specific actions to help people come together as a team as they go through the team development process. The team-development process, just as the PRCC leadership process, is characterized in a four-stage model. The four stages typically occur in sequence, but they can overlap. Each stage has its own set of unique problems and challenges for leaders and team members.

The first stage is forming. The forming stage is a period of member orientation and getting acquainted, which is characterized by high uncertainty because no one knows what is expected of them or what the ground rules are. The role of the leader is to facilitate communication and interaction among team members. The leader is to set guidelines and make everyone feel comfortable and part of the team. The leader must give special attention to shy or quiet team members to help them establish relationships with others.

The second stage is storming. The storming stage is a period where individual personalities and assertive behaviors emerge as team members seek to clarify their roles. This stage is marked by conflict and disagreement, jockeying for positions, and formation of subgroups based on common interests. At this stage, teams are characterized by a general lack of unity and cohesiveness from which they will not be able to achieve high performance without moving past the issues. The leader's role is to encourage each member to participate and help them find their common vision and values. Members must actively work their way through this stage by debating ideas, surfacing conflicts, and disagreeing with one another—with the ultimate goal of getting to the next stage of team development (norming).

The third stage is norming. The norming stage is a period where conflict has been resolved, resulting in team unity and harmony. A consensus has developed about the natural team leaders. Members' roles are clear. Members understand and accept one another and work to resolve differences. A sense of team cohesiveness has emerged. The team leader must continue to emphasize openness with the team and facilitate communication by clarifying team roles, values, and expectations. This stage is typically short and moves quickly into the next stage.

The fourth stage is performing. The performing stage is a period where the major emphasis is on accomplishing the team's goals. At this stage, members are committed to the team's mission. Frequent interaction and coordination of actions characterize team engagement. Disagreements are handled maturely and productively by confronting problems in the interest of task accomplishment. The leader's role at this stage is to concentrate on facilitating high-task performance and helping the team self-manage to reach its goals.

Team conflict—hostile or antagonistic interaction in which one party attempts to thwart the intentions or goals of another—occurs naturally in any and all group settings and can occur at any of the four stages in the team-development process. While conflict occurs in all teams and organizations, Daft warns that too much conflict can be destructive, tear relationships apart, and interfere with the healthy exchange of ideas and information needed for team development and cohesiveness. Effectively handling team conflict must be seen as a priority for leaders.

Leaders can be more effective in dealing with conflicts when they are aware of the causes of the conflicts. Daft lists a variety of typical causes of conflict within and among individuals and teams. Conflict may arise from competition for scarce resources. Unclear task responsibilities and pursuit of conflicting goals are also sources of conflict. The potential for major conflict occurs when two people do not get along with one another due to personality clashes or differences in values and attitudes. Daft suggests that, in some cases, the only solution for the conflict is to separate the individuals and reassign them to other teams where they can be more productive.

Conflict resolution is important to the ability of a team to meet its performance objectives and goals. According to Daft, the way individuals approach their willingness to resolve conflict is based on the desires of the individuals in the conflict to satisfy their own needs (the *assertiveness dimension*) or the needs of others (the *cooperation dimension*). As a result, Daft identifies five conflict resolution styles and notes that "effective team leaders and team members vary their style to fit a specific situation, as each style is appropriate in certain cases."

The competing style (high assertiveness and low cooperation) is seen in persons who insist on getting their own way. It has its advantages when quick, decisive action is vital for important issues or unpopular actions, such as during emergencies or urgent cost cutting. However, it should be used cautiously because it may become viewed by team members as offensive and dictatorial.

The accommodating style (low assertiveness and high cooperation) is used by persons when they want to get along with other team members. It works well when people realize they are wrong, when an issue is more important to others than to oneself, and when building social credits for use in later discussions or maintaining cohesiveness is especially important.

The *compromising style* (neither high nor low assertiveness and neither high nor low cooperation) suggests a moderate amount of assertiveness and cooperativeness. Compromising is appropriate when the goals on both sides are equally important, when opponents have equal power, and when both sides want to split the difference. It is also a useful conflict-resolution style when people need to arrive at temporary or expedient solutions under time pressure. A drawback is that each side feels like it had to give up something. This feeling of loss may surface and cause problems at a later time.

The *avoiding style* (low assertiveness and low cooperation) reflects neither assertiveness nor cooperativeness. This style is very useful when an issue is trivial, when there is no chance of winning, when a delay to gather more information is needed, or when a disruption would be costly.

Lastly, the *collaborating style* (high assertiveness and high cooperation) demonstrates a high degree of assertiveness and cooperativeness. It is highly effective in building team camaraderie because it enables both parties to win, although it may require a longer time to resolve the issue due to substantial dialogue and negotiation. If the concerns of both sides are too important to be compromised or commitment of both sides is needed for a consensus, collaboration is the best option.

Whole-Brain Leadership and Leadership Theory

Hughes, Ginnett, and Curphy, authors of *Leadership: Enhancing the Lessons of Experience*, make the following observation about leadership research:

> Scholarship may not be a prerequisite to leadership effectiveness, but understanding some of the major research findings can help individuals better analyze situations using a variety of perspectives. That, in turn, can give leaders insight about how to be more effective. Even so, because the skill in analyzing and responding to situations varies greatly across leaders, leadership will always remain partly an art as well as a science.

The need for an effective twenty-first-century leader to blend people skills and task skills is undisputable. It will take both art and science. The whole-brain design of the PRCC leadership process supports this need by presenting a reciprocal relationship between the art/practice of leadership and the science/theory of leadership. As a result of its strong theoretical foundation, PRCC is an invaluable tool for leaders in the practice of leadership. The discussion that follows presents the leadership theories and modern approaches to leadership that informed the identification of the PRCC leadership process.

The work of researchers and scholars of leadership divide the scientific study of leadership into three periods: the *trait period* (late 1800s to World War II), the *behavioral period* (World War II to the late 1960s), and the *contingency period* (the late 1960s to the present).

The trait era is defined as the period in which leadership observers in the nineteenth century focused their understanding of leadership success on the leader's personal traits. Traits are the distinguishing personal characteristics of a leader, such as intelligence, honesty, self-confidence, and appearance. This nineteenth- and early twentieth-century research examined leaders who had achieved a level of greatness. This became known as the *great man approach*. Central to the great man theory was the idea that leaders were born rather than made. Another premise of the great man theory was great leaders will arise when there is a great need.

These great leaders in America have traditionally been male, Anglo-Saxon, educated in a few elite institutions, wealthy, and members of the Protestant faith. One example of this group of great leaders is the forty-three presidents from George Washington, 1789–1797, to George W. Bush, 2001–2009. The goal of early leadership researchers was to identify the traits leaders such as these possessed that distinguished them from people who were not leaders.

Ralph Stogdill conducted one of the first comprehensive studies of leadership traits in 1948. He reviewed more than 120 trait studies in an attempt to identify a reliable and coherent pattern. He concluded that no such pattern existed; traits alone do not identify leadership because of the enormous amount of variation in leadership situations. Leadership theorizing must include personal and situational characteristics. The election of the first African American president, Barack Obama, in 2008 as the forty-fourth president is one example that demonstrates a fallacy of the trait theory based on race in its application to twenty-first-century leadership.

Without definitive success in identifying the personal traits that led to effective leadership, researchers begin to look at the behavior of leaders to determine how it might contribute to leadership success or failure. The researchers' goal during the behavioral period was to be able to say that anyone who adopts the appropriate behavior, i.e., conduct and deportment, can be a good leader. Numerous advantages to the behavioral approach over the trait approach were identified, including that behaviors can be observed more objectively than traits, behaviors can be measured more precisely and more accurately than traits, and—as opposed to traits, which are either innate or develop early in life—behaviors can be taught.

As a result of the leadership researchers' work, the behavioral period identified two ways to classify leader behaviors: styles of leadership and factors of leader behavior.

Three leadership styles were identified: *autocratic* (characterized by leader control of group activities and decisions), *democratic* (characterized by group participation and majority rule), and *laissez-faire* (characterized by very low levels of any kind of activity by the leader).

Two factors of leader behavior were identified: people (concern for the employee) and task (concern for the work). The people factor included items relating to interpersonal warmth, concern for the feelings of subordinates, and the use of participative, two-way communication. The people dimension—also referred to as the employee-oriented or socio-emotional dimension—was called *consideration behavior.* The task factor included behavior that stressed directedness, goal facilitation, and task-related feedback. The task dimension, also referred to as production-orientated dimension, was called *initiation of structure.*

While the study of leaders' behavior from the style and factor views showed promise in the study of leadership, it did not definitively provide the answer to the question of the "best" style of leadership. Examples of leadership success could be found among leaders who possessed any of the three leadership styles and exhibited either of the two factors of leader behaviors. The answer to the question of whether there is an universally accepted best way to lead across all situations and environments, consistently leading to important organizational outcomes such as group productivity, follower satisfaction, and attainment of organizational goals was yet to be discovered.

Both the trait approach and the behavior approach to leadership concentrated on the leader's personal qualities and behaviors. These approaches resulted in a very simplistic view of the complex phenomenon of leadership because they disregarded powerful situational elements.

Over the past six decades, theoretical approaches to the understanding of leadership have been classified under the contingency period. According to Afsaneh Nahavandi, the primary assumption of the contingency view is that the personality, style, or behavior of effective leaders depends on the requirements of the situation in which the leaders find themselves. For the purposes of this book and its intended outcomes, the most salient observations made by Nahavandi regarding the current status of leadership research findings, classified in this era and also referred to as "situational" is as follows:

> This approach suggests that there is (1) no one best way to lead; (2) the situation and the various relevant contextual factors determine which style or behavior is most effective; (3) people can learn to become good leaders; (4) leadership makes a difference in the effectiveness of groups and organizations; and (5) personal and situational characteristics [traits] affect leadership effectiveness.

The most recent approach to the understanding of leadership focuses on the relationship between leaders and followers as well as the impact of charisma and visioning on leadership effectiveness. Some researchers have named this approach the *neo-charismatic school*. Robert Lussier and Christopher Achua identified this approach as *integrative leadership theories* that attempt to combine the trait, behavioral, and contingency theories to explain successful, influencing leader-follower relationships.

The research attempts to identify traits and behaviors of effective leaders and explore why the same behavior by the leader may have a different effect on followers depending on the situation. Because this book focuses on developing effective leaders for the twenty-first century, a few of the most contemporary theories from the contingency period will be summarized here. These new models of leadership, which fall into the contingency era of "neo-charisma, inspiration, and relationship," are transactional leadership, transformational leadership, charismatic leadership, servant-leadership, ethical leadership, and citizen leadership.

Whole-Brain Leadership and Twenty-First-Century Evolving Theories of Leadership

Leadership research has evolved with great speed since the middle of the twentieth century. An abundance of leadership theories and approaches have been discovered, discussed, and published. An exhaustive review of this work is beyond the scope of this book, but I will present six theories and approaches to leadership that are viewed by leadership scholars and researchers as meeting the needs of our twenty-first-century global society.

The six theories and approaches are divided into two organizational categories. The first organizational category, leader-follower-based theories (transactional, transformational, and charismatic leadership), are built on the relationship between leader and followers resulting from the leader's personal qualities and/or leadership style, followers' needs, and the organizational situation.

James MacGregor Burns is credited with the discovery of the transactional model and the transformational model of leadership in the late 1970s, and they are now considered the two foundational models of the contingency era. Bernard Bass, a disciple of Burns, continued to explore these two theories in the 1980s and 1990s and provides the basis from which much empirical research has been performed. According to Gary Yukl, the two theories are distinguished in terms of the component behaviors used to influence followers and the effects of the leader on the followers. Yukl explains as follows:

With transformational leadership, the followers feel trust, admiration, loyalty, and respect toward the leader, and they are motivated to do more than they originally expected to do. According to Bass, the leader transforms and motivates followers by (1) making them more aware of the importance of task outcomes, (2) inducing them to transcend their own self-interest for the sake of the organization or team, and (3) activating their higher order needs. In contrast, transactional leadership involves an exchange process that may result in follower compliance with leader requests but is not likely to generate enthusiasm and commitment to task objectives.

Yukl also notes Bass's view that the two leadership theories—transformational and transactional—are distinct but not mutually exclusive processes. Transformational leadership will increase follower motivation and performance more than transactional leadership, but effective leaders use a combination of both.

The *transactional style* of leadership is based on a transaction or exchange process between leaders and followers that may result in the followers' compliance with the leaders' requests, but it is not likely to generate enthusiasm and commitment to goals. This leadership style, when used successfully, is particularly effective at keeping the organization running smoothly and efficiently by promoting stability and focusing on the present. It is not effective in the generation of innovation and organizational change.

In contrast, the *transformational style* of leadership is characterized by leaders being able to bring about significant change by inspiring followers to share the leaders' vision and ideas through personal values, beliefs, qualities, and visionary foresight. When used effectively, transformational leadership outcomes include developing followers into leaders, encouraging followers to move from lower-level physical needs in the workplace to higher-level psychological needs, inspiring followers to go beyond their own self-interests for the good of the organization, painting a vision of a desired future state, and communicating it in a way that makes the pain of change worth the effort.

The final leader-follower-based leadership theory to discuss is *charismatic leadership*. Of great interest to researchers who study political leadership, social movements, and religious cults is charismatic leadership. Recently, the study of charismatic leadership has occurred in the organizational setting. Charismatic leaders have the ability to inspire and motivate people to do more than they would normally do—despite obstacles and personal sacrifice. They have an emotional impact on people because they appeal to both the heart and the mind.

According to Yukl, some theorists treat charismatic and transformational leadership as essentially equivalent, and some view them as distinct but overlapping processes. Yukl writes the following:

> Many of the leadership behaviors in the theories of charismatic and transformational leadership appear to be the same, but there may be some important differences as well. Transformational leaders probably do more things that will empower followers and make them less dependent on the leader, such as delegating significant authority to individuals, developing follower skills and self-confidence, creating self-managed teams, providing direct access to sensitive information, eliminating unnecessary controls, and building a strong culture to support empowerment. Charismatic leaders probably do more things that foster an image of extraordinary competence, such as impression management, information restriction, unconventional behaviors, and personal risk taking.

Charismatic leadership is built on a relationship between the leader and the followers; the leaders' source of power stems from the person and not the position. Followers see them not merely as bosses but as role models and heroes who are larger than life. The development of charismatic leadership is based on the interplay between leader characteristics, follower characteristics, and leadership situation. Characteristics of charismatic leaders include high degree of self-confidence, strong conviction about ideas, high energy and enthusiasm, expressiveness, and excellent communication skills. Characteristics of followers of charismatic leaders include a high degree of respect and esteem for the leader, loyalty and devotion to the leader, affection for the leader, and unquestioning obedience. Elements of charismatic situations include a sense of real or imminent crisis and perceived need for change.

Any discussion of charismatic leadership must include its downside. Because of charismatic leaders' strong emotional hold on followers, the chance to abuse their power and do as much harm as good is always present. Leaders who have used their charismatic power for good include Sir Winston Churchill, prime minister of the United Kingdom; John F. Kennedy; Mohandas Gandhi, preeminent leader of the Indian independence movement in British-ruled India; and the Reverend Dr. Martin Luther King Jr.

In contrast are charismatic leaders such as Jim Jones, a cult leader who convinced thousands of his followers to commit suicide; Adolf Hitler, leader of the Nazi Party of Germany and responsible for the Holocaust; Charles Manson, a cult leader convicted of committing a series of nine murders at four locations over a period of five weeks; and Idi Amin, 1970s president of Uganda whose reign was characterized by human rights abuses, political repression, ethnic persecution, nepotism, corruption, gross economic mismanagement, and the killings of hundreds of thousands of his people. The main difference in these two groups of leaders is their use of and need for power. The latter group focused on personal goals (a personalized need for power). The former group focused on societal and organizational goals (a socialized need for power).

The second organizational category for leadership theories and approaches is ethics-based theories (*servant, ethical*, and *citizen leadership*) involving values and implicit assumptions about proper forms of influence as they relate to social, political, and economic issues.

Servant leadership (also discussed in chapter 9) is viewed as "leadership upside-down" because servant-leaders put their self-interests aside and seek first to serve the needs of others, help others grow and develop, and provide opportunity for others to gain materially and emotionally. In the organizational setting, servant-leaders' top priority is service to employees, customers, shareholders, and the general public.

Yukl explains that the servant-leader takes a stand for what is good and right—even when it is not in the financial interests of the organization. The servant-leader opposes social injustice and inequality and treats the weak and marginalized members of society with respect and appreciation.

The service model of leadership comes from the modern servant-leadership movement in America, which was developed and popularized by Robert K. Greenleaf in 1970. The idea of servant-leadership has been around for thousands of years, stemming in part from the teachings of Jesus. Jesus taught his disciples that servanthood is the essence of worthy leadership, exemplified through his actions of washing their feet. By his actions, Jesus demonstrated the service model of leadership (a servant-first model) as opposed to the power model of leadership (a leader-first model).

In *The Case for Servant Leadership*, Kent Keith identified several problems with the power model of leadership, namely the use of power as an end in itself with the focus being on *having* power as opposed to using it wisely. Accomplishing goals in service to the organization or community is not the focus of the power model of leadership and promotes conflict caused by leaders focusing on building a power base and not on the problems to be solved. The power model of leadership often results in the unethical use of power because of leaders' focusing on what *they* want instead of what the people need.

In contrast, the service model of leadership does have a moral base. According to Keith, "The whole point of the service model is to be of service—to identify and meet the needs of others. It is about paying attention to others and treating them right." The servant-leader's goal is to identify and meet the needs of others. It uses power as one of many tools, including listening and coaching, which are all needed to accomplish the goal.

Keith also notes a paradox around servant-leaders and power—a servant-leader can gain power without seeking it. People give power to people they trust. People trust servant-leaders because they know they will use their power to benefit everyone. People want to follow servant-leaders because they work on the problems and opportunities and not their own egos, personal status, or prestige. As a result, servant-leaders can more easily build teams and partnerships and get the work done.

Ethical leadership as a theory is not as straightforward of a construct as servant-leadership. It could refer to the ethics of the individual leader or the ethics of specific types of behavior. The focus of our ethical-leadership discussion is on an approach to leadership based on values related to socially responsible behavior that responds to critical needs in our society, especially as they affect the unfair and unjust treatment of marginalized and disadvantaged populations of the world. All three of the ethics-based approaches discussed in this book—servant, ethical, and citizen leadership—fit this description.

In *Ethical Leadership: The Quest for Character, Civility, and Community*, Walter Earl Fluker defines and describes his ethical leadership model. "Not only is society in crisis; leadership itself is in crisis." Fluker explains the rationale for the effectiveness of his model of ethical leadership.

> The critical issue at stake is the need for leadership to envision itself as a community of discourse and practice that is attuned to the kind of networking and decision-making that uses all available resources to respond to the crisis at hand. A community of leaders who are adept at communicating with one another requires more than the traditional approaches that highlight individual leaders as the center of authority. It requires the identification and training of a new generation of leaders who are able to look,

listen, and learn together at the intersections. Moreover, it requires certain virtues, values, and virtuosities (*moral excellencies*) that encourage collaborative leadership. The skills we are recommending revolve around three pivotal concepts: character, civility, and community, which are the defining concepts of ethical leadership.

Each of the three pivotal concepts of Fluker's ethical leadership model contain three interrelated dimensions or values: character (integrity, empathy, and hope), civility (recognition, respect, and reverence), and community (compassion, justice, and courage). Fluker states, "The task of the ethical leader is to inspire and guide others in the process of transformation through courageous acts of defiance and resistance against systems of injustice," especially those affecting African American life and culture.

The final ethics-based leadership theory to discuss is *citizen leadership*. In 1992, the Kettering Foundation, a nonprofit organization founded in 1927 "to sponsor and carry out scientific research for the benefit of humanity," published *Public Leadership Education: The Role of the Citizen Leader*. The publication speaks to the need to call upon all Americans to help solve the problems of society. Contributor Richard Couto observes, "There are not enough officials, elected or appointed, to even begin to get the job done," hence the need for citizen leaders. He defines citizen leaders as individuals who "facilitate organized action to improve conditions of people in low-income communities and to address other basic needs of society at the local level." The goal of citizen leadership, according to Couto, is "making a political, economic, and social system accountable for what it serves and fails to serve." Citizen leaders "act from the conviction that we, as a society, are responsible for redressing the conditions that undermine and understate the human dignity of any of its members."

Couto also observes that citizen leaders typically do not choose to serve. Their usual "first action" is to approach the people in charge to get something done about a specific problem.

If the problem is not resolved or if they feel dismissed by authority, they take further actions that eventually will lead to the achievement of their original purpose. As a result of their work and faithfulness to the achievement of the task at hand, followers bestow on them, according to Couto, the truly distinguishing characteristic of leadership: the gift of trust. From there, citizen leaders may establish or become part of a formal organization, such as "Concerned Citizens of ..." dedicated to the cause of citizen rights.

Two citizen leaders who exemplify the great work described by Couto are Mrs. Fannie Lou Hamer and my father, Mr. Benjamin Johnson. Allow me to share a little of each of their stories.

Citizen Leadership in Action

Many decades before Senator Barack Obama energized hundreds of millions of ordinary citizens to action with his "Yes, We Can" mantra, citizen leadership was alive and well in our neighborhoods. Citizen leaders are plentiful in the local community, but rarely known by the national public. A select few are fortunate enough to receive national recognition for their years of dedication and sacrifices to bring equality of services to their community. One such person is Fannie Lou Hamer.

Ms. Hamer, the granddaughter of a slave and the youngest of twenty children born in 1917 to sharecroppers in Mississippi, began working in the fields at age six and was only educated through the sixth grade. At the age of forty-six, she was arrested, jailed, and beaten to the point of disability for attempting to register to vote. She then joined the civil rights group that created the Mississippi Freedom Democratic Party (MFDP) to focus greater national attention on voting discrimination.

This new party sent a delegation, which included Fannie Lou Hamer, to the Democratic Party National Convention in 1964 in Atlantic City. Ms. Hamer spoke to the credentials committee to challenge the all-white Mississippi delegation because it didn't fairly represent all the people of Mississippi since most black people hadn't been allowed to vote. Because the convention was nationally televised, all of America was able to see Ms. Hamer and hear her impactful and moving description of the African American struggle for civil rights in the Mississippi Delta.

In contrast to Ms. Hamer's participation in the 1964 Democratic National Convention, citizen leaders' stories are more likely to mirror that of my father, Benjamin Johnson. Born in 1916 in Lowndes County, Alabama, my father was the second oldest of six children and formally educated through his early high school years. In 1942, he joined the US Army, proudly fought in World War II, and was awarded the Bronze Star Medal by General George C. Patton.

Upon returning from the army, Dad settled in Birmingham, Alabama, married my mother, Ozelle Sanders in 1949, and they became the proud parents of two daughters, Rebecca and me. In 1962, Dad moved the family to Hueytown, Alabama, a small rural town, twelve miles west of Birmingham, to be closer to his place of employment, US Steel Fairfield Works in Fairfield, Alabama. Because of the lack of many of the basic public services, my father became a founding member of the Concerned Citizens of Hueytown. As a member of this organization, my father worked tirelessly to improve the quality of life for blacks in Hueytown.

My father spent countless hours canvassing the neighborhood and collecting signatures on petitions to take to the Hueytown City Hall to get the streets in the black community paved, street lights installed, sewer lines laid, and public land designated for a community park. On several occasions, my father received awards from the Concerned Citizens of Hueytown in their efforts to recognize and show appreciation for his sacrifices to improve the quality of lives for all citizens of Hueytown, including African Americans.

Citizen leaders like Ms. Fannie Lou Hamer and my father, Mr. Benjamin Johnson, a veteran of World War II and Bronze Star Medal recipient, do not receive the grand public recognition for the great works they do and may not want the recognition. The goal of citizen leaders is simply to ensure that our local, state, and national government and elected officials of all communities live up to America's pledge of "justice for all."

Chapter Summary

The chapter begins with quotes from James MacGregor Burns, a founding researcher in leadership who states, "Clearly, no one best way to lead exists," and other researchers who agree that "leadership is both an art and science." As a result, twenty-first-century leaders will need to possess TASKBs that allow them to engage complex people in solving complex problems with virtuosity and deportment ("whole-brain leadership").

Bennis writes in his leadership classic *On Becoming a Leader* that a dire need in executive-level leadership is "whole-brained" leaders, capable of using both sides of their brain—the logical left side and the imaginative, values-based right side. Additional research by Daft in the area of whole-brain leadership complements the work of Bennis. The work of both Bennis and Daft is built on Herrmann's whole-brain concept, which proposes that the brain is divided into two hemispheres—the creative right side and the logical left side.

In response to Bennis and Daft's call for whole-brain leaders, this chapter outlines the PRCC leadership process—a way in which whole-brain leaders are able to accomplish the goals and objectives of their organizations via an appropriate blend of the art and science of leadership. This feat is accomplished through a whole-brain conceptualization of leadership that divides the brain into two halves—the people-oriented right side and the task-oriented left side.

The people-oriented right side of the PRCC process is comprised of partnership (visioning and communicating the desire for something better) and relationship (securing committed followers and building capable teams). The task-oriented left side of the PRCC process is comprised of companionship (working alongside the followers with fortitude and fervor) and championship (accomplishing the win).

Other concepts relevant to twenty-first-century effective leadership covered in this chapter include the four stages of team development: forming, storming, norming, and performing. The five styles of handling team conflict—competing, compromising, avoiding, accommodating, and collaborating—are also discussed. Effective team development and handling of team conflicts are important skills for twenty-first-century leaders.

This chapter ends with an overview of the history of leadership theory and six theories of leadership that seek to describe, explain, produce, and predict the type of leadership needed to address the myriad issues faced by humanity in the twenty-first century.

The history of leadership theory is categorized under three eras, spanning from the late 1800s to the present: the trait era, the behavioral era, and the contingency era. Throughout this period, the goal of each era remained consistent: to discover the "best way" of effective leadership. The consistent findings from all three eras also remained constant, leading to the conclusion that there is no "one best way to lead."

Additional findings of the contingency era approaches to leadership show that the situation and the various relevant contextual factors determine which style [behaviors] is most effective; that people can learn to become good leaders; that leadership makes a difference in the effectiveness of groups and organizations; and that personal and situational characteristics [traits] affect leadership effectiveness. Therefore theories of the contingency era are the most relevant approaches for twenty-first-century leadership, encompassing factors and findings from all three theoretical eras of leadership.

Six leadership theories from the contingency classification are presented and discussed in this chapter. Three of the leadership theories (transactional, transformational, and charismatic leadership) center on leader-follower relationships, and the remaining leadership theories (servant, ethical, and citizen leadership) center on values-based leadership. These six theories provide the theoretical foundation for the PRCC leadership process and the JWLM.

My overarching premise regarding successful leadership in the twenty-first century can be summarized as "Leadership without relationship is a sinking ship. Leadership *with* relationship is a championship." Effective leadership in the twenty-first century will result from the leader's ability to "be whole" and balance the art and science of leadership into a personal leadership style that takes into consideration follower characteristics and needs along with the situation. The PRCC process built on leadership practice *and* leadership theory is presented as a framework to assist leaders in accomplishing the art and science of *noble leadership.*

Leadership and Professional Development Exercises

Key Terms

- assertiveness dimension
- behavioral era
- charismatic leadership
- citizen leadership
- contingency era
- cooperation dimension
- ethical leadership
- five styles of conflict resolution
- four stage team development process
- Noble leadership-based big act of being and doing
- PRCC leadership process
- servant-leadership
- team versus group
- trait era
- transactional leadership
- transformational leadership
- twenty-first-century effective leadership
- whole-brain leadership style

Questions to Discuss

1. What is the fifth competency domain of the ACTION module? Explain.

2. According to Bennis and Daft, what is a whole-brain leader? What are the differentiating characteristics of a whole-brain leader?

3. What are the components of the PRCC whole-brain leadership process? Define and differentiate each of the four stages of the PRCC process. Is whole-brain leadership a process, a position, or both? Why?

4. What are the three major eras in the study of leadership and their contributions to modern leadership? What are the major similarities and differences between the trait, behavior, and contingency theories?

5. What are the six leadership theories and approaches named in the book that researchers feel are most likely to address the needs of the twenty-first-century global society? Define and differentiate each of the six leadership theories and approaches.

Questions to Consider

1. Is leadership based on principles and ethics, reflective of universal values, classical virtues, and moral maturity needed to achieve success and significance in one's personal and professional life?

2. Which of the leadership theories, styles, and behaviors do you feel best describes your leadership approach and demeanor?

3. Are you satisfied with the outcomes of your leadership style? Which of the leadership styles do you feel would give you better outcomes?

4. Do you believe that having a principled, ethical leadership style honors your faith as well as other components of your winning support system?

5. What traits and behaviors will you eliminate from your leadership style *today* because it hinders your ability to become a more principled, ethical leader? What traits and

behaviors will you integrate into your leadership style *today* to assist you in being a more principled, ethical leader?

Books to Stimulate Your Mind

- *On Becoming a Leader* by Warren Bennis (1989)
- *Ethical Leadership: The Quest for Character, Civility, and Community* by Walter Earl Fluker (2009)
- *The Servant: A Simple Story About the True Essence of Leadership* by James C. Hunter (1998)

The Johnson White Leadership Model

Module 3 Great Leadership

Introduction

The crisis of leadership today is the mediocrity or irresponsibility of so many of the men and women in power, but leadership rarely rises to the full need for it. The fundamental crisis underlying mediocrity is intellectual. If we know all too much about our leaders, we know far too little about *leadership*.

—James MacGregor Burns, "The Crisis of Leadership"

The final module of the JWLM is *Great Leadership*. Its purpose is to allow you to bring focus and action together in order to achieve a goal. This module challenges emerging leaders to view leadership, framed by a commitment to faith, ethics, and diversity, as "an influence process between team members (leaders and followers) resulting in the attainment of group goals for the betterment of the group, the organization, and/or society as a whole." In order to do so, you will put your *FOCUS in ACTION* by participating in a great leadership experience.

You will be guided through a team service-learning project with the goal to make a positive difference in your world by actively engaging in your leadership-development journey. Your engagement is described as the triple-E method of leadership development: education, experience, and examination.

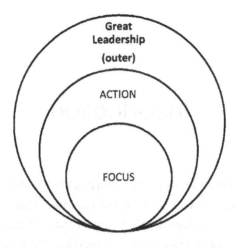

Figure Module 3-1. JWLM Summary

Leadership development depends not just on the kinds of experiences one has but also on how one uses them to foster growth. From my two decades of research on effective leadership development for emerging leaders, I have found that quality leadership development consists of three stages: education, experience, and examination.

My research shows that a three-step process is critical to leadership development for emerging leaders. The first step is education, grounded in theory and practice, on the necessary TASKBs (traits, abilities, skills, knowledge, and behaviors) of effective leadership. Secondly, emerging leaders need an opportunity to utilize their education through experiences designed to foster their leadership development. And lastly, emerging leaders must examine the outcomes by reflecting on the consequences of the experience, its significance and meaning, and adjusting behaviors based on the outcomes. This model of education, experience, and examination calls for repeated developmental opportunities. Growth for emerging leaders comes not just through time but through the opportunity to encounter repeated movements through all three phases: education, experience, and examination.

The triple-E method provides the pedagogical structure that allows students to maximize their leadership development and growth, creating a "safe" environment in which participants can develop effective leadership behaviors and skills through directed education, personal experience, and reflective examination. This method suggests a purposeful way of supporting emerging leaders as they put their focus into action, guiding them to achieving the ultimate outcome of the JWLM: Great Leadership.

Figure Module 3-2 triple-E framework demonstrates the circular developmental process.

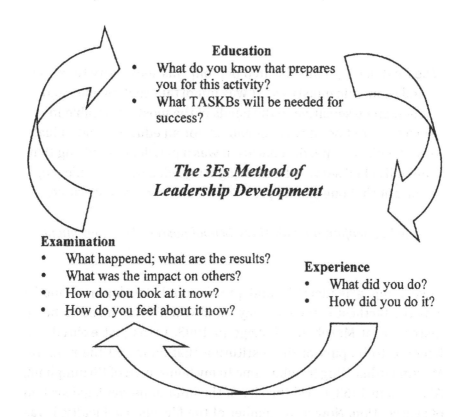

Education
- What do you know that prepares you for this activity?
- What TASKBs will be needed for success?

The 3Es Method of Leadership Development

Examination
- What happened; what are the results?
- What was the impact on others?
- How do you look at it now?
- How do you feel about it now?

Experience
- What did you do?
- How did you do it?

Figure Module 3-2. Triple-E (3Es) Framework

CHAPTER 11

Faith, Ethics, and Diversity

The final mark [of an educated person] was sensitivity to "social and economic injustices." It was important that an educated person be sensitive to the needs of the most vulnerable in society. For Mays, it was not enough for an educated individual to serve his own needs; education was a privilege requiring that an individual serve others. Being truly educated, he believed, meant that one should practice altruism and self-sacrifice.

—Jelks, *Benjamin Elijah Mays: Schoolmaster of the Movement*

Developing a leadership and professional development model was the farthest thing from my mind when I was hired to be an instructor at Morehouse College in 1993. I was just excited and honored to be part of the institution that educated the man, Dr. Martin Luther King Jr., who came to my hometown of Birmingham, Alabama in 1963, to rid the city of the inhumane, yet legal system of segregation. Now as a member of the Morehouse faculty, I was eager to do my part to continue its world-renowned legacy of developing "great leaders."

Quickly after my arrival at Morehouse, I became aware that there was a "specialness" in the place—a specialness that resulted in the making of leaders not by accident but by design. As many will agree, the specialness was due to the hard work, dedication, and twentieth-century visionary educational philosophy of Dr.

Benjamin Elijah Mays, sixth president of Morehouse College. According to Randal Maurice Jelks, author of *Benjamin Elijah Mays: Schoolmaster of the Movement,* Dr. Mays believed that "education was more than professional certification."

Dr. Mays, born in 1894 just three decades after the end of the Civil War, was inspired by his deep roots in Christianity from which grew his desire to work tirelessly to end segregation. While serving in a variety of local, regional, and national leadership roles throughout his nine decades, Dr. Mays was most famously known for his position as president of Morehouse College (1940–1967).

Orville Vernon Burton, who penned a revised forward in the 2003 edition of Dr. Mays's autobiography, *Born To Rebel*, quotes Dr. Mays as saying, "I will serve this institution as if God Almighty sent me into this world for the express purpose of being the Sixth President of Morehouse College." And in doing so, Burton writes of Dr. Mays's efforts in defining the mission of the College, "Morehouse ... was dedicated to the task of building men; first by enlightening their minds, then by freeing them from the shackles of a psychological conditioning brought about by nearly two hundred and fifty years of slavery."

Dr. Mays was a mentor and trusted friend of Dr. King, a 1948 graduate of Morehouse College. During the trying times of the civil rights movement, Dr. King often turned to Dr. Mays for advice and counsel. During one of these times, Dr. King asked Dr. Mays to give his eulogy should the occasion arise. Without doubt, Dr. Mays's contribution to the world as mentor, advisor, and spiritual role model to Dr. Martin Luther King Jr. is and will forever be a gift to all of humanity. Burton states,

> King's fame overshadows Mays's, but I believe there could not have been a Martin Luther King Jr. if there had been no Benjamin Elijah Mays. From their days together at Morehouse, through the years of the civil rights struggle, and until King's death, the pair shared the same philosophy and goals.

The conclusive positive influence that Dr. Mays had on the institution of Morehouse College and her students, from the start of his presidency in 1940 and continuing into the twenty-first century and ultimately to the global society, is incontestable to me. Under his twenty-seven-year stewardship of the college, the Morehouse way of leadership and professional development was institutionalized. The Mays model of great leadership provides lessons that still remain relevant today for the development of twenty-first-century emerging leaders.

For this reason, I was moved to construct a leadership and professional development model based on the legacy of Dr. Mays. His philosophy, along with current research, scholarship, and practice in the fields of leadership and professional development exemplify and epitomize the essence of my leadership model, which I named the Johnson White Leadership Model (JWLM).

The JWLM represents a far-reaching view of the "educated" leader that is in concert with Dr. Benjamin E. Mays's twentieth-century visionary educational philosophy that "education was more than professional certification." Mays's view of educational outcomes frames the definition of "great leadership," which is "an influence process between team members (leaders and followers) resulting in the attainment of group goals for the betterment of the group, the organization, and/or society as a whole." The Maysian educational philosophy was chosen as the blueprint for the JWLM because of Dr. Mays's example of leadership and professional excellence through a commitment to faith, ethics, and diversity.

The essence of whole-brain noble leadership is exemplified in Dr. Mays. His skillful comingling of the art and science of leadership resulted in unprecedented success at Morehouse College. He fulfilled his legitimate role as college president with intellectual acuity, taking Morehouse to heights of international recognition as a top-ranked private liberal arts college for black men. He possessed personal fortitude undergirded by strong intrapersonal skills and masterful execution of interpersonal skills and leadership skills.

Dr. Mays is one of the best examples of the positive outcomes that can derive from charismatic leadership. Dereck J. Rovaris

Sr. provides evidence that supports Dr. Mays's role in taking a struggling college for black men and transforming it to a college of distinction for black men in his 2005 book, *Mays and Morehouse: How Benjamin E. Mays Developed Morehouse College, 1940–1967.* "Mays did not have to force his ideas on anyone to bring about this change. Those involved with the college simply followed his lead." Rovaris notes that this kind of leadership does not come as a result of the traditional legitimate position, but because others are attracted by what the leader stands for and represents.

> Improving the lives of the students with whom he came in contact so that they might go out and improve the world in which they lived was what Mays sought to do at Morehouse. ... he was quite successful in developing Morehouse, its faculty, and students that led to success in his efforts for human betterment.

Dr. Mays saw the unification of diverse people and ideas as an imperative in the twentieth century and worked tirelessly through education to force the eradication of segregation in the United States. As we move swiftly through the twenty-first century, unifying diverse people and ideas continues to be an imperative; tireless efforts through education must continue to be employed to address global issues and challenges. I developed the JWLM as a contribution to the global effort of developing of ethical leaders. As such, I hope that you do not view the JWLM as skills and competencies to be used solely for the purpose of professional gain.

The great leadership vision of the JWLM is to prepare emerging leaders to hold true to a faith-based, ethical value system that addresses the needs of the diversity of all humankind. The JWLM is designed as a leadership-development model that results in social justice across all occupations, fields of study, and societal social constructs. The JWLM is for everyone who believes that "all lives matter" in quantity of years and quality of life. Entrenched also in its ethos is "all *minds* matter," in agreement with Dr. Mays's belief that "the life of the mind is the most important weapon that one has to overcome vestiges of institutional barriers found throughout our global society." The JWLM extends Dr. Mays's concept of the life of the mind to include the necessity of the whole-brain approach to twenty-first-century leadership.

As evidence of your understanding of great leadership that results in the betterment of society, born out of a commitment to faith, ethics, and diversity, I ask you to act now! Commit to leading a service-learning project to address a social issue in your community. The execution details for a service-learning project are outlined below. I extend thanks and give credit to the Institute for Leadership Advancement, Terry College of Business, University of Georgia, for providing a modifiable model that could be used for the design of this project.

The Service Learning Project: A Civic Engagement/ Social Responsibility Assignment

The purpose of the service-learning project (SLP) for you is threefold: 1) to experience firsthand the leadership concepts of contributing to the community by giving back to others and the positive impact it will have on your life and the lives of others; 2) to integrate the five principles of FOCUS and five competencies of ACTION into a deliverable whole that accomplishes a set of predetermined goals; and 3) to learn more about your own and others' leadership styles, skills, and competencies.

The intended outcomes of your project include the development and implementation of a meaningful project in collaboration with the leadership of a community service organization; firsthand experience in effective team-building and collaborative work; and presentation of project results to project stakeholders.

The PRCC leadership process (see chapter 10 for details) is the guiding framework for your SLP. The SLP is designed to be a team project. The ideal team size is five to seven members. Identify a small group of your associates and invite them to be part of your service project. Ideally, they too would have read this book and been educated on the FOCUS and ACTION modules of the JWLM. If not, you should design and deliver a workshop to introduce your group to the material.

As a team, identify a desirable nonprofit organization in which to serve. In collaboration with the leadership of that organization, your team will design and implement a meaningful project. This is not a short-term (one-day, eight-hours or less) activity where you and your team members show up and volunteer for a prearranged community service event (such as walk-a-thons, Habitat for Humanity, etc.).

This SLP requires project identification, planning, coordination, and execution of effort from all team members over an eight-to-ten-week period. Ultimately, the service project you design should benefit the organization in a meaningful way, utilize your team's resources in a creative way, and help you integrate the leadership and professional development concepts you have learned through the JWLM.

Brainstorm with your team regarding your personal passions in the area of service and the needs you see in the community. Use your board of directors (see chapter 3) to identify a suitable site. Your school counselors and teachers, church mission and outreach group, and community mentors are great resources for assistance for site selection. Also, ask someone to serve as your team's mentor/SLP-accountability coach. There will be times when you need guidance and encouragement to ensure the success of your efforts.

Six deliverables will be required of your team. They are outlined via the PRCC process as follows:

Step 1. Establishing Partnership and Building Relationship: Visioning, Connecting, and Planning

Deliverable #1: Team Contract

During the initial planning stage, have a team meeting to discuss team organization and document a team contract. Review the section in chapter 10 that covers team development and conflict resolution. Remember that a group of individuals is not a team.

Effective teams don't happen by chance. The team leader has to drive the process of team formation. It takes work and focused leadership on the part of all team members to achieve team cohesiveness that results in attainment of team goals. The team contract will be a two to three-page document containing the following:

- Team name, mission/purpose, and expected outcomes
- Team members' names, titles, and roles. Team roles to include team leader, team co-leader, record keeper, and communicator. Other roles should be identified as needed.
- Team organizational chart
- Team code of conduct and rules of engagement, including consequences for neglect of duties and responsibilities
- Team communication plan
- Team statement of agreement to fully participate in all aspects of the SLP with signatures of all team members

Review the contract with the team mentor/SLP-accountability coach. Give the team mentor a copy of the completed and signed contract.

Deliverable #2: Team SLP Proposal

This is a separate document from the team contract. Whereas the team contract outlined the team members' responsibilities to each other, the team SLP proposal outlines your responsibilities to your service site. Once the team has agreed on the service site, meet with the site official who will serve as the service site coordinator for your project.

The information contained in the team SLP proposal is to be created in collaboration with your service site coordinator. The team proposal will be a two-to-three-page document containing the following:

- Team information: team name, team member names, phone numbers, e-mail addresses, and team roles

- Team mentor/SLP-accountability coach information: name, title, place of employment, phone number, and e-mail address

Project Service Client Information

- Service Site: name, address, phone number, and website address
- Service Site Coordinator: name, title, phone number, and e-mail address

Project Outcomes and Scope Statement

- What will you do at the service site? Identify the specific tasks your team will perform and when they will be performed.
- What will you accomplish at the service site? Identify expected outcomes of your participation.
- What are the boundaries of your project? Identify time and resource limitations of your project.
- How will you assess the achievement of your outcomes? Assessment instruments such as pre- and post-tests; end of project survey; pre- and post-focus groups with the participants, etc., will need to be designed and conducted.
- Project timeline: Each member of the team is expected to complete twenty hours of service at the site, spread evenly over an eight-to-ten-week period. (The time commitment for your project is a decision that will be made by the team and the site coordinator. However, based on my twenty-plus years of experience with this assignment, this is the minimum time commitment from the participants that will result in the achievement of the learning outcomes.)

Timeline and Dates

- Project kickoff date

- Dates and times of participation for each team member
- Proposed date/time for team mentor/SLP-accountability coach to visit the site
  - Visit #1: one-third of the way through the project
  - Visit #2: two-thirds of the way through the project
  - Visit #3: end of service project (the date of your project celebration event at service site)

Step 2. Sustaining Companionship: Doing the Work and Achieving the Goals

Deliverable #3: SLP Update/Status Reports

Your team will compile three status reports on the progress of the SLP. Include a copy of the team's participation log (a record of each team member's dates and times at the service site) with your status report. A copy of the report covering the designated time period, signed by all team members, will be given to the service site coordinator and the team mentor/SLP accountability coach on each of the visit dates identified in the SLP proposal timeline.

The written status reports will summarize how you are progressing on your project. Include successes as well as challenges—and the team's plan to overcome challenges. The written summarization will be two pages in length, with the team participation log (summary of all team member hours served at the site) attached as a third sheet, resulting in a three-page status report.

Step 3. Create Championship: Celebrating the Success

Deliverable #4: Celebration

This will be a fun event at the service site coordinated and delivered by the team to celebrate the goals accomplished, friendships and relationships created, and to say thank you to the service site participants. Secure outside resources to make the event extra special. Invite your team mentor/SLP-accountability coach, church pastor and members, board of directors, and local media outlets. Take pictures and videos. Write an article for your community newsletter on the success of your SLP. Submit it to several outlets for publication, including the World Wide Web (www).

Deliverable #5: Team Oral Presentation

Your SLP will culminate with a formal presentation of your work with all team members dressed in business attire (see chapter 9). You will present to the leadership team at your service site and your team mentor/SLP-accountability coach. Other members of your support network can also be invited. This presentation should occur no later than two weeks after the SLP celebration.

The presentation assignment is to create a fifteen-minute, multimedia presentation (PowerPoint with pictures and video of the team serving at the site) to "show and tell" your service project. End the session with a five-minute question/answer and feedback time in order to interact with your audience.

The expectation is that you will use the JWLM (*FOCUS in ACTION Is Great Leadership*) as the framework for the team presentation to address the following:

- *Project Team Identity:* Team name; team members' names, and pertinent personal information; mission and goals of team; organizational structure of team
- *Service Organization Background:* What is your organization's name, location, mission, history, founders, etc.?
- *Project Criteria and Selection:* How and why did you select this organization? What criteria/values did you use to help guide your selection?
- *Project Planning:* What were the goals between your team and service site? What did you want to accomplish by the end of this project? What would success look like at the end of your project?

- *Project Roles and Ground Rules:* What role(s) did each team member play on the project? How was the leadership role defined in the team? How did you communicate with each other? How were decisions made? How did you deal with conflict? How did you integrate the expertise, skills, and interest of your team members with the outcomes of the community organization? What were your main ground rules for working together with your community agency?
- *Project Execution and Results:* How did you execute/ implement your project? When you completed your project, what evidence did you have that your team delivered the results/outcomes the organization wanted? What was each team member's story of involvement, achievement, and impact in the project?
- *Project Outcomes:* What were your project outcomes? What did you see, hear, and feel to know that you had met the goals identified in your proposal? (Provide assessment evidence.) What did this project do for the organization, the community, and the team?
- *Celebration:* How did you celebrate your team's efforts? What are your plans to continue to serve at the service site?
- *Worthwhile Check:* What did the organization gain by partnering with your team on this project? What did it lose? Was it worthwhile for the organization? Was it worth your team's effort? On a scale of one to ten, rate the value of the project to the organization and the team. (One represents a waste of time; ten represents a worthy use of time.)
- *Lessons Learned:* What were the three most important lessons your team learned about leadership from this project experience?

Deliverable #6: Final Documentation

At the conclusion of your presentation, present a hard copy of the final presentation to your site coordinator, followed within twenty-four hours by an electronic copy via e-mail. Be gracious leaders and publicly thank your service site coordinator, other people who worked with you at the site, the service site leadership team, and your team mentor/SLP-accountability coach for their time, expertise, and support in making the project a success.

Take a group picture for your records. Within five days, send a thank-you card signed by all members of the team to your service site coordinator. This is a touch of *noble leadership* they will never forget!

The culminating activity of the SLP is for each team member to write a personal reflection essay. It provides you the opportunity to engage in the final stage of the triple-E (education, experience, examination) framework of leadership development, maximizing your leadership and professional development growth via the JWLM.

Share a copy of your essay with your team mentor/SLP-accountability coach and your service site coordinator. Also keep a copy for your personal leadership-development portfolio. It may be useful in applying to colleges, scholarships, internships, and jobs.

The Service-Learning Project Reflection Essay Assignment

You have engaged a significant amount of your personal resources (intellectual, physical, emotional, social, financial, and time) in order to participate effectively in a service-learning project (SLP). You have given immensely and hopefully you have gained even more. The purpose of the SLP reflection essay assignment is to provide you an opportunity to spend time in critical reflection on your involvement in the SLP. The assignment is to write a three-to-five- page essay using the triple-E (education-experience-examination) framework as detailed below:

Introduction: Where did you serve?
- Describe the service site: name, location, population demographics, and mission
- Describe your service site coordinator: name, title, and something memorable about him or her

Education: What did you know?

- What had you learned about leadership and professionalism TASKBs (FOCUS principles and ACTION competencies) through the JWLM that prepared you for success in the planning and execution of your SLP?

Experience: What did you do?

- Describe the activities in which you were involved.
- What did you expect to happen and what happened as you did the action?
- How did you feel about the people and place?
- What assumptions (feelings, beliefs, judgments, and attitudes) about the people and place did you bring to the experience?
- What expectations (based on your assumptions) did you have about the people and place?
- What biases, prejudices, stereotypes, etc., did you hold regarding the people and place?
- How did the people react to you?

Examination: Were your expectations met? How do you look at it now? How do you feel about it now?

- How did the whole-brain and PRCC leadership processes contribute to your effectiveness in the service-learning project?
- Critically reflect on your assumptions by questioning and examining your views in terms of where they came from, the consequences of holding them, and why they are important to you.
- As a result of your critical reflection, did you hold a limiting or distorted view of the people/place? Are your values and the way you make meaning of the world substantiated? Did you hold a limiting or distorted view of the people/place?
- Do you need to revise your assumptions and perspectives to make them more open and better justified?
- What alternative points of view are you now open to?

New Start: What, if anything, will you do differently?

- Has this experience demonstrated a need for you to be more inclusive, perceptive, and self-reflective? Why or why not?
- Have you changed the way you see the people/place? Describe the change or provide your reasoning for no change.
- Will you act on your revised assumptions and/or alternative points of view through behaving, talking, and thinking in a way that is congruent with transformed (changed) assumptions or perspectives? Give examples of what you will do differently *or* do the same.

Chapter Summary

The final module of the JWLM is *Great Leadership.* Its overarching goal is to make real for you the definition of great leadership—"the influence process between team members (leaders and followers) resulting in the attainment of group goals for the betterment of the group, the organization, and/or society as a whole."

This chapter begins with a discussion of the origins of the JWLM. The JWLM reflects the educational philosophy of Dr. Benjamin E. Mays, sixth president of Morehouse College, who believed that education was a privilege requiring that an individual serve others by practicing altruism and self-sacrifice. You are asked to practice altruism and self-sacrifice through an assignment to design and execute a service-learning project using the triple-E framework of leadership and professional development.

The triple-E framework—education, experience, and examination—was developed as a result of my intensive involvement in the past twenty-plus years of educating undergraduates in the art and science of leadership. The triple-E represents three critical components of leadership growth for emerging leaders:

- *Education*—acquiring a solid knowledge base of leadership and professionalism terms, concepts, theories, and approaches; knowing the TASKBs (traits, abilities, skills, knowledge, and behaviors) required of a twenty-first-century leader.

- *Experience*—being directed and guided through a structured community-based activity providing students the opportunity to demonstrate the TASKBs of effective leadership.
- *Examination*—having the opportunity to engage in reflective, outcome-based introspection about their experiences and resulting TASKBs, and capturing these thoughts in journal writing and/or essay writing.

As a result of the triple-E model, emerging leaders have the opportunity to engage in a holistic leadership-development process that culminates in meaningful self-reflection. To remember and relive the happiness brought to someone else's life as the result of a service-learning experience is one of the joys of *great leadership!*

Leadership and Professional Development Exercises

Key Terms

- great leadership
- service-learning
- triple-E

Questions to Discuss

1. What is the third module of the JWLM?
2. What is great leadership? How is it defined?
3. What role, if any, should faith, ethics, and diversity play in achieving success and significance in one's personal and professional life?
4. What is a service-learning project?
5. What is the purpose of the triple-E leadership and professionalism framework for emerging leaders? What are

the components of triple-E? Explain their role in the triple-E method of leadership development?

Questions to Consider

1. What role, if any, does faith, ethics, and diversity play in achieving success and significance in your personal and professional life?
2. What makes a leader and/or leadership great? Why?
3. Do you believe striving for great leadership honors your faith as well as other components of your winning support system?
4. Pick at least one principle of FOCUS as a developmental area for the next year. Which will it be? Why? What will you start to do *today* to incorporate that principle into your leadership style?
5. Pick at least one competency of ACTION as a developmental area for the next year. Which will it be? Why? What will you start to master *today* to make that competency a part of your leadership style?

Books to Stimulate Your Mind

- *The 8th Habit: From Effectiveness to Greatness* by Stephen Covey (2004)
- *What Makes the Great Great: Strategies for Extraordinary Achievement* by Dennis P. Kimbro, PhD (1998)
- *Born to Rebel: An Autobiography* by Benjamin E. Mays (1971, 2003)

CHAPTER 12

The Twenty-First-Century Global Leader Challenge

Our quality of life depends on the quality of our leaders. And since no one else seems to be volunteering, it's up to you. If you've ever had dreams of leadership, now is the time, this is the place, and you're it. We need you.

—Warren Bennis, *On Becoming a Leader*

Developed through decades of research and teaching emerging leaders the art and science of leadership, the Johnson White Leadership Model is a powerful, holistic leadership and professional development model, organized in a practical, three-module framework (Figure Chapter 12-1. JWLM Summary).

The JWLM contains hundreds of TASKBs (traits, abilities, skills, knowledge, and behaviors) that you will need to be an effective twenty-first-century global leader. It is designed to guide emerging leaders along the pathway to becoming great leaders. The pathway begins inward with self and connects externally with others, resulting in the outer manifestation of positive outcomes in the larger societal system in which we live and operate.

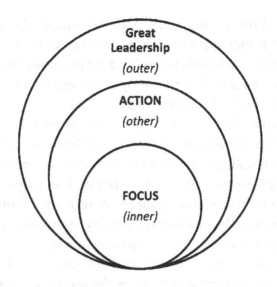

Figure Chapter 12-1. JWLM Summary

Great leadership is not a new phenomenon. Stories of great leadership dating back to 2000 BC are told in the biblical accounts of Moses, Joshua, Esther, Jesus, and the Apostle Paul; the stories of America's Key Founding Fathers in the eighteenth century including John Adams, Benjamin Franklin, Thomas Jefferson, and George Washington; the stories of nineteenth-century abolitionists Frederick Douglass, Harriet Beecher Stowe, Sojourner Truth, and Harriett Tubman; and the stories of Nobel Peace Prize recipients Reverend Dr. Martin Luther King Jr., South African President Nelson Mandela, and Mother Teresa, known in the Catholic Church as Saint Teresa of Calcutta, in the twentieth century. Great leadership demonstrated as "an influence process between team members (leaders and followers) resulting in the attainment of group goals for the betterment of the group, the organization, and/or society as a whole" amply describes what these leaders accomplished.

With intentionality, I chose to state the desired leadership pathway simply as *"FOCUS in ACTION Is Great Leadership."* It is easy to remember but challenging to do. The challenge is driven by the word *great*. Leadership is a neutral term, but great—the ability, quality or eminence considerably above the normal or average—is not a neutral term. The JWLM pathway dictates a commitment to a kind of leadership excellence that results in the "authentic" you—the "great" you God created and purposefully designed. That greatness is committed to the recognition and development of the greatness in others through service.

My humble desire is that the JWLM presents a fresh, new approach to the time-honored tradition of leadership development at Morehouse College that can be shared with emerging leaders in our global society from all walks of life, eager to become great servants in their four spheres of influence (home, place of worship, community, and workplace). My approach addresses the unmet need in leadership-development literature of a leadership model that intentionally combines leadership development and professional development *and* shares the secrets to executive-level leadership.

The JWLM is based on both the theory and practice of effective leadership and professionalism. Consequently, the five principles of FOCUS and the five competencies of ACTION are collectively referred to as "the ten tenets of leadership and professional excellence." Webster defines tenet as "a principle, belief, or doctrine generally held to be true, *especially* one held in common by members of an organization, movement, or profession."

A lifestyle of leadership and professional excellence, driven by the ten tenets, does not happen by accident. It's a mind-set that can be best described in the words of Apostle Paul: "Whatever is true, whatever is noble, whatever is right, whatever is pure, whatever is lovely, whatever is admirable—if anything is excellent or praiseworthy—think about such things" (Philippians 4:8, NIV). The ten tenets link by building on each other and through cross-referencing the TASKBs (see Figure Chapter 12-2. Ten Tenets of Leadership and Professional Excellence).

---

10 Tenets of Leadership & Professional Excellence

FOCUS	+	ACTION	=	Great Leadership
Find Your Power Source		Awesome Professionlism		"An influence process between team members (leaders and followers) resulting in the attainment of group goals for the betterment of the group, organization, and/or society as a whole."
Open Your Internal Systems		Courageous Character		
Connect to External Systems		Tenacious Inclusion		
Understand the Big Picture		Optimal Service		
Sell Yourself as Excellence		Noble Leadership		

Figure Chapter 12-2. Ten Tenets of Leadership & Professional Excellence

The JWLM is a leadership model with a holistic view—combining the surface, what people see of you, your actions and behaviors (the source of perceptions), and the soul, what's in your mind and heart, your thoughts, attitudes, and values (the source of your character). Woven throughout the JWLM are big and small acts of being and doing that capture the essence of great leadership. The big acts of being and doing—"be the authentic you, be likable, be strategic, be whole"—result from the small acts of being and doing—"be engaging, be interested and interesting, be prepared, be organized, be helpful, be humble, be nice, be kind, be truthful, be honest, be trustworthy."

The JWLM is a model that includes the blue suit, white shirt, striped tie, black socks leadership uniform *and* goes beyond to include Dr. Benjamin E. Mays's focus on social justice, driven by faith, ethics, and diversity. The JWLM challenges emerging leaders to embrace the social conscience focus evident in Dr. Martin Luther King Jr.'s cry for "a revolution of values to accompany the scientific and freedom revolutions engulfing the earth."

In his last book, *Where Do We Go From Here: Chaos or Community?* Dr. King passionately shares his view that the only way to address the global issues of racism, poverty, excess population in relation to resources for most of the large undeveloped nations of the world, and war is through an uprising of values. The revolution of values he so desperately spoke about comes from his deep and abiding faith in something bigger than ourselves. He had faith in a power higher and greater than the power of fragile humans who since the beginning of mankind have struggled to live in peace and harmony but too often failed.

The faith needed to address twenty-first-century challenges is not a faith in the size of our military and warhead schemes created by our ethically challenged, partisan governmental systems, our GDP created by our economic systems, or our technology advancements spun by innovative business people, entrepreneurs, and scientists. Faith in God drives us all to demonstrate our love for him through our *service* as business people, politicians, scientists, and educators who are tackling King's four monumental problems—racism, poverty, excess population in relation to resources, and war. In particular, we in America are called to lead the way in the revolution of values. It is on you—the global millennial generation—to stand up and be counted. It is your time. Will you answer the call?

Throughout this book, you have been presented with leadership challenges of epidemic—and in some cases, pandemic—proportions. In addition to those previously mentioned by Dr. King—racism, poverty, excess population in relation to resources, and war— global leadership challenges include human rights battles, systemic and institutionalized diversity oppression, social class conflicts, health disparities, lack of quality education and equal opportunity, economic recessions, financial illiteracy, famines, the reclamation of our communities from drugs and violence, and resource allocation.

Not discussed but equally horrific are the twenty-first-century challenges of nuclear proliferation, ethical dilemmas presented by technological advances in science, genetics, and health care, and the technology divide. Reading this list will induce one of three responses: indifference, complacency, or focus and action. I truly believe that your response is one of focus and action. (A great way to record your progress toward the incorporation of focus and action TASKBs in your leadership development journey is by engaging in the "coat of arms" exercise in Appendix A.)

If given the right tools, in the right way, for the right reasons, people will spring into action in order to solve the challenges that we face as a global society. The action may not happen immediately, but it will happen eventually. It will happen as a result of the natural law of sowing and reaping.

As a leadership educator, my hope is grounded in what I call the "SEEDS" process—sow expectations of excellence, dignity, and service. When the time is right, the "seeds" will sprout and the world will be a better place for generations to come. These seeds are found in the pages of this book. Continue to read and reread this book with the goal of internalizing and operationalizing the JWLM into all phases of our life.

The challenge for the diverse millennial generation of emerging leaders is whether you will lead from a place of universal values, classical virtues, and moral maturity. Embody the words of one of the greatest leadership educators of the twentieth century, Dr. Benjamin E. Mays, and *"serve as if heaven sent you and give as if your very existence depends upon it."*

Allow the JWLM, built on the educational philosophy of Dr. Mays, mentor to Dr. Martin Luther King, Jr., to guide you on your pathway forward. You can become a twenty-first-century global leader who achieves success and significance through service to society.

Success and significance in life happens when you have

- a plan, a brand, and a belief that you can;
- a drive to thrive, a yearning for learning, a passion for action, a place in the space, and a zeal to close the deal;

- a voice that commands and a desire to lend a helping hand;
- a head that is led by a heart that is smart.

Such that at the end of the day, when you kneel down to pray, you can honestly say, "Thank you, God. It was done your way."

Peace and blessings to you,
Belinda Johnson White, PhD

APPENDIX A

Leadership "Coat of Arms" Exercise

You should be beaming with excitement and desire to exemplify and share with others the principles and competencies of the JWLM. I have designed this "coat of arms" exercise to help fortify and reinforce your commitment to live a life of leadership and service. Dating back to the twelfth century, a coat of arms has been used to identify a warrior dressed in armor. See yourself as a twenty-first-century warrior, leading and serving for the betterment of mankind.

This exercise uses the triple-E—education, experience, examination—leadership-development framework for emerging leaders (see chapter 11).

Step 1: Education

Use the Johnson White Leadership Model Summary that follows in Appendix B to reinforce your knowledge and understanding of the intrapersonal principles of the FOCUS module; the interpersonal competencies of the ACTION module; the outcome of the Great Leadership module; and the corresponding TASKBs (traits, abilities, skills, knowledge, and behaviors) for all three modules.

Step 2: Experience

Identify an activity in one of your four spheres of influence (home, workplace, community, place of worship) you feel would allow you to utilize the principles, competencies, and TASKBs, resulting in the great leadership module outcome—attainment of group goals for the *betterment* of the group, the organization, and/or society as a whole. The activity should allow you to engage in all four components of the PRCC leadership process— partnership, relationship, companionship, and championship (see chapter 10).

Step 3: Examination

Keep a journal of your involvement in the activity. Specifically make note of the TASKBs you use in the activity, how people react to your use of the TASKBs, and how you feel about the strength and limitations of your intrapersonal, interpersonal, and leadership skills. At the conclusion of the activity, create your leadership coat of arms based on what you learned about yourself in the area of leadership and professionalism. The coat of arms template is found at the end of Appendix A.

The coat of arms has five parts to complete:

- *Top Banner.* Write your family name. Include the last names of as many ancestors as you know. As an example, the family name of my banner is "Johnson, Sanders, Shuford, White. Johnson is my father's family name; Sanders is my mother's family name; Shuford is my maternal grandmother's family name; and White is my husband's family name.
- *Left Side of Shield (FOCUS).* Summarize the intrapersonal TASKBs you excelled in during the activity and those you desire to improve.
- *Right Side of Shield (ACTION).* Summarize the interpersonal TASKBs you excelled in during the activity and those you desire to improve.
- *Bottom Section of Shield (Great Leadership).* Summarize the outcome of the activity.

- *Bottom Banner.* Create a personal motto (one to three words, an acronym, or an acrostic) that represents FOCUS, ACTION, and Great Leadership for you. As an example, JWLM is the acronym on the bottom of my banner. For me, it has two meanings: Johnson White Leadership Model and Jesus will lead me.

Feel free to decorate and embellish your coat of arms with meaningful symbols and icons. This is an exercise you will want to do repeatedly. Make copies of the coat of arms for later use. Be sure to date your sheets. Before entering a new "battle" (activity), review your coat of arms to determine what TASKBs you will utilize again because they proved effective, which TASKBs you need to improve or relinquish because of their ineffectiveness (and in some cases, counter-effectiveness), and what new TASKBs you will employ.

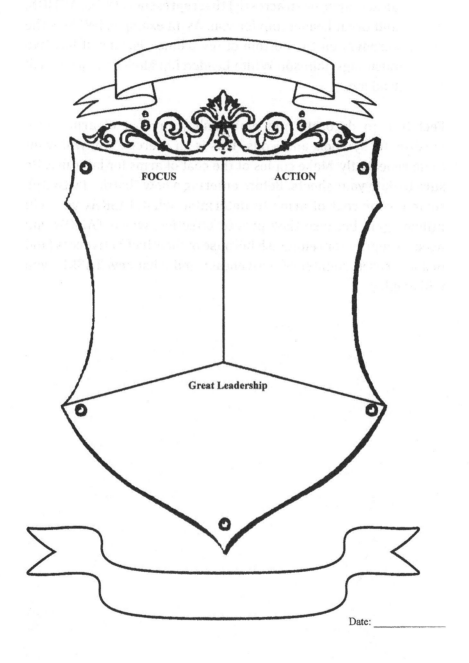

FOCUS   ACTION

Great Leadership

Date: _____

The Johnson White Leadership Model Summary

Module 1 FOCUS Principles: Intrapersonal TASKBs

#1. Find Your Power Source

Knowing, developing, and using your power source is step one in becoming an effective leader. Your power source is where you will derive your strength to accomplish the tasks and manage the stress of leadership in order to achieve the goals of the people and organizations you serve.

Twelve areas are identified as sources of power and comprise the "F" series: faith, fitness, finances, freedom, future, family, friends, forgiveness, forgetting, fulfillment, failure, and fun.

#2. Open Your Internal Systems

Possessing self-awareness, self-confidence, and self-identity is critically important to your ability to become an effective twenty-first-century global leader and derive from four states of being and doing: values (ideals considered by the individual to be important), attitudes (positive or negative feelings about people, things, and issues), personality (unseen structures and processes inside a person that explain his or her behavior), and principles (natural laws and governing social values of every great society and responsible civilization).

Leaders use Kidder's universal social values—love, truthfulness, fairness, freedom, unity, tolerance, responsibility, and respect for life—as the guiding force in their lives, integrating them into their internal operating system consisting of their life purpose, calling, life goals, mission, and vision.

#3. Connect to External Systems

The most effective and efficient way of getting what you want out of life is by developing meaningful relationships with others who are willing and able to assist you in making your personal and professional dreams come true. The key to being able to develop meaningful relationships with others is found in three big acts of being and doing: "Be the 'authentic you,' be likeable, and be strategic." This enables the emerging leader to construct networks that lead to increased net worth and net reach.

Networks should include a personal board of directors (sponsors, mentors, life coaches, and advisors); mastermind groups; brain trusts; professional organizations; and nonprofit boards. Net reach includes the people and organizations in which you serve.

#4. Understand the Big Picture

War, poverty, mortality, and health disparities are just a few of the many problems that comprise the twenty-first-century big picture. They are strongly rooted in the economic, political, and social structures of the world. Leaders must acquire a sensitivity and awareness of the span of environmental, political, regulatory, societal, technological, globalization, and competitive trends and forces that affect all demographic groups of developed and developing economies, local and foreign.

While many of the problems of the world are caused by "generation-old" vestiges of the classical "isms," including racism and sexism, the solution to the problems is in "generation-new" attitudes and a revolution of values.

#5. Sell Yourself as Excellence

Emerging leaders start their careers by adding value to an organization and strategically positioning themselves to become viewed as "value-add" in an organization, which leads to consideration for higher levels of responsibility within organizations. They add value by becoming unconsciously competent in demonstrating the specific TASKBs (traits, abilities, skills, knowledge, and behaviors) of professional excellence summarized as the ABCs of professional presence—appropriateness, believability, and credibility through appearance, body language, communication skills, deliverables (work ethic and work product), and etiquette (business and social skills). These ABCs are also referred to as the "secret code" of corporate culture exhibited through a balanced excellence of style and substance.

The small acts of being and doing are: "Be engaging; be interested and interesting; be prepared; be disciplined; be organized; be punctual; be helpful; be humble; be nice; be kind."

Module 2 ACTION Competencies: Interpersonal TASKBs

#1. Awesome Professionalism

To be considered for senior-level positions, emerging leaders must possess competencies that go far beyond the ABCs of professional presence. Executive-level professionalism goes past being a good candidate to being an elite candidate through phenomenal conscientiousness, which demonstrates readiness for senior-level leadership.

These competencies include making success look effortless, not being labeled political, and consistently exceeding performance expectations through challenging assignments while adhering to the cultural norms in the organizational setting.

#2. Courageous Character

Twenty-first-century global leaders consistently examine their character to ensure their ethics, values, morals, and principles line up with the seven classical virtues of courage, faith, justice, prudence, temperance, love, and hope, as well as Kohlberg's highest stage of moral reasoning—level three post-conventional. At this level, the leader is doing what is right because it is the right thing to do.

Necessary leader competencies in the area of character include the ability to consistently demonstrate ethical behaviors of integrity, trustworthiness, sound judgment, courage, conviction, and personal accountability; possessing an unquestionable personal brand; and wise and judicious use of power and influence. The small acts of being and doing advocated in the competency domain of courageous character are: "Be truthful; be honest; be trustworthy."

#3. Tenacious Inclusion (Diversity and Global Awareness)

The twenty-first-century global leader overcomes the challenges of working and leading in the global society by understanding and practicing cultural inclusion—a term used to describe the intrapersonal, interpersonal, or intercultural skill sets needed to cross cultural lines in order to bring diverse others together. Competencies of tenacious inclusion include the ability to embrace, appreciate, develop, and serve all people.

Leaders who operate from a position of cultural inclusion are open to using the gifts and talents of all people in the organization so they can contribute, add value, and possess a feeling of belonging in the organization. These leaders purposely strive to be personally free from stereotypes, prejudices, and biases, and they accept none of these attitudes from employees or customers.

#4. Optimal Service

Three concepts and competencies are associated with service: 1) corporate social responsibility (CSR), including the triple-bottom line's attention to profit, people, and the planet; 2) Robert Greenleaf's servant-leadership model; and 3) civic engagement through volunteerism, community service, and service-learning. The competencies associated with all three models focus on giving back to others, which is demonstrated through a personal commitment to helping improve the community in which you live and work and helping your organization address social needs in the communities they affect.

Stewardship of the planet through the protection of natural resources is an expectation of organizations in delivering optimal service in the twenty-first century.

#5. Noble Leadership

Researchers agree that no one best way to lead exists and that leadership is both an "art and science." As a result, twenty-first-century leaders will need to possess TASKBs that allow them to engage complex people in the solving of complex problems with virtuosity and deportment (whole-brain leadership). Whole-brain leadership activated through the PRCC leadership process divides the brain into two halves—the people-oriented right side and the task-oriented left side. The people-oriented, right side of the PRCC process is comprised of partnership (visioning and communicating the desire for something better) and relationship (securing committed followers and building capable teams). The task-oriented left side of the PRCC process is comprised of companionship (working alongside the followers with fortitude and fervor) and championship (accomplishing the win).

Competencies of noble leadership include the ability to guide, direct, steer, and navigate the twenty-first-century leadership process effectively through the ethical and prudent use of power and influence, resulting in the attainment of shared goals and positive outcomes. Effective leadership in the twenty-first century will result from the leader's ability to be whole and balance the art and science of leadership into a personal leadership style that takes into consideration follower characteristics and needs along with the situation.

Noble leadership holds as a truism, "Leadership without relationship is sinking ship. Leadership *with* relationship is a championship."

Module 3 Great Leadership: The Overarching Goal of the JWLM

The JWLM reflects the educational philosophy of Dr. Benjamin E. Mays, sixth president of Morehouse College and mentor to Dr. Martin Luther King Jr. who believed that education was a privilege requiring that an individual serve others by practicing altruism and self-sacrifice. Dr. Mays stated, "We are all called by God to human betterment and enrichment. If we fail on those scores, we disappoint God, break his heart, and make Him cry."

The overarching goal of the JWLM is the development of emerging leaders who can effectively participate in "an influence process between team members (leaders and followers) resulting in the attainment of group goals for the betterment of the group, the organization, and/or society as a whole."

References

Bennis, W. (2009). *On Becoming A Leader* (revised and updated). New York: Basic Books.

Burns, J. M. (1995). "The Crisis of Leadership." In J. T. Wren (Ed.) *Leader's companion.* New York: The Free Press.

Daft, R. (2005). *The leadership experience* (3rd edition). Canada: Thomson South-Western.

Dubrin, A. (1998). *Leadership: Research findings, practice, and skills.* Boston, MA: Houghton Mifflin Company.

Gardner, H. (1993). *Frames of mind: The theory of multiple intelligences* (2nd ed.).New York: Basic Books.

Gardner. J. W. (1995). "The Cry for Leadership." In J. T. Wren (Ed.) *Leader's companion.* New York: The Free Press.

Hughes, R., Ginnett, R. and Curphy, G. (2009). *Leadership: Enhancing the lessons of experience* (6th ed.). Boston: McGraw-Hill.

Keith, K. (2008). *The case for servant leadership.* Westfield, IN: Greenleaf Center for Servant Leadership.

Kets De Vries, M. (2001). *The leadership mystique.* London: Prentice Hall.

Kidder, R. (1995). "Universal Human Values: Finding an Ethical Common Ground." In *The leader's companion: Insights on leadership through the ages.* New York: The Free Press, p. 502-506

Kolp, A. and Rea, P. (2006). *Leading with integrity: Character-Based leadership.* Cincinnati, OH: Atomic Dog Publishing.

Lussier, R. and Achua, C. (2007). *Leadership: Theory, application, skill development* (3rd ed.). Canada: Thomson South-Western.

Nahavandi, A. (2009). *The art and science of leadership* (5th ed.). Upper Saddle River, NJ: Pearson Prentice Hall.

Rovaris, D.J. (2005). *Mays and Morehouse: How Benjamin E. Mays developed Morehouse College, 1940-1967.* Silver Spring, MD: Beckham Publications Group, Inc.

Yukl, G. (2002). *Leadership in organizations* (5th edition). Upper Saddle River, NJ: Pearson Prentice Hall.

Index

About the Author

After a thirteen-year career with the IBM Corporation in marketing, sales, and training, Belinda White answered the call to pursue her life mission and personal passion for leadership development. In 1993, she began her second career as a business instructor at Morehouse College in Atlanta, Georgia. Dr. White is currently associate professor and management program director in the Department of Business Administration, where she developed and teaches Bus 321 Leadership and Professional Development, a core course in the business program, and is co-designer of the leadership studies minor. Dr. White's research interests are effective leadership pedagogy and executive leadership development—with special interest in executive development for minorities.

Born in Birmingham, Alabama, Dr. White holds a BS from Spelman College, an MS from Georgia Institute of Technology, and a PhD in higher education policy and leadership from Georgia State University. She has done further study in leadership development at the John F. Kennedy School of Government, Harvard University; the Institute for Leadership Advancement, Terry College of Business, University of Georgia; and the Salzburg Seminar, Salzburg, Austria. Her professional organization memberships include the Academy of Management (AOM), Southern Management Association (SMA), and Omicron Delta Kappa National Leadership Honor Society. She has served as a faculty fellow in leadership at Baxter Healthcare and Operation HOPE.

In 2009, Dr. White founded BuildingLeaders, LLC through which she delivers training and consulting services in the area of leadership and professional development for educational, nonprofit, entertainment, and corporate organizations across industries. She is an avid traveler and has conducted leadership training sessions for students in more than twenty countries, including Greece, South Africa, Australia, France, China, Brazil, Spain, and Norway.

Belinda lives in Atlanta, Georgia, USA, with her husband Bob and two adult children, Robert and Bethany. Her contact information is as follows:

- Email: Belinda@belindajohnsonwhite.com
- Website: www.belindajohnsonwhite.com